A GROUNDBREAKING, SCIENTIFIC APPROACH TO
A HEALTHY LIFE WHILE RECOVERING FROM ALCOHOLISM

THE
RECOVERY
DIET

INCLUDES
12 WEEKS
OF MEAL
PLANS

REVERSE LIVER DAMAGE • PREVENT DIABETES • CONTROL
HEART DISEASE • ALLEVIATE ARTHRITIS PAIN • LOSE WEIGHT
RESIST CRAVINGS • MANAGE MOOD SWINGS • STAY THE COURSE

Renée Hoffinger, MHSE, RD

A adamsmedia

AVON, MASSACHUSETTS

Published by
Adams Media, a division of F+W Media, Inc.
57 Littlefield Street, Avon, MA 02322. U.S.A.
www.adamsmedia.com

ISBN 10: 1-4405-3026-2
ISBN 13: 978-1-4405-3026-5
eISBN 10: 1-4405-3126-9
eISBN 13: 978-1-4405-3126-2

Printed in the United States of America.

10   9   8   7   6   5   4   3   2   1

Library of Congress Cataloging-in-Publication Data
is available from the publisher.

This publication is designed to provide accurate and authoritative information with regard to the subject matter covered. It is sold with the understanding that the publisher is not engaged in rendering legal, accounting, or other professional advice. If legal advice or other expert assistance is required, the services of a competent professional person should be sought.

—From a *Declaration of Principles* jointly adopted by a Committee of the American Bar Association and a Committee of Publishers and Associations

Many of the designations used by manufacturers and sellers to distinguish their product are claimed as trademarks. Where those designations appear in this book and Adams Media was aware of a trademark claim, the designations have been printed with initial capital letters.

This book is intended as general information only, and should not be used to diagnose or treat any health condition. In light of the complex, individual, and specific nature of health problems, this book is not intended to replace professional medical advice. The ideas, procedures, and suggestions in this book are intended to supplement, not replace, the advice of a trained medical professional. Consult your physician before adopting any of the suggestions in this book, as well as about any condition that may require diagnosis or medical attention. The author and publisher disclaim any liability arising directly or indirectly from the use of this book.

The information in this book should not be used for diagnosing or treating any health problem. Not all diet and exercise plans suit everyone. You should always consult a trained medical professional before starting a diet, taking any form of medication, or embarking on any fitness or weight-training program. The author and publisher disclaim any liability arising directly or indirectly from the use of this book.

This book is available at quantity discounts for bulk purchases.
For information, please call 1-800-289-0963.

This book is dedicated to my parents, Edna and "Wild Bill" Hoffinger, who imbued in me a love for wordplay, and taught by example that the best things in life are not things.

Acknowledgments

Major stockpotfuls of thanks to my various cheering squads for inspiration, moral support, and feedback. Friends Leslie Sahler, Heath Lynn Silberfeld, and Jean Michelson, MS, RD, gave me the confidence to accept the task of writing this book. My fellow Substance Abuse Treatment Team members at the North Florida/South Georgia Veterans Health System, have taught me huge helpings about recovery and continue to support the role of nutrition in recovery, often happily sampling the results of our weekly cooking classes. Pam Coughlin, MHSE OTR, my co-leader in cooking classes since the beginning, has broadened my horizons by illuminating the occupational therapy perspective on hands-on cooking classes. Larry Condra, MDiv, CAP, former officemate extraordinaire, has shared the wisdom of his experience giving me greater insight into the process of recovery. It has been enjoyable to have the youthful enthusiasm of Lindsey Lankowsky, MS, RD, a recent addition to the world of hands-on nutrition education, reinforce my wild and crazy teaching style.

A burrito wrap stuffed with thanks for the folks at Adams Media who gave me the opportunity to put it all down on paper: Victoria Sandbrook, acquisitions editor, for birthing the book and Wendy Simard, development editor, for guiding it to fruition. And a large punchbowl of appreciation to my fellow dietitians and others who created recipes used in this book.

A large pressure cooker full of love to Baila and Dennis Scott who have been as family, cooking and sharing innumerable dinners together since B.C. (before children) and turned me on to pressure cooking.

Big salad bowls of gratitude to my family! My sweetie, Dennis, always the cooperative taste tester, encouraged me to write and has been phenomenally patient with the process. The ever-helpful Yosef has guaranteed me a lifetime contract of technical support, which I take him up on frequently, often on an emergency basis. A very special appreciative fair trade, organic chocolate bar goes to Meira, my capable, trusty assistant, for her expert, detailed assistance with the recipe section, being a delightful kitchen playmate, an amazing daughter, and inspiring human being.

Large wokfuls of respect and appreciation (although they often might prefer buckets of fried chicken) to the thousands of veterans who have been good sports, cooking and tasting weird foods in the teaching kitchen, who taught me most of what I know, and have shared their journeys of recovery over the past 18 years.

Contents

Introduction: The Edible Step vii

CHAPTER 1: **Damage Control—and a Healthier Future** 1

CHAPTER 2: **Recovery Diet Goals** 9

CHAPTER 3: **Eating to Manage Common Medical Concerns** 25

CHAPTER 4: **Putting It All Together in the Kitchen** 41

CHAPTER 5: **Recipes for Recovery** 53

Appendix: Resources for Recovery 231

Index 235

INTRODUCTION

The Edible Step

Congratulations! You are in recovery! You have taken a major, positive leap, meeting one of life's challenges head on by embracing change. You should already feel better about yourself, your body, and your life. You feel better—physically and emotionally—think clearer, and look younger. The hard work continues: meetings, continually making amends, lifestyles changes to match the internal shifts. So many new leaves to turn over—but there's a very important one left to tackle: Diet. What, exactly, does food have to do with your recovery? Everything!

Simply put, your diet can either support or sabotage your program of recovery. When you understand how food affects your physical, emotional, mental, and spiritual health—and apply these principals in your kitchen—you can give yourself the best odds at staying in recovery and living the rest of your sober years as healthy as possible.

What to Expect from This Book

Informed people are able to make informed decisions. And, as they say, "inquiring minds want to know." I have learned an immense amount from the people in recovery whom I have been privileged to work with over the past 18 years. They have taught me, among a million other things, that when they understand the "why" it is much easier for them to implement the "how." Therefore, this book will provide the background information you need to build your own case for eating well to support your recovery.

This includes a review of alcohol's impact on your nutritional infrastructure and function, how best to counteract the damage, the science behind mental and emotional health, and straightforward guidelines for applying these to your life. We will address dietary interventions for medical conditions specific to folks in recovery. Most importantly, we will tackle the seemingly immense hurdle of how to go about the process of dietary change. By understanding your own psychology and how it interacts with situations and environments and overcoming the obstacles in reaching your dietary goals, you'll be empowered to have edible, nutritious, delicious food on your table.

What to Expect of Yourself

Just as Rome wasn't built in a day, your current food habits—as compulsive or erratic, premeditated or predictable as they may be—took a lifetime to build. The way you eat has been molded by family and upbringing, ethnicity and geography, finances, friends, aptitudes, and addictions. Much of what we consider to be inborn tastes are actually acquired preferences. Just as tastes are acquired, they can be modified and changed. I encourage you to be confident yet patient with yourself as you learn and apply the principles of nourishing yourself for successful recovery.

Although you may have more physical and psychic energy for focusing on nutrition and food preparation once you are more solidly grounded in your recovery, it is never too early to learn about and incorporate good nutrition into your program of recovery.

Many Americans suffer nutrition-related maladies such as heart disease, cancer, and diabetes. Many more are just plain overweight, or even obese. Most are aware of, even if not willing to state aloud, the dissonance between their lifestyle and the health they seek. They might even say that they want to make some dietary changes to alleviate or prevent disease or lose weight, but they may never act on their own values. As a person in recovery, you are already one step ahead of the game. Your personal experiences, plus the lessons learned and skills you've developed in becoming sober, can be transferred to the food realm of your life. By aligning your dietary practices with your heart and your health, you can take your recovery up a notch, reinforcing your success and fortifying a foundation for all of your life's goals.

May you be blessed with the power to nourish yourself, in all the realms.

CHAPTER 1

Damage Control— and a Healthier Future

Excessive alcohol takes an immense toll on your health. As our nation's third leading cause of premature death, alcohol lops off an average of 30 years of life for each alcohol-related death. Aside from the immediate health concerns due to increased incidence of unintentional injuries, violence, and alcohol poisoning, alcohol is associated with a host of long-term chronic diseases. These include heart disease, a variety of cancers including liver, breast, ovaries, and pancreas, as well as cancers of the entire gastrointestinal tract, neurological and psychiatric problems, gastrointestinal maladies, and of course, liver disease. Excessive alcohol can also interfere with reproductive health, leading to impotence in men and fetal alcohol syndrome in the offspring of pregnant women. One effect of alcoholism, in particular, intertwines with every other symptom, health complication, and psychological struggle: malnutrition. It's easy enough to forget about what you've been feeding yourself while you're beginning your recovery and planning your healing process, but nutrition is a cornerstone in the damage that's been done—and in the road back to health

Malnutrition

The quantity and quality of the food alcohol abusers eat is usually less than ideal. Clouded judgment and other priorities means an alcoholic's typical diet is rarely healthy. People under the influence are more likely to consume processed frozen dinners, doughnuts, soda, and fast-food takeout than broccoli, brown rice, and fresh fruit. In general, moderate drinking adds calories to the usual diet while heavy drinking replaces calories from food. The former may lead to some weight gain; the latter to weight loss and muscle wasting. Binge drinking is also associated with disordered eating patterns such as bulimia and anorexia, especially in women. Heavy alcohol use actually increases your requirements for protein as well as some vitamins and minerals, while at the same time your intake of these nutrients is dampened and the efficient processing of these in your liver is hampered.

Poor Intake

When you consumed massive quantities of alcohol, you literally crowded out more nutritious calories. Heavy drinkers may easily consume up to half their calories as alcohol. Considering that one beer contains approximately 150 calories, that means that a six-pack adds up to 900 calories. A pint of 80-proof vodka contains 1,035 calories. Just for comparison, the average person needs about 2,000 calories a day. Add these figures to high-calorie, low-quality food, and there's little room left for nutrient-dense food to keep you healthy.

Alcohol also depressed your appetite, so alcohol may have started to replace much of the food in your diet altogether. If you smoke, cigarettes also dull your sense of taste. Even mild malnutrition can affect your desire for food, while poor health, dental issues, and gastrointestinal pain may have also served as deterrents to eating. And well, if things don't taste good and just make you feel worse when you eat them, why bother eating?

Bottom line: Whether you ate too much or began eating too little, you haven't been feeding yourself well.

Maldigestion

What food you did consume when using alcohol may not have been digested well. Strong teeth are vital for good digestion. Chewing breaks food down to smaller pieces, thus increasing the surface area exposed to the enzymes that digest it. Your teeth may not be in prime condition after abusing alcohol. Brushing, flossing, and regular dental care may not have been at the top of your "to-do" list, resulting in cavities, loose or missing teeth, and sore gums. Many people in recovery also find that their teeth have been damaged in accidents and fights caused by poor coordination and judgment under the influence. Compromised dentition tends to steer you away from crunchy or slightly tough foods, restricting the variety of foods, and thus the variety of nutrients, that you consume.

In addition, your body may be producing fewer enzymes that break down fats, proteins, and carbohydrates into simpler compounds that can be absorbed from your gastrointestinal tract into your bloodstream. This makes it even more difficult to digest everything you eat, and you may face digestive problems including indigestion, nausea, and diarrhea—in addition to the nutrition-related issues. Bottom line: You've been making your body work harder for fewer rewards, and it's time to reverse that trend.

Malabsorption

Alcohol is cruel to the gut. It breaks down the lining of the intestinal tract, limiting the nutrients your body can absorb. Your body also secreted excess acid when you abused alcohol, possibly damaging your stomach lining by causing alcoholic gastritis and eating away your pancreas. Alcohol also relaxes the sphincter leading to the stomach, preventing it from stopping food and the acid from heading back up into the food pipe and causing reflux esophagitis (a.k.a. GERD). Plus, alcohol-related diarrhea rapidly flushes nutrients through your GI tract before they have an opportunity to be absorbed. This "Roto-Rooter" effect also sends enzymes—including lactase—on their way, rendering you temporarily lactose intolerant. Diarrhea often leads to dehydration and electrolyte imbalances.

Bottom line: These gastrointestinal issues are painful deterrents to eating and absorption, continuing the cycle of malnutrition until you decide to stop it.

> **Common Nutrient Deficiencies**
> The malnutrition cycle sets alcoholics up for multiple nutrient deficiencies. Some of the most common nutrient deficiencies caused by alcohol include B vitamins (folate, thiamin, B6), fat-soluble vitamins (A, D, E, K), and the minerals calcium, selenium, iron, and zinc. Much of this is due to the dysfunctional relationships of these nutrients with the alcohol soaked liver.

Let's Talk about Your Liver

Ask anyone "What does the liver do?" and the immediate answer is something to the effect of "It acts as a filter." While this is certainly true, it is only part of the truth. The liver is the original multitasker. In addition to neutralizing drugs (both legal and illegal), contaminants, and other unwanted substances that have found their way into your bloodstream, the liver serves many other vital functions. Among these is the production of lymph (another of the body's waste disposal systems), recycling iron from red blood cells, the synthesis of immune and clotting factors, and, most important to our current discussion: its role as a nutritional clearinghouse. The liver is where fats, proteins, and carbohydrates are broken down, stored, re-synthesized, and sent out to do their respective tasks. Vitamins A and D are activated in the liver. Bile is formed and sent to the gallbladder. Cholesterol is manufactured. It's all happening in the liver. But here's the rub: Its job of filtering trumps everything else. So when we give the liver lots to do when it comes to filtering the blood, its work on these other functions slack. This results in inefficient use of the nutrients you are consuming, compromised immune function, muscle wasting, anemia, low energy, increased risk of heart disease, and osteoporosis.

Alcohol as the Spoiled Brat of Nutrition

Although the stomach breaks down some alcohol (with alcohol dehydrogenase, or AD), most is dealt with by the liver, the body's main source of this enzyme. (Remember: If it ends in *-ase*, it's an enzyme.) Once in circulation, alcohol gets preferential treatment by the liver, demanding to be quickly absorbed. When the amount of alcohol in our system exceeds the liver's production of AD (it can detoxify about ½ ounce per hour), the alcohol continues to circulate, wreaking havoc in its path.

Alcohol is used in disinfectant cleaners because of its ability to dissolve the fatty membranes of living cells, murdering microbes by splitting open their cell membranes. Nondiscriminatory, alcohol does the same to human tissues. An intermediate step in alcohol breakdown is the formation of acetaldehyde (a.k.a. vinegar). While this also waits to be metabolized to a safely excreted compound, it continues to circulate in the bloodstream, pickling all in its path. In the process it also changes the liver structure, leading to fatty liver. So it is this cell destruction, organ pickling, and the structural changes to the liver that account for much of the damage done by alcohol.

The metabolism of alcohol overtakes other metabolic processes for various vitamin-requiring transactions. This disrupts the body's acid-base balance and energy pathways, creating a cascade of fiascos in its wake, including disruptions in fat synthesis, nutrient and oxygen distribution, glucose production, protein synthesis, hydration, etc. Metabolism of other prescribed drugs may slow as well. All this, plus the insidious changeover from healthy liver tissue to fatty liver tissue—and possibly on to cirrhosis and fibrosis—compromise the body's ability to efficiently metabolize most nutrients. The result is malnutrition, even when ample nutrients are consumed.

Road to Recovery

The moment you stopped drinking was the moment your body began to heal. Although timing is individual and depends on how much you drank, how long you drank, and your unique genetic makeup, you can expect to see positive changes over the first days, weeks, and months.

Your face will become less puffy, your skin will clear, any yellowish tinge should recede, and you will lose the bags under your eyes. Your eyes will brighten as the red of bloodshot evaporates. Some people even report improvement in eyesight! You will feel less bloated as edema disappears.

After the initial unpleasantness of withdrawal, your mind will clear. You will feel brighter and be less prone to mood swings, anxiety, and depression as your neurotransmitters kick in, more brain cells are produced, and your brain recovers from the physical changes caused by alcohol.

Your digestive system will be a lot happier as alcohol-related reflux, acid indigestion, and diarrhea retreat. Your blood test results will normalize as liver enzymes and blood lipids (such as cholesterol), blood sugar, and markers of anemia come back into balance. Blood pressure should also stabilize. Other positive reports have included lower levels of overall pain, less hot flashes in menopausal women, and improvement in sleep patterns. In summary, your sobriety will bring you more healthier and happier years. And the longer you are in recovery, the more time your body will have to recuperate from the damaging effects of alcohol. So it's important

to every aspect of your health to *stay* in recovery.

So, What Can Diet Do for Me?

Diet—along with continued abstinence from alcohol, and getting outside treatment, support, and exercise—can help to repair the damage and set the stage for future health. We *all* need protein, vitamins, minerals, and even some fat to maintain our bodies' integrity and keep the machinery running well—but in recovery these things become even more important. Eating well supplies the nutrients you have been missing to restore your gut and get your body and mind back into shape. All the stuff that makes up your body and the substances responsible for chemical reactions, from digestion to nerve impulses, is made from the raw materials of your food. So good food equals a stronger, healthier body that operates at its best and has the resources it needs to repair physical damage from alcohol abuse.

What you eat also affects your emotions via neurotransmitters and blood sugar levels. Learning what, when, and how to eat can optimize your mental and emotional health and can play an important role in preventing and resisting triggers and cravings. Another vital building block of successful recovery is self-image and self-motivation. In recovery, you have the opportunity to discover healthier ways of being in the world that are consonant with your sobriety. A healthy lifestyle includes a commitment to exercise, healthy emotional relationships, and sober leisure time activities. Consuming a healthy diet completes the picture, complementing and supporting your new overall healthy lifestyle.

How to Use This Book

Just as addiction education is needed to learn relapse-prevention strategies, nutrition education is vital to implementing dietary strategies supportive of recovery. This book's sidebars aim to answer the "everything you always wanted to know about nutrition but were afraid to ask" questions that I've heard directly from people in recovery. You've already seen some basic ways in which alcohol contributes to malnutrition, but the rest of the book will concentrate on teaching you specific approaches to improving your nutritional status and increasing the effectiveness of your recovery, day-by-day.

Chapter 2, Recovery Diet Goals, outlines the essential objectives of *The Recovery Diet* and practical guidelines for achieving these goals. No matter where you are in recovery, these goals will be the foundation of your new nutritional beginning. Replenishing nutrients by eating nutrient-dense foods helps your body and mind to recover and operate at their best. Supporting a

positive emotional state by paying attention to timing and quality of intake serves helpings of relapse prevention. Viewing diet as part of your overall healthy lifestyle seals the deal, securing your place at the sober dining table.

Chapter 3, Eating to Manage Common Medical Concerns, arms you with information about medical problems you may be facing and how to leverage nutrition to tilt the scales in favor of optimum health outcomes. Even if you're not dealing with any of these concerns now, you'll find plenty of information about how to head off some of these conditions in early stages and how to help friends and family who are. Use the information in this section along with data from your lab work, blood pressure readings, and blood glucose monitoring to track your progress. Remember: It is vital to communicate with your health care provider to tweak doses of medications as lifestyle changes decrease or negate the need for drugs. **The advice in this book cannot and should not replace the individualized advice and instruction of your health care provider.**

In Chapter 4, Putting It All Together in the Kitchen, you'll find practical strategies to reinforce what you've learned about eating well—from market to stove to table. You'll learn how to navigate the food market and restaurants. You'll get advice on how to set up your kitchen and learn basic food preparation skills so you can easily nourish yourself with great tasting food that is supportive of your recovery. Along the way you'll be encouraged to take charge of this important aspect of your life. Choose strategies that resonate for you first, and as you master those, you will gain confidence in the kitchen and move on to other strategies that at first may have seemed more challenging.

In Chapter 5, Recipes for Recovery, you'll get down to brass tacks and make concrete menu plans, both easy and elegant, familiar and innovative. Twelve weeks of menus—complete with healthy recipes—will be there any time you're in need of guidance and inspiration. Let these be a jumping off point for your own creativity.

CHAPTER 2

Recovery Diet Goals

When setting out on a journey it is helpful to know your destination. To have a vision of how things would be if they were "just right" helps a vision become reality. So envision yourself in successful recovery: You look younger, feel physically vital, are free of cravings, emotionally confident, and have a pervasive sense of well-being.

Over the years I've found that the three main goals set out in this chapter lay out a path that has worked for many people in recovery. You may want to add some goals of your own, such as controlling your weight, feeling more energetic, managing health concerns such as diabetes and hypertension, improving your complexion, and so on. But, in the end, you will likely find that those goals fit under the three biggies, which are: Replenishing nutrients, managing moods with foods (to keep yours on an even keel), and considering your diet as part of an overall healthy lifestyle.

Goal No. 1: Replenish Nutrients, Reverse Damage

Depending on how far into recovery you are, you may be feeling "out of sorts." The "liquid diet" may have supplied calories but is notable for being totally devoid of useful nutrients (the idea that beer is full of B vitamins is nonsense). In addition, the process of metabolizing alcohol requires B vitamins, while alcohol intake—along with inactivity—works to accelerate muscle breakdown and protein losses. Nothing in, lots used up, adds up to depletion of nutrients. Plus, if the diet also consisted of the typical fast-food, overprocessed standard American diet, it didn't exactly contain a treasure trove of nutrients.

Now that you're in recovery, you should concentrate on replenishing the nutrients your body needs and reversing the damage done, especially to your GI tract and nervous system. Eating well is your best revenge on the scourges of alcohol. Selecting foods high in nutrients and avoiding "empty calories" can restore your system to optimum functioning.

How It Works

For optimum recovery, strive to be the optimal you! When you are at your best cognitively, you stand to gain the most from addiction education classes. When your mind is clearer, you are more likely to be open to insight and less prone to impulsivity. When your emotions are on an even keel you are less prone to mood swings and those low emotional spaces that may serve as triggers. This is the bedrock of successful recovery. So while eating well may not make you as smart as Einstein, as even-tempered as the Dalai Lama, or as buff and healthy as Serena Williams, it can go a long way in helping you fulfill your optimum physical, mental, and emotional potential.

Good nutrition affects everything about you, structurally and functionally. To be at your best requires good-quality raw materials. As an adult, you may think that your body is fully formed, when in fact your body is continually being broken down and rebuilt. Skin sloughs off, bones demineralize, red blood cells die, hormones, enzymes, and neurotransmitters are used up in reactions, and the list goes on. This will all happen, regardless of what you do. But what you do on the other end really impacts your health. To create new cells, re-mineralize bones, and keep up with the steady need for building materials and regulating chemical compounds—all those little things that make such a big difference—the raw materials needed to make these up must be supplied in sufficient quantities in the foods you eat every day. If this all works the way it should some say that every seven years we are an entirely new person with a whole new set of body cells!

To take on this goal, you'll need to start making crucial decisions about the quality of your food—and learn how to make every bite count. Your main strategy is to eat a variety of nutrient-dense foods. The vitamins, minerals, and phytochemicals in these foods will facilitate the process of bodily repair and preventative maintenance of the optimum you.

Nutrient Dense, Your Best Defense

In order to help define our terms, visualize a gooey, chewy, chocolate-covered candy bar alongside a bowl of steamed collard greens. The candy bar has approximately 300 calories, a lot of fat and sugar, but is low to nil on vitamins, minerals, and protein. A cup of fresh cooked collards has approximately 50 calories, no fat (assuming it wasn't cooked with fatback), lots of vitamin C, vitamin A, calcium, iron, fiber, a little bit of protein—all things that your body needs and loves.

"Nutrient density" refers to the amount of nutrients per calorie. The candy bar is a nutritional bust—lots of empty calories. The collard greens, on the other hand, deliver a multitude of good nutrients at a relatively small caloric "cost." When we choose nutrient-dense foods, such as fruits and vegetables, whole grains and beans, we maximize the availability of nutrients to rebuild, nourish, and support our body's structure and function. Other "five-star" vegetables include most greens (kale, collards, turnip greens) as well as sweet potatoes, broccoli, carrots, winter squashes, and tomatoes. Excellent fruit choices include berries, melons, citrus fruits, papaya, and apricots. But honestly, any fruit or vegetable wins hands down against any bag of chips, cookies, doughnuts, or candy.

Focus on the Real B Vitamins

B vitamins include several water-soluble substances that provide a variety of vital functions in sort of an "assist on the serve" manner. As part of coenzymes, they are indispensable to energy production, protein metabolism, and cell division.

The B vitamin most prescribed in recovery is folate (a.k.a. folic acid or folacin). In adults, it is necessary for cell division. Therefore, its lack is most noticeable in places where there is relatively rapid cell turnover such as the epithelial cells that line the digestive tract and red blood cells (which have a three-month life span). Chronic alcohol abuse causes major folate deficiency as the liver is unable to retain it. This deficiency in turn decimates the GI system, rendering it less able to absorb

nutrients, contributing mightily to severe malnutrition. As you focus on replenishing and repairing, remember to add fol*ate* to your diet through fol*iage*. (Hear the similarity in the word? It's a great mnemonic device!) Leafy greens such as collards, kale, and bok choy are excellent choices, as are beans, peas, lentils, and seeds.

This inability to absorb nutrients leads to another well-known deficiency: thiamin (also known as vitamin B1). Thiamin is present in most foods but is lost when foods are preprocessed and packaged (a good example is brown versus white rice). Heavy alcohol users lose thiamin in their urine. Thiamin is necessary for energy metabolism in all the body's cells, especially nerve cells. In its most advanced state, thiamin deficiency leads to Wernicke-Korsakoff syndrome, a classic condition of long-term alcoholics characterized by poor muscle coordination, damaged nerves, and impaired memory. Good sources of thiamin are as varied as pork, soymilk, watermelon, green peas, acorn squash, and fortified cereals.

Vitamin B6 (or pyridoxine), also destroyed by alcohol, is of particular interest in recovery due to its role in the synthesis of the neurotransmitter serotonin, which helps in the regulation of mood, appetite, and sleep. While some people use it to treat carpal tunnel and other nerve problems, large doses of vitamin B6 may be toxic. Dietary sources are easy to come by; it's found in green leafy vegetables, whole grains, purple fruits, bananas, as well as most meats, fish, and poultry.

Phytochemicals Are Your Friends

"Phyto" is Greek for "plant." These bioactive compounds, naturally found in plant foods, literally "fight" off ill health by inserting themselves in reactions in our body's systems. While we are going about our lives, phytochemicals are busy lowering blood pressure, fighting off cancers, boosting our immune function, and saving our lives. More than 900 phytochemicals have been discovered in recent years, mostly in brightly colored fruits and vegetables. For example, various carotenoids (a family of phytochemicals), found in carrots, sweet potatoes, spinach, cantaloupe, and others, may help to slow the aging process, improve lung function, reduce cataracts and macular degeneration, and reduce the incidence of some cancers. Other phytochemical families have been shown to fight cavities, decrease tumor formation, dissolve gallstones, lower cholesterol, reduce symptoms of menopause and allergies, inhibit blood clots . . . the list goes on. Learning about phytochemicals helps us to understand why it's not good to get into a vegetable "rut"—each plant food has its own unique complement of phytochemicals. By including a variety of plant foods—richly colored fruits and vegetables, nuts, seeds, fresh herbs, green tea, whole grains, soy and other beans—you

increase your odds of allowing them to protect your health.

> **Cooked or Raw?**
>
> People often ask: Is it better to eat vegetables cooked or raw? The answer is "yes!" It is best to eat a variety of vegetables prepared in a variety of ways. While cooking may destroy some nutrients, by breaking down thick fibrous walls it also renders other nutrients more accessible. Also, just as heat affects chemical reactions in a lab, it changes some of those phytochemicals to slightly different forms. For example, cooked, not raw, tomatoes are associated with a reduced incidence of prostate cancer in men.

Goal No. 2: Manage Moods with Foods

Steady blood sugar levels are vital to recovery. Your body wants them to obey the "Goldilocks Theory"—not too high, not too low; the ideal is "just right." When your blood sugar spikes high or dips low, you open the door to a whole host of problems—and triggers.

Your body does its best to regulate your blood sugar level on its own. The food you eat is broken down into simple sugars and absorbed through the intestinal wall into your bloodstream. As blood sugar rises, the hormone insulin is secreted from the pancreas to usher blood sugar into the body's cells, especially the brain, where it serves as fuel. Thus the concentration of blood glucose stays relatively constant, and all is well. When you don't eat for a while, the supply of glucose in your bloodstream is depleted and you end up with low blood sugar, or hypoglycemia. How you react will vary depending on your body chemistry, but the symptoms of hypoglycemia will always wreak havoc on your mood. You may feel depressed, irritable, sleepy, and uninspired. You'll have a harder time handling problems as they arise, and you'll be more likely to use emotional and mental crutches to get by. These symptoms are your body's way of screaming "I need energy!"

You can't just solve a low blood sugar problem by feasting on a few doughnuts and a super sweet coffee. Eating lots of sugar all at once will cause your blood sugar to rise rapidly. Your body will respond quickly, and your pancreas will send in a flood of insulin to manage the sugar. While the insulin is trying to do its job, you'll feel the "buzz" and may even get the jitters. But this spike is always followed by a precipitous drop in blood sugar. It won't be long before you're feeling tired, sluggish, and depressed again. This rollercoaster will leave you mentally, emotionally, and physically exhausted.

It doesn't help that you're particularly susceptible to these crashes. Alcohol is a type of sugar, so your body likely understands blood sugar swings well. (You may feel like the spikes and dips are like a familiar old hat, but don't be fooled.) Staving off one kind of craving by feeding another will just keep you running in circles instead of moving forward through recovery.

On top of the physiological problems, don't forget that your mood will involuntarily swing with your blood sugar. In the past, you may have used alcohol as a way to extricate yourself from this negative space, but that is no longer an option!

There are ways to avoid these negative, biochemically induced states of high and low blood sugar. Follow these simple food rules and plan your diet to eliminate triggers to avoid cravings.

Glycemic Index

The glycemic index (GI) is a means of measuring the effects of various carbohydrate-containing foods on blood sugar levels. The concept and GI ratings were originally developed by Dr. David Jenkins and colleagues in the '80s to be applied to diabetic patients. Since that time studies have revealed high GI foods to be a risk factor for atherosclerosis (hardening of the arteries), macular degeneration (a major cause of blindness in the elderly), kidney disease, and obesity, as well as diabetes. In general, most fruits, vegetables, whole grains, beans, and nuts are low GI foods, while processed foods, such as white bread, cornflakes, and sugar, are high GI foods. In actual practice, blood sugar depends on the amounts and mix of foods we eat. For example, fiber and fat slow absorption, thus lowering GI.

White Versus Sweet Potatoes

Potatoes are ubiquitous; they're baked, fried, mashed, added to soups, stews, casseroles—they are everywhere. Unfortunately, white potatoes have a high glycemic index (raising your blood sugar more quickly than foods with a lower glycemic index), not a whole lot to offer nutritionally, and also tend to inspire fatty add-ons. Sweet potatoes, although similar to their white relatives in calories, protein, and fiber, count among those "superfoods": they have a much lower glycemic index and are chock full of beta carotene, vitamin C, and phytochemicals. My suggestion: Replace those whites with sweets. Leftover baked sweet potatoes can even be a convincing palliative for sweet tooth cravings.

Don't Get Hungry!

The standard Alcoholics Anonymous adage "HALT" (don't get Hungry, Angry, Lonely, Tired) has truth to it, but the solution for remediating hunger is not candy. Eating regular, healthy meals and snacks keeps your blood sugar level and helps you avoid unnecessary mood swings. What does this mean in real life? Just as you plan ahead for relapse prevention—avoiding or role-playing in advance of dicey, triggering situations—you can practice dietary relapse prevention, forestalling low blood sugar by planning to have appropriate food available when needed. (The meal plans in Chapter 5 are a great way to get started!)

When It Comes to Carbohydrates, Get Complex

Carbohydrates can be simple (candy and other sweets, including presweetened cereals) or complex (think brown rice, oats, pasta). Carbohydrates can also be high in fiber (think whole wheat bread, vegetables) or low in fiber (white bread, "minute" white rice). These two variables determine how a food will affect your blood sugar. Simple carbohydrates require only minimal processing by your body and basically pour sugar straight into your bloodstream; complex carbohydrates make your body work for the energy. Fiber helps "cushion" the effects of both types of sugar. Therefore, choosing more complex, higher fiber carbohydrates slows down the process, giving you more of a sustained release effect. You'll have more steady, sustained energy over a longer period of time, without the lift-off and let-down of spiking and crashing blood sugar levels.

Eat Regular Meals and Snacks

Timing is every bit as important as content—make sure you eat something healthy every three to four hours.

1. **Breakfast.** You're busy. You like to sleep late. You're not hungry in the morning. But your excuses just won't cut it if you're serious about controlling your blood sugar! Breakfast can be easy, and—if you plan it right—will give

your blood sugar levels solid footing for the rest of the day. Breakfast doesn't have to be fancy, complicated, or time-consuming. Indeed, a bowl of high fiber cereal and low-fat milk (or soymilk) with some fresh fruit provides you with all you need to be at your best for several hours. Just be sure to have a bit of protein (milk, soymilk, cheese, egg, or nut butter) and some complex carbohydrates (whole wheat bread or bagel, hot or cold whole grain cereal), and both your blood sugar and brain chemistry will be grateful and happy. Need more motivation? Studies have revealed that eating breakfast is one of the key habits associated with living a long, healthy life. Each breakfast is an investment in your future, so take it seriously!

2. **Lunch.** Many of us are at work, on the road, meeting deadlines, too busy to eat, at the mercy of vending machines or fast-food joints, feel social pressure to eat out with coworkers at places we'd rather not frequent, or (fill in the blank with your own excuse). But again, let's do lunch—simply. Consider your "relapse prevention lunch bag"—what can you put in it? This will be somewhat determined by whether or not you have a place to reheat food. In either case, be sure to include some vegetables, whole grains, and some lean protein. The possibilities are endless: Leftovers from the previous evening's healthy dinner (plan for leftovers and always cook extra), a hearty sandwich, a homemade burrito, a fresh salad, a healthy frozen meal . . . the sky's the limit! If you are eating out, you can arm yourself with sober ways of navigating a restaurant menu (more on this in Chapter 4).

3. **Dinner.** I know, you've had a hard day at work and just want to have an instant dinner and relax, but your relapse prevention, delicious, nutritious dinner can be on the table in less than 20 minutes (with some minor kitchen and mindset reorganization). We'll delve into the details of how to do this in later chapters.

4. **Between-meal snacks.** Just in case the time between your meals is long enough for low blood sugar to sneak in, be proactive. People in recovery, especially if they've also quit smoking, tend to want to put something in their mouth to nibble and chew. Some ideas for easy, healthy snacks to have on hand include a piece of fresh fruit, a slice of juicy melon, a handful of unsalted nuts, a glass of diluted juice, a low-sugar yogurt, and whole grain crackers with nut butter or preserves. If weight gain is a concern, aim for the low-calorie choices, such as fresh fruit, and go easy on the nuts and juices. Either way, stick to the nutrient dense options and keep the chips and cookies out of sight.

5. **Choose decaffeinated beverages.** I know you're thinking, "No, anything but that!" But consider that caffeine has similar effects to sugar: after every lift-off there's a letdown. By using caffeine to provide the "up" that would more naturally come from adequate sleep, exercise, and nourishment, you are destined to come back "down" again when the caffeine wears off. You may also become prey to an old pattern: calming your hyper-excitable caffeinated state with alcohol. The other downside of caffeine is that it is a diuretic (it causes you to urinate more), which can lead to dehydration. These effects hold true regardless of your caffeine of choice, whether you get it from coffee, iced tea, or massive amounts of diet soda. So what's left to drink?

The ideal hydrator is water—good old fashioned H2O. There is a wide variety of herbal, non-caffeinated teas on the market (some of which are coffee-like) that can be enjoyed hot or cold. An excellent stand-in for soda is the natural "spritzer": Mix ⅓ glass juice (100 percent juice, not juice cocktail or "juice drink") and fill the rest with seltzer water (which is simply carbonated water). This satisfies your desire for sweet and fizzy without the sugar, caffeine, or artificial sweeteners. Plus you get a few good vitamins from the juice!

Sports Drinks and Hydration

Dehydration is dangerous. But unless you are a professional athlete, plying your trade under the hot sun, sweating quarts at a time, the hydrating beverage of choice is water. Sports drinks contain calories, sodium, sugar, and artificial flavorings—none of which support you in reclaiming your health. To improve the drinkability of water, add a squeeze of lemon or a small amount of real fruit juice.

Goal No. 3: Diet as Part of a Healthy Lifestyle

A colleague of mine on the substance abuse rehabilitation team often says, "It's hard to eat wheat germ for breakfast and snort cocaine for dinner." You understand the mindset: Once you are doing something healthy and wholesome, other healthy, wholesome activities tend to follow. Recovery is a time to develop a whole new constellation of sober habits, one reinforcing the other, all working to seal recovery. Diet is a pivotal element among these habits. Healthy food is emblematic of a healthy lifestyle. The folks who eat at fast-food "restaurants" are not usually the portraits of good health. By choosing to eat in a way that optimizes your health, you are saying to yourself and others that you value your life enough to nourish yourself properly. It's an overall healthy lifestyle package deal: sobriety, exercise, honest relationships, reconnecting with nature, art, your highest values, service to others—and healthy diet!

Is "Diet" a Four-Letter Word?

For some of us the word "diet" has a huge, negative charge. The original meaning simply refers to what you regularly eat. But it's taken on the connotation of adhering to a restrictive menu plan, most commonly for the purpose of losing weight. To most people, being "on a diet" feels like being in prison. And prisons are places from which you want to bust out. So using the word "diet" may not bode well for encouraging most people to follow a plan. I'd like to suggest a bit of cognitive reframing (a fancy term for changing the way you think about something) What if a diet was your chariot of liberation? The freely chosen means for getting you where you want to be? That is my perception of diet: by making certain food choices you can free yourself from disease, gain control over your health and environment, fulfill your potential, feel the way you prefer to feel, even make a political statement. I'm hoping that by the time you finish reading this book, the word "diet" will have taken on new meaning for you.

Food Groups as Your Roadmap to Health

By eating a variety of foods, you not only succeed in replenishing nutrients but bring your diet and yourself back into balance. Once you become friendly with these major food categories, you'll be well on your way to making better food choices in recovery and adopting a healthy diet for life.

- **Grains.** Whole grains are an excellent source of fiber as well as *beaucoup* B vitamins and trace minerals, which are needed for replenishing and keeping your neurotransmitters in happy mode, and are the essence of those complex "sustained-release" carbohydrates. Focus on a variety of whole grains for best glycemic control. Our standard grains in the United States are wheat and corn. If you haven't yet, expand your horizons to encompass brown rice, quinoa (actually a seed), oats, millet, barley, spelt, buckwheat, and all their grainy relatives.

- **Fruits and Vegetables.** Fruits and vegetables are the sources of the vitamins that keep you healthy—vitamins C and A—plus a variety of other vitamins, minerals, fiber, and phytochemicals, all of which are needed for optimum health. Vegetables, in general, are more nutrient dense than fruits.

- **Dairy Products.** These foods obviously include milk, cheese, and yogurt. All are rich in protein, calcium, and riboflavin. But a simple comparison of caution: A cup of whole milk has 150 calories; a cup of skim milk has only 90 calories. It adds up. Also, an ounce of Cheddar cheese has about 200 mg of sodium, while a cup of cottage cheese has more than 900 mg sodium. For optimum health, choose the low- or non-fat versions and use high-sodium cheeses sparingly. Also keep in mind that if you are lactose intolerant or vegan, there are plenty of other ways to meet your calcium requirements without using dairy products (see Chapter 3).

- **Protein.** This group includes beans, nuts, eggs, fish and poultry, and, of course, beef and pork. The nuts and beans are good sources of soluble fiber—and none of the other foods in this category can make that claim! And beans (except soy) are virtually fat-free! A handful of nuts a day is good for lowering triglycerides and providing useful nutrients and phytochemicals. If you do eat meat, be sure to choose low-fat, leaner cuts of meat, trim all visible fat (including poultry skin), and opt for low-fat cooking methods such as baking, broiling, grilling, and boiling instead of frying.

- **Fats and Oils.** Are these frowned-upon foods really necessary for well-rounded nutrition? Yes, healthy fats are vital, but in moderation. We need some fat and oil in our diet to ensure membrane integrity, absorb fat-soluble vitamins, build hormones, give us a bit of a cushion (it would hurt to sit on bare bones), and for some energy storage. There is a more thorough discussion of "good" versus "bad" fats in Chapter 3, but regardless of the type of fat, they all contain nine calories per gram, so use sparingly. Better ways to use your fat "quota" include the aforementioned nuts and seeds, as well as avocados, olives, and olive oil.

- **Sweets.** Yes, they are up there—the peak experience atop the old Food Pyramid. The occasional treat is truly unnecessary, but oh so much fun! So while sweets don't fit your nutrient-dense goals, and you are now aware of the peril of blood sugar seesawing, it's okay to indulge if you only eat sparingly. Dean Ornish, MD, in his book *Eat More, Weigh Less*, describes the "Häagen-Dazs meditation": Take just one bite of whatever constitutes your bliss, close your eyes, fully experience the feel of the food in your mouth, take your time, and savor it to the fullest.

Substance Substitution

Often people in recovery consume massive amount of sweets. The theory is that without alcohol your body "craves" sweets. But overdoing sweets can put recovery at peril by messing with your blood sugar levels. Solution: Plan ahead by eating regular nourishing meals and snacks. By including complex carbohydrates for sustained energy and fruits and sweet potatoes to satisfy your sweet cravings, you can reprogram your brain to appreciate food that feeds your body, not your impulses.

Spotlight on Fiber

Fiber is the Zen nutrient. Its quality of nothingness is what makes it so essential. Lacking the "sex appeal" of protein or vitamins, fiber is mostly the butt of bathroom humor, formerly referred to as mere "roughage." Yet, it is the single most important nutrient lacking the most in the American diet, which, if consumed in recommended amounts, can have the most beneficial effect. Dietary fiber can aid in the control of high cholesterol, blood sugar, and hypertension. Fiber intake is associated with a lower risk of most cancers, especially prostate and breast cancers. Low fiber intake is a risk factor for metabolic syndrome, a constellation of symptoms that includes abdominal obesity, blood lipid anomalies, high blood pressure, and poor blood sugar control. Due to fiber's nothingness in the calorie department, it has the ability to make you feel full with a minimum of calories, which can be very helpful when you are trying to lose weight. And, true to its roughage reputation, fiber does "keep America moving." Unfortunately, the average American consumes only less than half the daily recommendation for 20–40 grams of fiber, thanks to our highly processed ideas about food. White bread, white rice, meat, milk, cheese, eggs, and soda are not ideal sources—none contain an iota of fiber.

The most complicated thing about fiber is that there are two main types. Insoluble fiber—which, as its name implies, does not dissolve in water—is chiefly responsible for the "roughage" effects. Good sources of insoluble fiber include most whole grains and vegetables. Soluble fiber sponges up liquid to become pasty. Think oatmeal. This type of fiber takes most of the credit for the health benefits: controlling blood sugar and keeping cholesterol in check. Oats, barley, legumes, and fruits are all good examples of soluble fiber. Conveniently, foods that are high in fiber are more likely to be nutrient dense, so they are all excellent choices for your diet in recovery.

Here's how to increase your fiber intake:

1. Start slow and increase little by little. Do not go from eating no beans to eating two cups of beans overnight, as you may suffer a bit of discomfort.
2. Modify snacks. Change from eating processed foods to fruit, whole grain muffins, or homemade trail mix.
3. Change some of your usual foods to high fiber versions. Try whole wheat pasta and bread as well as brown rice.
4. Add high fiber foods such as vegetables, beans, and whole grains to your usual dishes of casseroles, soups, and salads. For example, add oatmeal to your meatloaf, barley to your soup, and chickpeas to green salad.
5. Graduate to meals based on high fiber foods such as bean dishes, high fiber breakfast cereals, and ethnic cuisines, such as Cuban (black beans and rice),

Indian (millet and lentils), Italian (polenta), and Greek (whole wheat couscous and white beans).

Remember: If you are taking medications for diabetes or blood pressure, be sure to monitor yourself for changes that might call for a decrease in dosage.

OMG: Omega-3 Fatty Acids

Omega-3 fatty acids are a subset of polyunsaturated fats and a hot topic of recent research. Found in fatty fish, flaxseeds, walnuts, and canola oil, omega-3s have been found to protect against heart disease and hypertension, aid depression, and reduce pain and inflammation, especially in arthritis. Medical experts also link the American diet's imbalance of omega-6 fatty acids (found in soybeans, corn oil, and all our fried foods) versus omega-3s with an increased risk for cardiovascular disease, cancer, diabetes, and neurodegenerative disease—further reason to replace soy and corn oils with olive and canola oils. Ground flaxseeds can be baked into breads, sprinkled into hot cereal and yogurt, and mixed with water to make a great substitute for eggs in baking.

Real Food for Real People

We live in a pill-popping culture. Whether it's the sniffles, too much weight, not enough sleep, or high blood pressure—there's a pill to solve your problem. Some people ask, why bother eating a healthy diet? Can't I just take a multivitamin with 100 percent of what I need, relax about the food, go out, and eat candy bars? Sorry, but there are no shortcuts. Supplements contain only those vitamins and minerals that our human minds have discovered over the past century. We don't know what we don't know yet. Also, vitamin supplements do not contain protein, fiber, and numerous other substances we do know are required in our diets.

Some advocate megadoses of particular nutrients in recovery; however, this can upset the metabolism of other nutrients and perpetuates the pill-popper mindset. In natural diets, vitamins and minerals come from varied foods in certain proportions that are exactly what our bodies need. This is why, for recovery, we recommend a nutrient-dense diet of *real* foods, plus a good, one-a-day type multivitamin-mineral supplement, and other supplements only as prescribed for serious deficiencies.

Take Time to Enjoy Your Meals

As part of embracing your new healthy lifestyle, it's essential that you slow down when it comes to food. Many Americans spend mealtimes alone, often chowing down a TV dinner aptly in front of the television. When they get up from the meal, still feeling hungry, they head back to the fridge, maybe the freezer, still wanting something to fill an empty space. What's happening is that when we wolf down our food, distracted from the full experience of the meal, we may barely recognize that we've eaten. Many of us have been trained to eat fast: to quickly refuel and move on to the next item on our "to-do" list, and the rest of our busy, busy lives. But this is hardly satisfying.

When you take time to enjoy your meal, it fills you up in countless ways. You've probably heard the axiom that it takes twenty minutes for our brain to figure out that our stomach is full. If you take only seven minutes to eat a normal plate of food, you run the chance of overshooting your calorie quota in the remaining thirteen minutes.

There is also the issue of chewing. Eating quickly obviates chewing, and chewing is necessary for ideal digestion and enhancing the nutritive value you derive from your food. Also, as you can see, food is more than the sum total of its biochemical parts. Food is imbued with infinite social, familial, emotional, cultural, and spiritual meanings. "Refueling" fails to capture the breadth of these qualities. When we eat in a more mindful manner, food tastes better, we feel more satisfied, and our food is actually better for us.

The Famous "Grape Meditation"

Becoming aware of the multiple meanings of food in our lives enhances our experience of food. We have been using the guided "grape meditation" in our residential rehabilitation program for many years to explore the breadth of our relationships with food. (It all started with grapes, but sometimes we use blueberries, melon, or banana chunks, or whatever is seasonally available.) Here's how this works:

The grapes are meant to represent all foods; have a minimum of seven available for this exercise. Start with a basic relaxation technique: Sit in a comfortable position, feet on the floor, legs and arms uncrossed, gently close your eyes, take some deep breaths allowing your breath to deepen, sending healing energy to relax your body. You will be eating four grapes, each representing a different aspect of your life: physical, emotional, mental, and spiritual.

Take the first grape, place it in the palm of one hand, and try to get a sense of the physical qualities of the grape. Quietly note its shape, temperature, texture, and other physical characteristics. Do the same as you put the grape in your mouth and allow yourself to "play with your food." Very slowly bite into, chew, and then swallow the grape. Make sure you fully experience the grape on the physical plane. Note anything that you may not have noticed before while eating a grape. Try to get a sense of how the grape incorporates into your body, how its nutrients are sent out to do their healing duties. Ask yourself: "How does what I eat affect how I feel physically? How does how I feel physically affect what and how I eat?"

Repeating this for the "emotional grape," make note of any feelings that arise: family associations, love, guilt, remorse, innocence. Try to get a sense of how the foods you eat affect your emotional state and conversely, how your emotional state affects what and how you eat.

With the third "mental" grape, consider this: What do we know about grapes? Food in general? How does what we eat affect our cognition and intellectual functioning? How does what we know about food affect what and how we eat?

At this point, you may want to return to your breath, recenter, and relax for a moment. Now it is time for the "spiritual" grape. Pay attention to any sense of connection to the divine that arises: gratitude, trust, forgiveness, transcendence. Ask yourself: "How might what I eat and how I eat it affect my spiritual being? How does where I'm at spiritually affect what foods I eat and how I eat them?"

Now, almost at the end, recognize that despite these different aspects of your life and your relationship with food, you are one non-compartmentalized, integrated, whole person: being, feeling, knowing, and divine. With this intention, slowly consume any remaining pieces of fruit, consolidating the thoughts and feelings that arose for you during this exercise. Take a few centering breaths, open your eyes, and return to this planet, bringing with you the fruits of this experience.

Volunteering in Food-Related Activities

One way of becoming more present around food is to combine diet and service to those less fortunate than yourself. Every community has homeless shelters, soup kitchens, and food banks. If you can't easily find one of these programs or organizations, call your local United Way agency for referrals. Such programs are always in need of extra pairs of hands. The work may range from cooking to serving, sorting cans, or driving to deliver meals. Your service goes miles further when performed with a smile.

By participating in these types of programs you will truly understand the oft-quoted "To give is better than to receive." One year our clients, as a group, still in residential rehab, opted to spend Thanksgiving Day serving dinner at a homeless shelter. Even while being so financially and emotionally broken themselves, it allowed them to experience gratitude for how far they had come.

Creating New Food Memories

As part of your new healthy lifestyle you can create new happy and healthy food experiences. Preparing and sharing food with friends can be a therapeutic, tasty, and fun way to overcome isolation and try out your new culinary skills. Plan a weekend brunch for new friends. Organize a potluck dinner. Meet friends at an outdoor concert with gourmet picnic baskets to share. Invite friends over for a sushi rolling party. Sharing good conversation with sober partners over nourishing food is a treasure. Be in awe at the power of food to bring people together and create new and joyful memories that encourage love, support, and healing.

A note of caution: While food can be part of healthy leisure time activities, do not let food become the total focus of these experiences, or a new obsession.

Edible Spirituality

Every religion has food-related rituals. A simple grace over the meal allows you to connect with your Higher Power—whatever that may be—three times day. Eating foods with spiritual meaning such as Catholic Communion, the symbolic foods of Passover, Moslem Eid, or Hindu Prasad literally internalizes spiritual lessons. Conceiving of your body as a holy temple, a vehicle with which to serve the Divine, almost guarantees a certain level of dietary mindfulness. Those who keep kosher, fast, consume a vegetarian diet, or any other dietary spiritual practice keep their spiritual path as close as their next meal. Some people create their own non-denominational rituals such as simply chewing the first bite of each meal as a grace, practicing mindfulness, or eating in silence. Such practices may reinforce your program of recovery by connecting you up with the Divine and creating community with like-minded people. Whatever works to fortify your recovery, do it!

CHAPTER 3

Eating to Manage Common Medical Concerns

As you saw in the first chapter, heavy alcohol use puts you at risk for a wide variety of medical conditions. This increased risk occurs as a result of how alcohol is processed by your body, the associated malnutrition, as well as your genetics and lifestyle factors, such as tobacco use and physical activity.

The beauty of dietary modification is that you can use it to manage an otherwise seemingly overwhelming medical condition in a deliciously simple manner. Diet is a radical approach in the true sense of the word. The Latin origin of "radical" is "root" (as in "radish"). Rather than going for symptomatic relief or putting a Band-Aid on the problem, with a healthy diet you often get to the root of the problem and heal it wholesale. For example, if you have hypertension or diabetes because you are overweight and you lose the weight, the "disease" often vanishes. In many cases, limiting sodium and increasing fiber can at least help to decrease drug dosages, thereby reducing your risk of unpleasant side effects (like erectile dysfunction). When making such dietary changes, be sure to continue self-monitoring blood sugars, blood pressure, or blood cholesterol (whatever applies to your situation) and consult with your physician before making any major changes in diet or medication.

Heart Disease and Hypertension

Despite all the press about AIDS and the dread over cancer, heart disease is still, far and away, the number one cause of death of Americans. The number of people dying due to hypertension alone is equivalent to one jumbo jet crashing each day (that's about 400 adults). Epidemiological studies (where large populations are compared) show that moderate and heavy alcohol drinkers have three to four times the frequency of strokes, coronary heart disease, and congestive heart failure as their non-alcoholic American counterparts.

The apparent mediator for these diseases in alcoholics is hypertension (a.k.a. high blood pressure). To understand hypertension, visualize your blood vessels as pipes made of elastic material. If these pipes are forced to carry more than the usual volume of fluid, the force of pressure on the walls of the pipes will increase. If the walls become brittle and inflexible, they may burst under the high pressure. The same might happen if the diameter of the pipe is narrowed due to buildup of waxy fats, which can happen with high cholesterol or if a blood clot blocks the way. When an insufficient amount of blood gets through the blood vessels to a specific body tissue, that tissue dies. If it is the heart muscle, this will cause chest pain, a heart attack, or ischemic stroke. If the blood vessel bursts in your brain it is called a hemorrhagic stroke. All can lead to permanent brain damage and/or death. Unchecked hypertension is also the leading cause of kidney disease.

Alcohol contributes to hypertension by affecting the production of hormones that control fluid balance and constriction of blood vessels. Alcohol-induced heart muscle disease may also lead to the formation of blood clots. Plus, the processing of alcohol by the liver results in an excess of circulating fatty acids. All these factors can be further complicated by lack of exercise and excess weight. Regular physical exercise helps keep blood vessels supple and able to withstand sudden changes in pressure.

Excess weight increases the burden on your heart and blood vessels.

Typically, your physician treats the symptoms of heart disease with an arsenal of medications: diuretics to shed excess fluid, beta-blockers to lower your blood pressure, statins to lower your cholesterol, blood thinners and aspirin to decrease your risk of blood clots, nitroglycerin to banish the pain of angina, and so on. If your arteries become severely blocked, a cardiovascular surgeon might perform bypass surgery. As you can well imagine, none of this in on the cheap, nor anyone's idea of a good time.

Actions You Can Take to Lower Your Blood Pressure

The good news is that there are a multitude of steps you can take to lower your risk for hypertension and heart disease. The first one is unrelated to dietary modification: If you're a smoker, quit. This is probably the single most effective lifestyle change you can make at this point in your life. There is not enough room here to recite the entire litany of tobacco-caused health maladies. Suffice to say that with every puff, nicotine constricts your blood vessels, driving up your blood pressure. This constriction results in poor circulation, which deprives body cells of their fair share of nutrients and other health-promoting substances. Also, cigarette smoke destroys vitamin

C, increasing your requirements for this nutrient.

Another seemingly non-diet-related factor is stress. Learning positive coping skills is vital to recovery as well as hypertension.

Dietary strategies for dealing with hypertension and heart disease are multipronged and include lowering dietary sodium and fat, increasing fiber and potassium, and above all, losing weight. Here, we'll look at the various dietary strategies.

Understanding Blood Pressure Readings

When you measure your blood pressure you get two numbers: the top one (systolic) is the pressure in your arteries as your heart contracts for a beat; the lower one (diastolic) is the pressure between beats, with the heart at rest. An accurate reading is best obtained after you have been sitting quietly for several minutes. The ideal blood pressure is 120/80 or below. Note that blood pressure generally rises with age due to stiffening of the arteries, so it's never too early to eat for prevention.

What Is Sodium and Where Do I Find It?

Sodium is a mineral our bodies need for fluid regulation, nerve transmission, and muscle contraction. Essentially, fluid follows sodium, so when blood sodium rises we get thirsty and also retain more fluid, leading to hypervolemia (excessive blood volume) and higher blood pressure. "Salt" is often used interchangeably with "sodium," but this isn't quite accurate. Table salt (a.k.a. "sodium chloride") is made up of only 40 percent sodium and actually has a greater effect on blood pressure than pure sodium.

Your body doesn't need much sodium—only 500 milligrams a day (less than a quarter of a teaspoon of salt). The major challenge is keeping your intake down to the American Heart Association's recommendation of 1,500 milligrams per day. Food in its natural state contains very little sodium. But processed food and fast-food restaurants make it easy for Americans to consume two, three, or even four times this amount. Even foods that don't taste salty—like white bread, Danish pastry, and Corn Flakes—contain surprisingly high amounts of sodium. My sense is that using a lot of salt often masks poor quality ingredients or betrays a lack of culinary prowess. Imagine the poor canned green bean: The process of heating canned foods up to very high temperatures to kill microorganisms surely renders the beans limp and tasteless. Salt to the rescue!

Of course you all know that perfectly healthy person who eats plenty of processed foods yet maintains a normal blood pressure. Evidently, some people are more sensitive to sodium than others, including alcoholics and, sorry to say, long-term alcoholics even after they are in recovery. Here are some ways to lower your sodium intake:

1. Taste your food before salting. I've seen people who automatically pour salt on everything on their plate. Taste it first! Maybe you'll find it tastes just fine without the salt.

2. Develop an awareness of how much salt you use. It's hard to see all those tiny grains once they're on your food. Shake the salt into the palm of your hand instead of directly onto your plate to get a clear visual of how much you're actually using.

3. Wean yourself. Salt is an acquired taste; we are not born with an appreciation of salty foods. Just as we have acquired the taste, we can lose the taste for salt by using other means of flavoring and gradually cutting back. Start by moving the salt shaker off the table.

4. Cut back on salt used in cooking. There is nothing magical about salt in rice, pasta, or hot cereal. You can just leave it out. The same thing goes for cakes and other recipes. Begin by halving, then cut out the salt all together.

5. Spice things up with herbs, spices, or lemon juice. Find recipes and experiment with new low-sodium main courses, vegetables, and grains. You'll find plenty to get you started in Chapter 5. You can also buy low- and no-sodium herbal blends such as Vegit, Mrs. Dash, and Frontier's salt-free curry and chili powders.

6. Read the nutrition facts label. This is your resource for discovering what is in your food. Compare sodium in similar products and you will discover, for example, that Shredded Wheat has 0 milligrams of sodium, compared to Corn Flakes, which has 260 milligrams of sodium. When doing this, pay attention to serving size: Ramen noodles lists nutrients for only half the seasoning packet!

7. Select fresh produce in season. Frozen is the next best. Canned vegetables should be used only as emergency provisions in your hurricane shelter. If you must buy canned foods, choose those marked "low-sodium" or "no salt added." Most canned foods, especially soups, are very high in sodium. Some, such as canned beans, can be drained and rinsed to vastly reduce the sodium content.

8. Limit intake of obviously salty condiments and foods. Soy sauce, bouillon, potato chips, processed meats, pickles, salad dressings, and sauerkraut all fall into that category.

9. At restaurants avoid dishes with dubious sauces, ask for the dressing on the side of the salad, and ideally, ask to have your food prepared without salt. This

works well at restaurants where your food is prepared fresh when you order it—such as in Chinese and most other Asian cuisines.

10. Balance your sodium levels within a day. If you do get caught by a barbecue, don't despair; merely eat lower-sodium foods for the rest of the day to average it out.

Deciphering Blood Lipids

A lipid profile can help determine your risk for heart disease by measuring different fats in your blood:

- Total cholesterol—best is < 200 mg/dL
- LDL (low density lipoproteins, a.k.a. "bad") cholesterol—the culprit in depositing waxy plaque in your arteries, best is < 130 mg/dL
- HDL (high density lipoprotein, a.k.a. "good") cholesterol—carries away LDL, clearing your arteries. Men should shoot for > 40 mg/dL, women > 50 mg/dL. Higher HDL is protective but alcohol can raise "HDL 2," giving a false sense of protection
- Triglycerides—another type of fat in the blood usually associated with eating excess calories and sweets. Keep it < 150 mg/dL

NOTE: Reference values may vary by laboratory.

Fight the Fat

Americans eat way too much fat, and it clogs arteries, widens waists, and promotes cancer and heart disease. So overall, the consensus is that collectively we need to cut down on dietary fats. But not all fats are created equal (see following sidebar). Calorically, they are all the same: 120 calories per tablespoon. Yes, even "light" olive oil and vegetable sprays. Americans consume approximately 35–40 percent of their total calories as fat. The American Heart Association recommends reducing this to 30 percent. Dr. Dean Ornish argues that no one has ever proved that 30 percent reverses heart disease, so he recommends a more prudent 20 percent.

Here are some guidelines for chewing less fat:

1. Use lower-fat cooking methods. Bake, steam, roast, grill, poach, or microwave foods. Stir-fry or sauté with a small amount of olive or canola oil. Air pop popcorn.
2. Prepare soups, stews, and gravies in advance, allow them to cool, and skim off the surface fat.
3. Create flavorful dishes with herbs and spices instead of high-fat gravies and cream sauces. Lighten your favorite recipes with the suggestions listed in Chapter 4.
4. Replace some or all of the oil in baking recipes with applesauce.

5. Use lower-fat versions of milk, cheese, yogurt, salad dressings, and frozen desserts.

6. Choose more meatless meals—beans and peas are virtually fat-free yet high in protein.

7. When you do eat meat, limit portions to 2–3 ounces, trim visible fat, and remove skin prior to cooking.

8. Read the labels! Compare absolute grams of fat.

9. Avoid trans fats altogether! Do not buy any product that lists "hydrogenated vegetable oil" in its ingredient list even if it has 0 grams of trans fat.

10. Include small amounts of healthy fats. Try incorporating nuts, seeds, avocado, nut butters, and fatty fish into your diet. Try avocado or hummus in your sandwich instead of mayonnaise.

11. Improve your omega-3 to omega-6 ratio by choosing more olive and canola oil and less corn, soy, and safflower oils.

The Good, the Bad, and the Ugly Dietary Fats

Fats and oils naturally come in varying degrees of "saturation" according to the number of hydrogen atoms saturating the carbon chain of the fatty acid: saturated, monosaturated, and polyunsaturated. Most fats and oils are a mixture of these three types of fatty acids with the preponderant fatty acid determining properties, health effects, and classification.

- Saturated fats, generally solid at room temperature, raise your cholesterol. These include most animal fats (lard, butter), as well as tropical oils (palm, coconut). But this just in—recent research on coconut oil finds it's mostly comprised of lauric acid, which increases the "good" HDL and may have antiviral properties.

- Monosaturated oils, generally liquid at room temperature, allegedly neither raise nor lower your blood cholesterol. These include olive, canola, and peanut oils. But, olive oil with 70 percent oleic acid raises the "good" HDL, which in turn raises its status, making monosaturates the top choice.

- Polyunsaturated oils, always liquid, tend to lower blood cholesterol. These include most vegetable oils (safflower, sunflower, and corn).

- Trans fats (or trans fatty acids) are formed when manufacturers hydrogenate liquid oils to make them solid or increase shelf life. Thus, margarine was invented as a cheaper and healthier version of butter. But, as it turns out, years later we find that trans fatty acids are even worse for your heart than naturally occurring saturated fats.

  Meanwhile, these killer fats have become almost omnipresent: in baked goods, crackers, fast foods, peanut butter, doughnuts, and so on. Its newly found notoriety has several cities banning trans fat and food industries and restaurants scrambling to reformulate their products.

Living with Liver Disease

The liver has an amazing ability to regenerate itself. But sometimes alcohol damages part of the liver beyond repair and one must learn to live in such a manner as to do no further damage and preserve what is left so it can function as happily and healthily as possible. You have already taken the most important step—stemming further damage. But what else can you do? Smoking has proven to be an independent factor in advancing liver disease, so again, if you smoke, quitting would be very helpful. Getting adequate sleep and exercise, as well as keeping a positive attitude, are also essential.

Food as Medicine

The nutrition prescription for the damaged liver depends on the current state of the liver and needs to take into account the liver's usual functions and its inability to do these in an efficient manner. This requires lots of some nutrients (to regenerate and make up for inefficient use) and less of others (that the liver is unable to handle and might cause toxicity). Good nutrition can help to regenerate liver cells, slow disease progression, improve your response to treatments, and make you feel your best. Nutrition recommendations for treating cirrhosis (a condition in which functional liver tissue is replaced by nonfunctional scar tissue due to damage) are similar to those for recovery in general, with some exceptions:

1. Consume a high-calorie, high complex-carbohydrate diet (50–60 percent of calories) to provide steady energy. This translates into whole grain cereals, breads, pastas, and beans.

2. Eat a high-protein diet, mostly from plant and low-fat dairy sources. The damaged liver has a difficult time tolerating the types of proteins in meat, which can lead to disease progression and encephalopathy (brain fog) caused by ammonia buildup. If and when brain fog does occur, a very low protein diet should be followed briefly, just until medical management can lower ammonia levels.

3. Avoid other foods high in ammonia such as bacon, ham, ground beef, gelatin, salami, and aged cheeses.

4. Limit sodium to <2,000 milligrams a day to avoid fluid buildup.

5. Limit high-fat and high-sugar foods. Fat clogs your liver and prevents it from functioning properly. Trans fats are *especially* difficult for the compromised liver.

6. Focus on consuming nutrient-dense foods—lots of fresh fruits and vegetables—for an abundant supply of nutrients and antioxidants to repair and protect your liver.

7. Maintain a healthy weight. Excess weight is another proven risk factor for disease progression.

8. If you have problems with low blood sugar, poor appetite, or digestion, you

may want to try eating smaller, more frequent meals.

9. Choose a multivitamin that does not contain iron. Avoid large doses of supplemental fat-soluble vitamins. You may need to take fat-soluble vitamins in water soluble forms.

Hold the Bologna, Hot Dogs, Sausage . . .

Nitrates and nitrites used to preserve bologna, pepperoni, bacon, hot dogs, ham, and similar deli meats are strongly linked to increased risk for several types of cancer, notably prostate, bladder, and stomach cancer. Experts seem to agree that there is no safe level of intake when it comes to such foods. Thankfully, uncured versions of these foods are becoming more widely available. Another solution is to simply explore the vast treasures of other items to make your sandwich: slices of leftover home-cooked chicken or roast beef, meatless bologna-type products (such as Tofurky slices, which come in a variety of styles), hummus and other bean spreads, nut butters, low-sodium cheeses, avocado, and more veggies (tomato, cucumber, mushroom slices, lettuce).

Diabetes

Due to the effects of alcohol on the pancreas, many people come to recovery with the diagnosis of diabetes—the pancreas does not produce enough insulin, a hormone responsible for moving glucose from your blood into your body's cells, where it is used as energy. This results in hyperglycemia (high blood sugar), which if left untreated can lead to coma and death. Sometimes diabetes can be managed or even "cured" with just diet, exercise, and weight loss. Oral hypoglycemic agents may be needed to assist whatever insulin you do have to do its job. If the insulin-producing part of your pancreas is totally kaput, you will require insulin injections to control your blood sugar. In all cases, diet is key.

The "diabetic diet" is basically the same healthy diet recommended to everyone in recovery, but the consequences for non-adherence are far more serious. Diabetics are at greater risk than the general population for heart disease, strokes, and blood sugar swings, so the recommendations of a low-fat, low-sodium diet, avoiding concentrated sweets, and maintaining an ideal body weight are key in preventing the long-term complications of diabetes. Chronically high blood sugars can lead to blindness, end-stage kidney disease, amputations, neuropathy, and all sorts of other unpleasant outcomes. Soluble fiber and exercise can both aid greatly in glycemic control. Timing of meals in relation to medications is vital.

If you are diabetic, you need to self-monitor your blood sugar to ensure that you are staying within the recommended range (generally <130 mg/dL glucose). If you are having difficulty maintaining glycemic control, a registered dietitian, especially one who is also a certified diabetic educator, can help you develop a plan for managing your diabetes.

Weight Management

No news here: Americans are overweight and it's hurting our health. The weight issue is especially relevant to those in recovery because a) you may have gained weight in recovery due to your newfound appetite, smoking cessation, and substance substitution; b) you are more likely to suffer from hypertension, diabetes, and liver disease, all of which are better managed by maintaining an ideal body weight; and c) if your self-esteem is weight-dependent and you've put on weight in recovery, this added weight could serve as a trigger to relapse.

So what is an "ideal body weight?" The official calculations give men 106 pounds for their first five feet of height, plus six pounds for every additional inch of height. For women, they get 100 pounds for the first five feet and five pounds for each additional inch. After you add that up, decide what size frame you have (if you can reach the thumb and middle finger of one hand around the wrist of the other, you are small-framed) and add 10 percent for a large frame or minus 10 percent for a small frame. Note that these standards were set by insurance companies, not health professionals, and do

not fit all population groups. Since IBW is based on height, it is important to have an accurate height measurement and not assume that it is still what it was when you were 18.

> **What Is a Calorie?**
>
> A calorie is a unit of energy. The parts of food that contain calories are called "macronutrients." These are easy to keep track of because there are only four: protein, carbohydrate, fat, and—you guessed it!—alcohol. Protein and carbohydrates each have 4 calories per gram, fat has 9 calories per gram, and alcohol has 7 calories per gram. This explains how eating fat and drinking alcohol can lead to putting on pounds and why the low-fat dairy products (skim versus whole milk, frozen yogurt versus full-fat ice cream) are a better choice if you prefer not to put on pounds.

Defining Weight

Medical journals and the popular press trot out terms like "overweight" and "obese." What do these actually mean? Well, there are at least three measures to interpret this: IBW, BMI, and WC.

Ideal Body Weight (IBW)

You might have calculated your ideal body weight above. Now you can compare it to these standards:

- To be officially "overweight," you must be at >110 percent of your IBW.
- To be officially "obese," you must be >120 percent of your IBW.

To put this in layman's terms, a medium frame 5'5" woman with an IBW of 125 pounds is considered overweight at 138 pounds and obese at 150 pounds.

Body Mass Index (BMI)

The BMI method plugs height and weight into a formula and comes up with a score that falls into a range of underweight, normal, overweight, or obese. The BMI is a bit kinder to our reference woman: She would not be considered overweight until she hit 150 pounds, and would be obese at 180 pounds. You can calculate your BMI at *www.nhlbisupport.com/bmi/*.

Waist Circumference (WC)

Waist circumference actually measures abdominal obesity, which is a risk factor strongly associated with type II diabetes and heart disease. The official waist is found by locating the top of your hip bone and measuring the circumference of your body at this level. Measure after the out breath but without "sucking it in." The alert points are >40" for men and >35" for women.

Overweight Versus Overfat

There are limitations to these standards. If you work out a lot and are muscular, your weight is likely higher than these standards, since muscle weighs more than fat, which is by no means unhealthy. Indeed, body composition is probably more important than absolute body weight. Imagine the 160-pound guy who is "all muscle" versus the one who is all flab. There are ways of measuring body composition but most of us can get a general idea by looking in the mirror. Even more important than looks is health. Muscle tissue is where metabolism occurs. The more you can maintain the better you will function and survive at every age. Increased muscle mass correlates positively with reduced side effects from medications, fewer disease complications, shorter hospitalizations, maintaining independence as you age, and so on. If weight loss is your goal, focus on losing the fat and keeping the muscle.

How to Build Muscle Mass

Building muscle mass, a popular topic among males in recovery, is fairly straightforward. You need four ingredients to build muscle mass: adequate protein, adequate calories (so the protein isn't used for energy), testosterone (not a problem unless there is some underlying disorder), and resistance exercise.

The amount of protein recommended for athletes depends on the type of activity in which they engage. Strength and speed athletes need slightly more than endurance athletes. Well-trained athletes need less protein than beginners, meaning a 180-pound athlete would need 123 grams of protein. The typical meat-based American diet easily exceeds this amount. Most of us are not serious athletes or even weekend warriors. If the average 180-pound person is walking a few miles a day or playing tennis for two hours a week, according to RDA standards, 65 grams of protein per day is more than adequate. The usual impediment to building muscle mass is actually doing the resistance exercises.

The Simple Science of Weight Loss

So how does one go about losing weight? It's not, as they say, "rocket science," but you have to be really motivated (more on this in Chapter 4). For now, let's look at the science of weight loss.

Simply put: If you take in more calories than you burn in your daily activities, the excess calories will be stored, as fat, on your body (most likely in the location you least prefer to see it). If you burn more calories than you eat, those fat stores will be used for energy and slowly disappear. *Voilà!* Weight loss. Another thing we know is that the ideal rate of weight loss is 1 to 2 pounds a week—such gradual weight loss has proven to be most likely to be maintained over time. So patience and persistence are key.

The best "diet" is one you can live with permanently. People who go on psychically and physically unsustainable food plans may initially lose some weight but are doomed

to regain. Here are some additional pointers that may help you on your way:

1. Focus on your motivation for losing weight. Do you want to fit into your old wardrobe? Feel healthy? Be able to enjoy vigorous activities? Control hypertension or diabetes? Live to see your grandchildren grow up? Feel sexier? I had one friend who tacked this saying on her fridge: "Nothing tastes as good as the feeling of being thinner." This worked for her. Find what works for you and keep it close by.

2. Focus on healthy new habits, not the numbers on the scale. Remember: diet as part of a healthy lifestyle.

3. Enjoy your food—just smaller portions of it. Chew every bite. Put your fork down between bites. Take at least thirty minutes to eat each meal. Serve yourself the amount you think you should be eating and then store the leftovers away before you start to eat so you won't be tempted to take seconds.

4. Live the mantra "Out of sight, out of mind, out of mouth." Don't purchase the foods you do not want to eat. Forget the excuses about having them available for kids and company. In the back of your mind, you'll know ice cream is waiting for you in the fridge.

5. Don't fall into the "Snackwell" trap—just because something is lower in fat or calories doesn't give you the green

light to eat the whole bag. That being said, fat is more calorific than protein or carbohydrates so by choosing the same amount of lower fat foods, you automatically consume fewer calories.

6. Eat higher fiber foods to feel full on fewer calories.

7. Drink a glass or two of water just before each meal. Filling your stomach with zero calorie liquid leads to early satiety and prevention of overeating.

8. Differentiate between "foods that hum and foods that beckon" to avoid emotional impulse eating. Quiet your mind and get in touch with what your body really needs at that moment—perhaps the crunch of an apple (humming), or a hug, or maybe you're just tired or stressed out. When you pass the French bakery and the napoleon in the window calls out to you, that is beckoning. (This concept is adapted from *Making Peace With Food*, an excellent book by Susan Kano.) Imagine how you will feel after eating a certain food or after those beckoning second helpings. We *all* remember those times we overate and lived to regret that ill feeling.

9. Beware of evening eating and mindless munching. These are the stumbling blocks of many. Distract yourself with non-food activities. Have low-calorie alternatives available. Avoid those activities that usually trigger an impulse to eat junk food mindlessly.

10. Trust trial and error. You may wonder "How many calories do I need?" and "How much exercise do I need?" The bottom line is that if you are not losing weight then you need to work on one end, the other, or both of the calorie equation. Keep track of your intake for several days (include one weekend day) and look up the caloric values of foods you consume to develop an awareness of what and how much you are actually taking in.

11. Exercise! The other side of the calorie equation is burning calories. Find something you enjoy doing that matches other needs so it doesn't feel like drudgery. Need more time to socialize? Walk your talk with a buddy. Enjoy nature? Hike in the woods or mountains, or kayak on a river. Get off on competition? Join a tennis league. Need some anger management? Try some martial arts. Into culture? Try some dance classes. There is something for everyone—seek and you shall find.

12. Reward yourself with non-food pleasures. Instead of thinking "As soon as I lose ten pounds I can afford to eat some (fill in the blank with the decadent food of your choice)," do something more appropriate. Celebrate with a new article of clothing for your slimmer body, a special outing, an inspirational movie, a

hot date with your sweetie, a new hairstyle . . . think along those lines.

Pain Management

While not a specific illness, a book about recovery would be remiss not to address the issue of pain. The trials and tribulations of life, injuries, and arthritis, and just plain aging bring chronic physical pain to many. In working with veterans in recovery, it became evident that many were self-medicating for pain with alcohol and drugs.

The good news is that there may be some tasty modalities to alleviate pain. Some foods quell inflammation (the source of most of what we perceive as pain), while others favor the production of inflammation-producing substances. As usual, the key is to discern the difference.

Here are several suggestions to ease the pain:

1. Do not exceed your IBW. Each extra pound of weight translates into a four-pound increase of stress on your joints; each ten pounds of excess weight increases your risk of osteoarthritis by 30 percent.
2. Avoid inflammatory foods. These include refined processed foods, omega-6 fatty acids (refined soybean oil, corn oil), high fructose corn syrup, and saturated fats (meat, lard, any fat that is solid at room temperature).
3. For some, consuming vegetables from the "nightshade" family (white potatoes, eggplants, tomatoes, bell peppers) may also contribute to arthritis.
4. Increase your intake of anti-inflammatory foods and substances. Antioxidants stop free radicals at the molecular level. Some of these include beta-carotene (found in sweet potatoes and carrots); vitamin E (found in whole grains, beans, and vegetables); selenium (found in whole grains and Brazil nuts); vitamin C (found in most fruits and vegetables); various phytochemicals (found in olive oil, white, green, and oolong teas, cumin, ginger, turmeric,

and garlic); and the enzyme bromelain (found in fresh pineapple).

5. Aim for a positive omega-3 to omega-6 fatty acid balance. Good sources of omega-3s are salmon, sardines, herring, flaxseeds, canola oil, walnuts, leafy greens, beans, avocado, berries, and soy (not soybean oil).

6. Consume less heme iron and more non-heme iron. This means eat less red meat and more leafy greens.

7. Be proactive against gout attacks by avoiding red meat (especially organ meats), seafood (especially shellfish and anchovies), and alcohol (duh!)

8. Capsaicin (from hot chili peppers) applied to the skin works by depleting substance P (the substance that nerves use to transmit pain signals), but produces moderate skin burning.

A Common Digestive Woe, Demystified

Does this sound familiar? You don't "do well" with dairy products but drink milk anyway. And shortly thereafter you notice rumblings, flatulence, feelings of bloating and cramping, and then loose stools. If so, here's what's happening: Cow's milk contains milk sugar, called "lactose." At birth most people are able to produce "lactase," an enzyme made in your small intestine that breaks down lactose into even simpler sugars which can then be absorbed

through the intestinal wall into your bloodstream.

Depending on your genetic makeup, and from where your ancestors hailed, your gut may produce less lactase as you get older. Depending on the degree to which the lactase production diminishes, you may be able to handle ½ cup of milk, ¼ cup—or not even a teaspoon. The undigested lactose remains in your gut and the microflora (usually friendly bacteria) that inhabit your intestines digest it for you. This might sound helpful, but the byproduct of their digestion is gas. The increasing pressure from their gas causes you cramping, bloating, and diarrhea. This same phenomenon may occur as temporary lactose intolerance in anyone with diarrhea caused by stomach flu, foodborne illness, or alcohol, as the lactase is flushed away. (Note: Lactose intolerance is not to be confused with milk allergy! Allergy is an autoimmune response to a protein whereas lactose intolerance is an inability to digest a carbohydrate.)

So What's a Lactose-Intolerant Person to Do?

If you are mildly lactose intolerant, you may find that you are able to tolerate yogurt (which is cultured with bacteria that digest some of the lactose), chocolate milk, ice cream, and cheeses (lactose is removed with the whey during processing). Depending on your degree of intolerance, you may be able to drink Lactaid-brand milk. This product has the lactose predigested so it is lower in lactose and less likely to trouble your tummy.

Some people who can't stomach dairy products often ask if they should consume them anyway and suffer the consequences. Consider this: There are plenty of cultures that do not include milk products in their diet (for example, China and parts of Africa) and they have endured for millennia. How do they survive? To understand, check out what dairy products provide: protein, calcium, and riboflavin (a.k.a. vitamin B2). Americans get ample, possibly even too much, protein, in our diets. Calcium can be found in many other foods including leafy greens, molasses, almonds, sesame seeds, beans, tofu, and in plenty of fortified products from OJ to soymilk, breads to cereals. Riboflavin is also present in meats, leafy vegetables, whole grains, mushrooms, and bananas, among other foods. Luckily, we live in a time when many lactose-free alternatives, such as milks, yogurts, cheeses, and even frozen desserts made from soy, rice, and nut milks, are available. Some may even be fortified with vitamins and calcium to mimic the nutritional value of cow's milk. Most brands of soymilk are fortified with calcium (as well as vitamins D and B12) up to the same levels found in cow's milk. Plus, soymilk is equivalent to regular milk in protein and serves the same purpose as milk over cereal and in recipes, such as soups, puddings, cakes, and sauces. So

don't cry over not drinking milk. Substitute with soymilk and focus on other calcium-containing foods.

What Is Tofu?

To some, tofu is a four-letter word with a reputation for blandness. But for those who can get past the bad PR, you may find tofu undeserving of derision. A staple food in the Orient for millennia, tofu is high in protein, calcium, iron, has some fat, but little fiber. Lower in fat and sodium than meat, tofu has no saturated fat or cholesterol, and the plant proteins are gentler on your liver. A white pillowy block with variable consistency (silken, firm, or extra firm), tofu takes on the flavor of other foods with which it is cooked. Tofu can be used in stir-fries (a.k.a. soybean curd on a Chinese menu), as an eggless scramble, stealthied into macaroni and cheese or lasagna, chilled in a cream pie, blended into smoothies, skewered for kabobs—the possibilities are truly endless.

Bottom line: By taking charge of what you eat you can make a huge difference in your health, your quality of life, and that of others whom you know and feed, thus adding years to your life and life to your years of sobriety.

CHAPTER 4

Putting It All Together in the Kitchen

If you're still with us by this point in the book, you have figured out that good nutrition is essential to recovery. Eating well replenishes nutrients, enabling you to fully engage—physically, mentally, emotionally, and spiritually—in the process of recovery, as well as more broadly, in the fullness of life. Timing and quality of food can help you avoid triggers and keep on keepin' on your program of recovery. Food is also "thy medicine," providing a measure of healing and safeguarding your future health. So, now that you are convinced and excited to make a change, how do we take all this theory into practice?

Empower Yourself—Food in the Larger Context

Traditionally, food was part of something much larger than what ends up on your table. People grew, harvested, prepared, and enjoyed food together as part of a cohesive community. The crops were close

by to where the people who ate them lived. Today, few of us grow our own food. A large percentage of meals are takeout or eaten outside the home. Not only are we not connected to the land or the people who grow our food, we are usually totally oblivious of our food's origins and the processes that took place to get that food to our table. This divorce from the means of food production has led to a sense of alienation and powerlessness around food. By reclaiming even a small piece of the process, you can re-instill a sense of ownership. Being able to choose a better diet is an important first step in creating a healthy lifestyle in recovery, and cooking is your means of empowerment.

David Kessler, the previously obese former commissioner of the Food and Drug Administration, explains in his book, *The End of Overeating*, how we have been conditioned to choose high-fat, high-sugar foods by the constant availability of these foods in our environment. "Chronic exposure to highly palatable foods changes our brains, conditioning us to seek continued stimulation," he writes. In other words, resistance to gooey foods becomes all but futile. Comfort foods leave a mark on our brain, setting up a spiral of wanting. If that doesn't sound familiar enough, he argues that the only way to free yourself from this cue-response cycle is via "Food Rehab." Only by reframing our perceptions of such foods, viewing them as negative, and learning new rewarding behaviors can you break the bonds of conditioned hypereating. To restore control, he recommends planned eating of satisfying, high fiber foods, and employing a variety of self-talk strategies that sound remarkably similar to the relapse prevention tools you use in recovery. Having the knowledge and skills to prepare delicious, nutritious, satisfying food for yourself is a necessary part of "food rehab" and a step on the path to wholeness.

Preparing a nutritious meal for yourself also signifies self-nurturance, taking responsibility, and choosing health, all steps that will help heal residual feelings of guilt and unworthiness. Food is so simple, yet cuts across so many aspects of our lives that it can serve as "grist for the mill," stirring up old wounds, taking you to delicate places and unresolved issues, as well as fortifying you with sweet reminders of good times, olfactory memories, bygone family and friends. Perceived as opportunities, food experiences are a blessing.

"Anyone Can Cook!"

One of my favorite movies is the sweet, animated Pixar film *Ratatouille*. It stars a wannabe chef named Remy who happens to be a French rat. The flames of his aspirations are continually fanned by visions of his hero, the famous Chef Gustave, exhorting (with a French accent, *bien sur*) "Anyone can cook!" From the many years of cooking classes with veterans in residential rehab, I can attest to the veracity of this statement. Our residents have included a diverse crew: homeless veterans, lawyers, handymen, and physicians, mostly men, due to the setting. Baseline skills have ranged from professional chefs to those who couldn't slice a tomato. Each participant who opted to be receptive learned something new, gained some skills, tasted something they never tasted before, and came away from the experience even more willing to try new foods and feeling more confident in the kitchen.

If you're in recovery, you've come through a lot. Through intelligence, perseverance, and adaptability you have survived. These same qualities can be a great asset when applied to new situations—even in a kitchen. So, yes, anyone can cook, including and especially you!

At the end of the day, it's all connected: Consciously taking charge of this vital aspect of your life and mastering the required skills builds competence and confidence and calls up inner resources that can spill over into other areas of your life, thereby enhancing your recovery. Now go out there and start playing with your food!

Navigating the Food Market

In the United States there is a plethora of choices when it comes to food. The modern American supermarket carries upward of 30,000 different products! Depending on where you live, you can also choose to shop at farmers' markets, health food stores, delicatessens, butcher shops, minimarts, bodegas, ethnic markets, or other local grocery and specialty shops. There is, indeed, an almost overwhelming crush of choices.

The supermarket used to be the main source of my family's food. But over the past several years, in the wake of reading several inspirational books, I've tweaked my diet, made some conscious decisions about how to spend my food dollars, and find myself buying less and less at chain supermarkets.

Your best bet for quality, tasty, fresh seasonal produce is a local farmers' market. Local food, often picked the morning of the market, is literally thousands of miles fresher—which is important since vegetables start losing nutrients as soon as they are harvested. Farmers' markets are also a good source for heirloom fruit and vegetable varieties, local honey and crafts, as well as the rich sensory input of vivid vegetables, fragrant fruit, and local character.

Food Neurobics

In the book *Keep Your Brain Alive* the authors explain how using our senses in novel ways actually builds new neural pathways in our brain! Smelling exotic spices, tasting new foods, changing the location of where you eat, even using your non-dominant hand to eat are all food-related actions that can improve our brain's fitness. Engaging multiple senses and creating emotional associations work even better. The sterility of our modern food system—with shrink-wrapping, automated checkouts, and TV dinners—deadens our senses with its stultifying predictability. So get creative and daring. Shop at an ethnic market, eat blindfolded, go to a pick-your-own farm, swap lunch bags at work. Because we can *all* use some extra neurons!

Spending Less, Eating Better

The question I've heard most often from people in recovery is "How can I eat well on a budget?" The assumption is that eating well requires spending more. This is simply untrue. But before getting to the "how-to" of eating well on a budget, remember that health is wealth. Can't afford two dollars for organic kale? Try spending $80,000 on a quadruple bypass. Check out the Centers for Disease Control and Prevention's website to find facts such as this: According to the American Heart Association, all cardiovascular diseases together were projected to cost $475.3 billion in 2009, including health care services, medications, and lost productivity. Then consider that according to the Center for Science in the Public Interest, "Government's annual budget to promote fruit and vegetable consumption is less than what McDonald's spends on ads in a day."

How many ads do you see for broccoli compared to glossy magazine ads by pharmaceutical companies for drugs that treat what might have been prevented by eating more broccoli? Produce is simply not profitable enough for companies to bother marketing. Unlike meat, which is artificially inexpensive due to government subsidies of animal feed.

In Marion Nestle's well-researched and delightfully written book *What to Eat: An Aisle-by-Aisle Guide to Savvy Food Choices and Good Eating*, she answers this exact question. She bought fresh green beans, trimmed, cooked, and measured them out to discover that the standard ½ cup serving cost only eleven cents. Dr. Nestle also exposes the nefarious designs supermarkets and the food industry use to part us from our money for meager nutritional recompense: why the milk is usually at the back of the store (you are forced to pass by thousands of other less useful products on the way there); that stores rent prime shelf space to companies for "slotting fees"; why so much of our food is laden with high fructose corn syrup (the corn industry is highly subsidized and this allows them to refashion corn into outrageous profits); and other facts that will make your blood boil but shout out "Consumer Beware!"

A Shopper's Guide

Here are some tips for smart shopping. Chose several to put into action this week, try more in the following weeks, and keep practicing until they become solid habits.

1. Plan ahead!
   - divide grocery money into weekly amounts and keep to your budget
   - create menus in advance
2. Check the newspaper ads
   - plan meals around specials
   - only stock up on sale items you need and can use
3. Shop with a list
   - check your inventory to avoid redundancy and waste
   - make a list based on your menus, inventory, and specials
4. Buy only what you need
   - eat before you shop
   - leave the kids at home
   - resist buying extras
   - only use coupons for foods you usually buy
5. Get the best price
   - choose one or two stores with the best prices (or you will just waste time and gas driving around)
   - buy generic/store brands
   - compare unit pricing (most supermarkets calculate the price per ounce and include it in small print on the price sticker in front of the item)
   - if an item is "buy one get one free," you have to purchase an even number to get the deal; if it is "three for $5," there is no penalty for only getting one
6. Beware of marketing techniques
   - bigger isn't always better (or less expensive, especially if most of it will spoil before you can use it up)
   - an apparent sale is not always a sale (it pays to be familiar with the usual price which is tricky since the actual package is not usually marked)
   - shop the perimeter of the supermarket—this is where your basic foods are usually found
   - beware endcap displays, items at the checkout, and items at child's eye level
7. Read the labels
   - ingredients are listed by weight in descending order
   - choose lower-sodium, lower-fat, and lower-calorie versions of your standard packaged items
   - avoid ingredients you can't pronounce
   - check expiration dates

8. Health is wealth
   - buy fruits and vegetables in season
   - choose whole grain breads, pasta, rice, and cereals
   - limit convenience foods
9. Eat less meat
   - beans, lentils, and soy products are healthy, less expensive protein sources
   - ground chicken and turkey have less fat and are more economical than red meat
   - buy with portion size in mind to pre-empt overeating; limit meat to three-ounce portions
10. Be savvy at the checkout
   - check the scanner for price errors—some chain stores will give you the item for free if you catch a mistake
   - check your receipt for accuracy
   - count your change before leaving the store

Choosing Choice Ingredients

What's better—organic or conventional? This is a case of weighing risks versus benefits. Organic fruits and vegetables are better for the planet and better for you. Studies show some actually contain higher levels of antioxidants! But, organic food usually costs more. As it turns out, some produce is sprayed more heavily than others—the most contaminated ones may contain residues of several pesticides. Luckily, the Environmental Working Group does the legwork for you, testing fresh produce from around the country and publishing lists of the "Dirty Dozen" and the "Clean 15." Some of the worst offenders include apples, celery, strawberries, peaches, spinach, and imported grapes. Produce least likely to test positive for pesticides include onions, avocados, asparagus, cabbage, eggplant, and sweet potatoes. For the EWG's latest list, check out: *www.foodnews.org/walletguide.php*. As more people "vote with their forks" for fewer pesticides and a cleaner environment, organic foods will be more readily available and less expensive.

Food Labeling 101

The "nutrition facts" label seen on food packages isn't perfect, but it's what we've got. Most of the information on it is fairly self-evident but some of it can be a bit tricky. The first item of note is the serving size. All the other information is based on this amount. If that's not the amount you eat (you take two cups of cereal instead of the official one-cup serving size), do the math. Another confusing part is the %DV (daily value). This is based on the nutritional needs of a reference person who may be quite unlike you. Your best bet is to simply go by the absolute amount of the nutrient of interest and ignore the %DV. The value for sugar can be misleading as there is no differentiation between natural and added sugars. Case in point: A banana might have the same number of sugar grams as a honey bun snack cake.

Fishy Business

On one hand, we are told to eat more fish—it's good for your heart and brain health. On the other hand, we are cautioned about contaminants and the perils of overfishing our seas. So what's the real fish story? Virtually all waterways are contaminated with methylmercury and other contaminants from industrial waste, coal-fired power plants, and runoff of agricultural pesticides. As small fish are devoured by bigger fish, these toxins are passed up the food chain, concentrating in the muscles and fat. You would think that farmed fish would be safe, but they are usually fed fish meal made from larger fish (the most contaminated species). There are some wild fish caught in some locations that may provide more health benefit than risk but, honestly, it's hard to keep up with all of it. For guidance, you can refer to the Monterey Bay Aquarium "Seafood Watch" pocket guide, which is updated regularly and gives the best choices: *www.montereybayaquarium .org/cr/cr seafoodwatch/download.uspx.*

Lightening Your Carbon "Food Print"

Kermit laments "It's not easy being green," but actually it's not so hard, and the future of our planet depends on our being as green as possible. Here are some environmentally friendly food-related actions you can take:

- Buy locally grown produce in season. Locate farmers' markets near you: *www .localharvest.org/farmers-markets/.*
- Start your own garden. Local Cooperative Extension offices can help.
- Minimize packaging by buying in bulk (the healthiest foods don't come in a package) and BYOB (which now means "bring your own reusable shopping bags").
- Eat lighter on the planet. Plant-based meals use less of our planet's limited resources. Factoid: It takes 40 calories of fossil fuel to produce one calorie of protein from feedlot beef; only two calories for the tofu.
- Conserve energy in the kitchen with Energy Star appliances, use a pressure cooker or slow cooker, cover the pot to heat food and water, cook larger quantities and freeze in one-meal size containers.
- Save water—it is predicted to be our scarcest future commodity. Don't let the faucet just run; repair leaks; soak dishes then rinse all at once; run the dishwasher only when it's full; install aerators on faucets.
- Decrease garbage by composting, not using disposable dishware, recycling food containers, and buying in bulk.

Now You're Cookin'

Kitchens are special places. Ever notice how people congregate in the kitchen? It may be the smallest room in a house full of nice sofas and airy porches, but when guests come over, they all seem to be mysteriously drawn to the kitchen. It's a place where magic happens— it's warm when it's cold outside, it's the hearth of the home, and alchemy happens there when raw materials are turned into delicious dishes, a source of sustenance and comfort.

A pleasant kitchen inspires cooking. No matter what the size, if the kitchen is well-lit, well-organized, well-stocked, and uncluttered you will be more motivated to cook than if it is cluttered, dark, and disorganized. It's a cinch to remedy most kitchen unpleasantries with hooks for hanging pots, replacing dim bulbs with brighter ones, and making room for a few new items by casting off the old and unused.

Equipping Your Kitchen

You could spend a *lot* of money on cookware and fancy kitchen accessories but it's not really necessary. Most cooks with cabinets full of stuff find that they really use only a fraction of the gadgets. A few saucepans and skillets of varying sizes, plus a wok, will do. Cast iron is safe, holds heat, and provides a workout without going to the gym. Stainless steel with copper clad bottoms heats evenly. Both are easy to wash. Since I've started using a pressure cooker a few years ago, I use it more than

anything else in the kitchen. Once you get the hang of it you'll appreciate that it saves time and energy and makes the food taste great. Other well-used equipment in my kitchen include: the microwave (mostly for reheating leftovers); the coffee grinder (for flaxseeds); a small food processor (for making Gourmet Sorbet, see Chapter 5); cutting boards (I like the feel of wood, but the jury is still out on which is safer—wood or plastic); a few knives; mixing bowls; my trusty microplane (a grater on a knife handle—mostly used for grating ginger); a colander; a steamer basket; a vegetable peeler; plus the usual measuring cups and spoons, spatulas, and mixing spoons (some wooden or plastic for use in metal vessels).

Cooking Under Pressure

How would you like to enjoy delicious, nutritious food, while saving money and the planet at the same time? Tall bill, but all attainable by using a pressure cooker. Put your pressure cooker phobia on the back burner for a minute and hear some praise for the new second-generation versions. Not your grandma's fear-inducing jiggle-top pressure cooker, these come with a stationary pressure regulator with a backup mechanism to prevent buildup of excess pressure. For $50–70 you can buy one that will last a lifetime. Pressure cooking is cooler and cleaner (kills germs), food achieves gourmet-level flavors as seasonings quickly meld, more nutrients are retained, and best of all, pressure cooking opens up entire new worlds of culinary delight. For me, the destination was the world of beans (presoaked dried pintos in three minutes!) but now my regulars include steaming vegetables (collard greens in three minutes that will melt in your mouth), and brown rice (takes 20 minutes and comes out with a texture I prefer). Most pressure cookers come with directions, recipes, and sometimes even an instructional DVD.

Safety First!

Foodborne illnesses make the news entirely too often, leading to food recalls, restaurant closings, even cruise liner quarantines. Keep your kitchen out of the news by following the basic rules of food sanitation and safety, much of which is simple common sense. Assume dangerous microorganisms are everywhere and minimize the conditions they need to multiply: time, temperature, moisture, and food.

1. Clean thoroughly—this applies to your hands (before food preparation, after using the bathroom, sneezing, touching your hair or nose, a doorknob, or meat) as well as kitchen work surfaces, cookware, and utensils. Wash with soap and warm water for at least twenty seconds. Alcohol wipes are not as effective and should only be used when soap and warm water are not available. (Plus the alcohol may be a trigger for some people.)

2. Avoid cross-contamination by not allowing uncooked meats to come into contact with food that will be eaten raw (for example: if you cut up chicken, sanitize the cutting board used before using it to cut up salad fixings—or even better, keep separate cutting boards). It is estimated that up to 90 percent of all chickens and eggs contain salmonella, so take special care to cook these foods thoroughly.

3. Wash dust and dirt from lids and jars before opening, rinse fruits and vegetables before slicing, and use different spoons for stirring raw and cooked foods.

4. Life begins at 40—degrees, that is. (At 135°F most bacteria are killed or at least slowed down.) So avoid keeping food in this danger zone for more than 2 hours—keep hot foods hot, and cold foods cold.

5. Marinate foods in the fridge. Also store foods properly and not too long in the refrigerator (use fresh fish within 24 hours, fresh meat 3–5 days, fresh poultry only 1–2 days, leftovers 3–4 days) or freeze.

6. Thaw beef, pork, chicken, and fish in the refrigerator. Never in the sink! And never leave it on the counter for more than two hours.

7. Do not use anything but glass or Corelle in the microwave! "Nuking" plastic releases chemicals into your food. Likewise, bleached paper plates and coffee filters contain dioxins, which are potent carcinogens.

8. Check all equipment for frayed cords, clean your stove hood to avoid a grease fire, and make sure you have a fire extinguisher handy in your kitchen.

9. Avoid steam burns by lifting the back of the pot cover first, turn pot handles in so you don't knock into them by accident, and use potholders. If you do get burned, the best treatment is immediate cold running water.

10. Don't submerge sharp knives in soapy water where you can't see them.

Safe Grilling

Grilling is often recommended as a low-fat cooking method for meats, but the dangers can outweigh the benefits unless certain precautions are taken. Cancer causing HCAs (heterocyclic amines) and PAH (polycyclic aromatic hydrocarbon) are caused by cooking meats at high temperatures and when fat drips down and smokes up coating the meat, respectively. To reduce risk turn down the heat, avoid smoking and charring meat, use leaner cuts, and trim the fat before cooking. Premarinating meats with a combination of olive oil and spices such as sage, oregano, rosemary, and thyme (the herbs are key!) has been shown to decrease HCA levels by about 70 percent Precooking meat for even two minutes in the microwave also limits HCA production. Grilled vegetables such as summer squashes, asparagus, eggplant, and red pepper are also savory, safe choices.

Safe Cooking Temperatures for Meat

In May 2011, the USDA updated recommendations for safely cooking meat:

- whole cuts of meat – 145°F
- all ground meats – 160°F
- all poultry, ground or whole – 165°F

These temperatures are as measured with a food thermometer placed in the thickest part of the meat, then allowing the meat to rest for three minutes before carving or consuming to ensure that any pathogens are thoroughly destroyed. The agency cautions that appearance is not a reliable indicator of safety or risk. When in doubt, call the food safety experts at USDA's Meat and Poultry Hotline: 1-888MPHotline.

Kitchen Tricks and Shortcuts

Cooking is therapeutic. There may be times when you may spend hours cooking up a storm, really enjoying yourself with the textures, aromas, and tastes, and being creative to your heart's content. But there are also times when you get home after a hard day at work and just want something nutritious to eat—but it better be on the table in fifteen minutes or less!

The best trick for saving time is to plan for leftovers. You can justify this with the knowledge that some foods, such as most soups and sauces, taste better after a day or two. Even just having some leftover cooked grain can be a major time-saver. Create a quick stir-fry and then add in the (rice, noodles, quinoa, whatever) to reheat and incorporate it into the new dish. Leftover steamed vegetables can be quickly recycled by adding them to green salad fixings. Just about any leftover can be incorporated into a wrap—add some cheese and/or sliced mushrooms and serve it cold or nuked for a minute. The possibilities are endless.

Here are some other easy ways to streamline kitchen work:

1. Arrange kitchen areas in ways that make sense to you: alphabetize spices, have specific areas in the refrigerator for different classes of foods, etc.
2. Store foods in see-through containers
3. Read recipes ahead of time to have all ingredients and utensils handy
4. Multitask in logical sequence: boil water for pasta while slicing vegetables, wash prep dishes while a casserole is in the oven, etc.
5. Do as much prep work ahead of time as possible: assemble baking mixes without the liquid, slice up vegetables, soak beans, prepare favorite spice blends
6. Thaw foods overnight in the refrigerator or defrost in the microwave and then finish cooking immediately
7. Save on clean up time by making one-pot meals or using the same pot several times for different dishes or steps in preparation

Sex and the Single Diet

After budget, this is the second most popular question I've gotten from those in recovery: "Are there foods that are good for sex?" The objective answer is that malnourished people usually don't feel too sexy. On the flip side, overnutrition (too much food) is also a mood killer. Fat-clogged arteries preventing blood flow to important extremities and chronic diet-related heart disease, obesity, and diabetes (along with cigarette smoking) are the major causes of erectile dysfunction and poor libido in men and women in America today. If you'd like to see the titillating research for yourself, search the National Library of Medicine's PubMed journal resources using those search terms: www.ncbi.nlm.nih.gov/pubmed/.

What's on the Menu?

Virtually every language has an expression that roughly translates into "There's no accounting for taste." Some tastes are acquired, others actually inborn (consider cilantro: people either love it or hate it—to the latter it tastes like soap). Menu planning should take it all into account: Taste, time, budget, creative energy, and above all, recovery.

Making the Best of Restaurant Menus

Although cooking at home is the ideal if you want to be sure of what is in your food, whether for business or pleasure, eating out is an inevitable part of life. Dodging the excess calories, fat, sodium, and other dietary pitfalls on your list is easier if you follow these general strategies:

- Be assertive. If you are not sure, ask the waiter about ingredients, methods of preparation, and anything else you'd like to know.
- Avoid dubious sauces that may be high in fat or sodium or request that they be served on the side so you can taste and decide how much you want. Same goes for salad dressings.
- Beware the salad bar. It may sound healthy, but prepared macaroni and other salads, dressings, and the like may add surprisingly large loads of sodium, fat, and calories.
- Be even more cautious about "all-you-can-eat" buffets. These should be called "all-you-shouldn't-eat" food bars.
- Some restaurants actually cook your food fresh when you order it so you can specify how you prefer it to be prepared. This is certainly true for stir-fries in Asian eateries and will vary for other restaurants.

- Some restaurants use symbols on their menus to signify the healthier choices. Let them know you appreciate this!
- Restaurant portions are usually large—order an appetizer as your main course, split a main course with a friend, or just eat half and "doggie bag" the rest for a later meal.

CHAPTER 5

Recipes for Recovery

So here you are where the rubber meets the road, or more aptly, the knife meets the cutting board. It's time to apply your newfound recovery diet strategies in your kitchen.

There is no expectation that you need to follow the twelve weeks of menus as written. They are here not as a strict road map but rather as suggestions to set you off in the right direction, inspire you to see some of the sights, and—if you get a little lost—welcome you back to get your bearings again. Along the way, perhaps you'll find some foods and dishes you'll want to take along with you on your journey, others you may visit once or twice, and still others that may give you an idea for a dish destination of your own.

In all cases, don't lose sight of the fact that the journey is recovery.

There are basic signposts, but each person's journey, and menu, will be different.

These menus follow strategies for recovery and kitchen shortcuts and include measures for managing or avoiding medical concerns. The standards for developing these menus include the following:

- A focus on foods that are nutrient-dense, high in fiber, phytochemicals, and complex carbohydrates, low in fat and sugar, moderate in protein, and are whole foods or only minimally processed. **Absolutely no alcohol is used in the preparation of these meals.**

- Realistic time frames for food preparation to enable you to prepare a weekday dinner in less than thirty minutes; dishes that take longer to prepare are restricted to the weekends.

- A reliance on built-in leftovers, to save time, energy, and expense.

- Ingredients chock full of a variety of colors, textures, and occasionally a very novel flavor to keep you expanding your palate.

- In general, beef or pork is on the menu maybe once a week; chicken or turkey, once a week; fish or seafood twice a week; with the remaining meals containing dairy-, egg-, or plant-based protein sources.

- No mystery meats and a minimum of processed products—no chicken nuggets, fish sticks, bologna, etc.
- Suggestions for preparing vegetarian versions of the meat, poultry, and fish dishes when feasible (by substituting with tempeh, tofu, edamame, gluten, beans, and minimally processed vegetarian "transition" products, such as vegetarian "soysages," burgers, etc).
- Use of base recipes with "variations on a theme" (vegetable medleys, stir-fries, lunch wraps).

It's a Bird, It's a Plane, It's Superfood!

The darlings of the nutrition world, superfoods are naturally dense in vitamins, minerals, and phytochemicals. The winner's list includes: sweet potatoes, mangoes, unsweetened yogurt, broccoli, wild salmon, crispbreads (hearty whole grain crackers), chickpeas, watermelon, butternut squash, and all the leafy greens (kale, collards, spinach, turnips, mustard, chard), berries, citrus fruits, tomatoes, whole grains, nuts, quinoa, and kiwis. You will see many superfoods incorporated into these twelve weeks of nourishing menus for a super recovery.

Your Daily Diet

As part of your Goals for Diet in Recovery (Chapter 2), you will recall that in order to proactively manage moods it's best to eat three square meals plus snacks. (Yes, all of them—no skipping!) This does not mean you have to consume tons of calories and overshoot your target body weight. Note that the recipes and menus say nothing about how *much* you should eat; this depends on your size and activity level. And while leftovers are great, you may want to adjust recipes for smaller yields to avoid too many leftovers or the feeling that you must "clean your plate" to prevent waste.

Breakfast

The breakfasts included in these menus try to provide a good boost toward your daily fiber needs with the use of high fiber, whole grain cereals, both hot and cold. Suggestions are made for Overnight Oatmeal, so that with only minimal preparation the night before you can have a hearty breakfast with even less effort in the morning. And of course, breakfast doesn't have to look like breakfast—in much of the world beans are on the breakfast menu—so as long as breakfast is high in fiber, nutrient dense, and includes some protein, go for it!

Breakfast is also a good opportunity to tank up on fluids. Once you leave the house in the morning, you're likely on the run and may forget about fluids until you suddenly notice that parched feeling. Herbal teas are an excellent, calorie-free way to get your fluid fill without the diuretic-inducing effect of highly caffeinated beverages. Be careful with fruit juice—½ cup is probably enough. Consider: an eight-ounce glass of grape juice contains 160 calories. Compare this to your overall calorie needs (likely around 1,800 to 2,200 calories) and you can see how more than one glass of juice can be a substantial contribution. On the other hand, diluting juice (as ⅓ of the glass) can encourage you to drink more water.

Lunch

Weekday lunches rely heavily on good quality leftovers from nourishing meals you've made for dinner. Most meals can be easily "recycled" into wraps or stuffed in pocket bread, or just toted along in containers. Of course, if you are retired or work a non-nine-to-five routine, you may prefer to have your main meal of the day at "lunch" time.

Snacks

Don't forget that nutritious snacks are important for keeping your blood sugar and mood on an even keel. Although the menus only have one snack listed each day, the intention is for you to have at least two. The one not listed is a piece of fresh fruit, the precise type best determined by where you live and what is seasonally available, as that is what will be the tastiest, most accessible,

and reasonably priced. Many of the other suggested snacks are healthy "grab and go" items that you can buy in bulk and repackage into single serving sizes using small containers: nuts, seeds, dried fruits, do-it-yourself trail mix. Nuts and dried fruits are intense packages of calories as well as nutrients, so if you are trying to lose weight focus more on the fresh fruits and vegetables and go easy on the nuts and dried fruits.

Other snacks can be as simple as a whole grain cracker with preserves or as "complicated" as making your own snack bars (as an alternative to commercially available "granola bars," which are so high in sugar they are basically cookies with a healthy veneer). By satisfying your sweet tooth with natural sweets you can avoid "sugar blues" and improve your overall intake of healthy nutrients.

Dinner

Dinners are the heartiest meals included in these menu plans. As you will see, with a little bit of planning, hearty does not have to mean time-consuming. This is an excellent meal time to make sure you get ample vegetables. Guidance from the USDA's new Choose My Plate campaign can cue you to proportion and balance: Fill half your dinner plate with vegetables, a quarter of the plate with whole grains, and the remaining quarter with protein. Don't take this too literally when it comes to mixed dishes—just go with the concept.

Healthy Convenience Foods?

It sounds like an oxymoron, but for those days that you can't even look at a recipe book, there are some lesser-evil convenience foods. Some suggestions include certain brands of frozen burritos (El Monterey), ravioli, pierogies (the Polish version of ravioli, usually stuffed with potatoes), vegetarian burgers, whole grain frozen waffles, Tabatchnick frozen soups (fairly unprocessed and lower in sodium than other commercial soups), and Kashi frozen entrees. Your key job here is to read the labels: check the sodium, fat, and make sure you can pronounce the list of ingredients.

Brown Bag It

Toting your lunch to work is a great way to save money and make sure that you eat what you really want and need. But to avoid getting sick from that food, please make sure that your lunch sack is not a breeding ground for bacteria. If refrigeration is available at work, claim a space for your lunch bag there. If not, packing your food in an insulated sack with an ice pack is a viable alternative. Save time, dish washing, and dioxin poisoning by transferring your dinner leftovers directly into a small glass casserole dish that you can pack in your lunch bag and use for reheating in a microwave at work. (Note that this is not recommended if you bike to work.)

Owning the Meal Plan

As incredibly nutritious as these menus may appear to be, you may find that certain dishes contain ingredients you just don't eat due to allergy, intolerance, taste, or world view. By all means, feel free to take artistic license, change out vegetables, substitute tempeh for the pork, or simply omit the offending ingredient. For the lactose intolerant, there are more and more very decent alternatives including a variety of plant-based milks, yogurts, cheeses, even frozen desserts. For those eschewing eggs, there are egg substitutes such as Ener-G egg replacer (made from tapioca flour). In addition, banana purée, oatmeal, and ground flaxseeds mixed with water (1 tablespoon plus 3 tablespoons of water replaces one egg) all make excellent binders, all lower in fat and calories than eggs. If the sodium content still doesn't look low enough for you, feel free to omit the salt all together.

Measuring Up

Although most recipes can do just fine with altering ingredients and amounts, it makes sense to follow the actual recipe the first time so you have a baseline from which to work. Measuring is probably most critical for baked goods such as cakes and cookies. Did you know there are two types of measuring cups? Glass or clear plastic measuring cups are used for liquid ingredients. You may have to lean over to check at eye level to make sure the ingredient is up to the correct line. Metal or plastic measuring cups with straight edges are used to measure dry ingredients. Use the flat edge of a knife to level off the excess. The same technique can be used for dry ingredients in measuring spoons.

> ### "Doesn't the Alcohol Burn Off?"
> Many well-intentioned cooks add various alcohol-containing substances (Grand Marnier, red wine, Burgundy) to their dishes to achieve authentic flavors, assuming that they are doing no harm to friends in recovery because "the alcohol burns off." Well, researchers have actually conducted studies on this matter and the answer is "No, it does not." Up to 78 percent of the alcohol may remain, depending on the source of alcohol, length and method of cooking. In classic dishes, alcohol is generally used as a meat tenderizer, or to add sweetness or acidity. A substitute can often be found by using fruit juices, vinegar (even if they are called "wine" vinegar, they are alcohol-free), and/or flavored oils to replicate the taste and effects of the alcohol-containing ingredient. For most of us, cooking an authentic Coq au Vin is not a concern in our daily lives; however, making baked goods that call for vanilla extract (35 percent alcohol by volume) is more of an issue. Fortunately, one can substitute imitation vanilla, powdered vanilla, and for the truly gourmet types, vanilla beans. And don't be put off by Bourbon-Madagascar vanilla beans—the Bourbon in the name refers to Bourbon Island, not the booze.

Edamame Who?

You may notice recipes calling for some unusual ingredients. Over the past several decades most of these "exotic" items have become more and more mainstream, and although they may be less expensive in an Oriental market, they can also usually be found in most urban chain supermarkets. Here's a rundown of some ingredients with which you may not be familiar.

Arrowroot Powder

Arrowroot is used as a thickener, similarly to cornstarch, but it's more neutral in flavor and works better at lower temperatures and more acid conditions. Its thickening power endures more cooking than cornstarch as well.

Bragg Liquid Aminos

Made from soybeans, this seasoning is wheat-free, a tad lower in sodium than soy sauce and tamari, and lends a savory flavor.

Edamame

Looking like large English peas, edamame are basically soybeans harvested before they reach the "hardening" time. They are often served at Japanese restaurants, steamed in the pod, and can also be purchased shelled and frozen and used in stir-fries and other dishes as the official protein component. Edamame is a great source of fiber and unprocessed soy protein.

Flaxseeds

Grown since ancient times as an oil seed, flaxseeds are a rich source of fiber, omega-3 fatty acids, lignans, and other antioxidants, including anti-cancer substances. Use freshly ground for ideal absorption and to prevent rancidity. Flaxseeds can be added to yogurt, hot cereals, baked goods, salads, smoothies, and when mixed with water can serve as an egg replacer in baked goods.

Miso

A traditional Japanese seasoning made of fermented soybeans, miso paste adds a hearty, savory flavor to soups and sauces. Many Japanese start their day with miso soup. There is quite a variety of misos made with different grains and beans that produce different colors, tastes, and textures. The end product can be high in sodium, so use sparingly.

Mochi

Another traditional Japanese food, mochi is made of whole glutinous rice pounded, cooked into a paste, and molded. It comes in a translucent block, can be cut into chunks and "melted" over vegetables to yummy effect, and is also an ingredient in sweets and ice creams.

Neufchatel Cheese

This is merely a fancy name for low-fat cream cheese despite the fact that it bears no resemblance to the original Neufchatel produced in France.

Nut Butters

Jazzing up the classic peanut butter experience, you can now diversify with "butters" made from almonds, cashews, and sunflower seeds. I've even seen expensive spreads made from macadamias, hazelnuts, and Brazil nuts. In all cases, best to buy the one with the least ingredients—look for just nuts without added salt, sugar, or hydrogenated oils. And again, unless weight gain is your goal, nuts are full of fats (albeit good ones), so use sparingly.

Nutritional Yeast Flakes

Known to its science buds as *Saccharomyces cerevisiae*, this yeast, grown on molasses, is deactivated (won't rise in your tummy), cornmeal yellow in color, has a savory cheesy flavor, and is a rich source of those B vitamins especially needed in recovery. Nutritional yeast can be used to enhance scrambled eggs, in "gravies" and "cheese" sauces, and sprinkled over air-popped popcorn, salads, and steamed vegetables.

Quinoa

Cooked like a grain but in actuality a seed, quinoa has bounded in popularity over the past decade. Held sacred by the Incas, quinoa is higher in protein and calcium than most other grains, cooks up quickly, and has a pleasant nutty flavor.

Sea Vegetables

Also known as seaweed, these veggies include wakame, nori, and arame. These are used in Japanese dishes, lend some interesting, sometimes fishy flavors, and are often referred to as "nature's mineral supplements" due to their high content of trace minerals. You are probably most familiar with nori—that's the seaweed that is compressed to form the flat sheets used to roll your sushi.

Seitan

Also called "gluten" or "wheat meat," seitan is made from the protein part of wheat so it's a good source of protein. Seitan has a fairly meat-like texture, so it can be used as a low-fat, higher fiber substitute in most beef, pork, or chicken dishes.

"Soysage"

These products are usually made from wheat gluten and/or tofu and are often flavored to taste like processed meats. Unlike real sausages, they do not contain carcinogenic nitrates or saturated fats and are usually lower in sodium. Some good ones are made by Tofurky and Field Roast.

Steel Cut Oats

Steel cut oats are oat groats (or kernels) that are cut up into "grit" size (as opposed to ground into flour or flattened into rolled oats), which amps up the fiber. This is an excellent choice in recovery and among diabetics due to its lower glycemic index.

Sucanat

A contraction of the French for "natural cane sugar" (sucre de canne naturel), Sucanat is pure dried cane sugar with the molasses still in it, so it's a fairly decent source of calcium, iron, and other useful nutrients and lower in sucrose than refined white sugar. Use it as you would brown sugar.

Tamari, Shoyu, and Soy Sauce

These are all made from soybeans. Traditionally there was an actual difference in these sauces: Tamari is a fermented wheat-free byproduct of miso production. Shoyu—translated into soy sauce as it came to the United States—contains wheat. The definitions of these seem to have blurred in the West. Bottom line: All are high in sodium, so read the label and use sparingly.

Tempeh

Made from whole cultured soybeans, tempeh has been the staple food of Indonesia for ages. It is high in protein and fiber and can be used in stir-fries, salads, wraps, mock "chicken" or "tuna" salads, and so on. The flavor of the tempeh depends on the manufacturer and can range from meaty or fishy to a mild nutty flavor.

Tofu

Tofu has been a staple protein source for much of southeast Asia for millennia. Tofu is to soymilk what cheese is to cows' milk. Basically the beans are ground with water and strained separating the liquid soymilk from the high fiber solids ("okara"). The "milk" is curdled, often with a high calcium agent, and the final texture depends on how much liquid is pressed out of the tofu. In the Orient one can find hundreds of different types of tofu textures and versions. Here in the States, tofu generally can be found as "silken" (good for smoothies and "cheesecakes"), regular or firm, and very firm (these two latter both can be used in scrambles, stir-fries, miso soup, and so on). Silken tofu is sometimes packaged in aseptic boxes that do not require refrigeration and has a shelf life of up to a year, unopened. Once any tofu container has been opened, submerge any unused portion with water in a container, cover, and refrigerate for up to a week.

Where's the Protein?

You may notice that there are a lot of meatless meals included in these menus and feel a) concerned about getting enough protein, and b) uncomfortable not eating meat several times a day just because that is what you are used to and what you know.

No need to worry! Meat is not the only source of protein. Beans, lentils, nuts, seeds, and soy products with funny-sounding names like tempeh, edamame, and seitan (a.k.a. gluten or wheat meat) are also excellent sources of protein and are widely include in the menus.

For example, a cup of soymilk, ½ cup of cooked beans, ⅓ cup quinoa, or 2 tablespoons of almond butter each contain approximately 7 grams of protein, the same as in one egg, one cup of milk, or one ounce of meat, poultry, or fish. Even vegetables, grains, and fruits contain some protein. Moreover, it will be difficult for you to follow those strategies for diet in recovery and manage those medical conditions on the typical meatlover's fare. Animal products are devoid of fiber and phytochemicals, and generally higher in fats, especially those that clog the heart and liver. Therefore, these twelve weeks of menus are planned to be moderate in the meat department, encouraging healthier preparation methods, and in combination with plenty of fresh vegetables, whole grains, and nuts.

Vegetable Variety

This "non-recipe" provides you with general instructions for unlimited combinations and permutations so you can customize your own vegetable dish.

1. First, steam your veggies. Using a vegetable steamer with a cup or two of water in the bottom and a tight lid, get the water heating, and add the firmer, long cooking vegetables first. Check for tenderness and don't overcook!

2. It's nice to have a colorful medley with complementary tastes—two or three is a good number. Remember, each type of vegetable provides different nutrients and phytochemicals, so eat a variety.

3. Get creative and invent your own favorite vegetable combo. Here are some suggestions:
   - Kale, sweet potatoes
   - Broccoli, cauliflower, carrots
   - Green beans, carrots, cabbage
   - Beets, sweet potatoes, greens
   - Carrots, zucchini squash, mushrooms
   - Asparagus, carrots, red bell peppers
   - Brussels sprouts, yellow squash, carrots

4. When tender, remove to a serving dish. Jazz up and vary the flavor while limiting fat and sodium by adding one of the following:
   - Nutritional yeast, Spike (Mrs. Dash), dab of butter/non-trans fat margarine
   - A drizzle of toasted sesame oil, tamari (or low-sodium soy sauce), and/or grated fresh gingerroot
   - A sprinkle of olive oil and/or balsamic vinegar
   - Tomato sauce and Italian herbs
   - Fresh lemon juice
   - OJ and low-sodium seasoning
   - A small amount of crumbled feta or shredded mozzarella cheese
   - Plain yogurt mixed with curry powder
   - Any low-fat salad dressing

Dancing Through the Menus

So how to get started? You may want to browse through the twelve weeks and see if any of the recipes call to you, pique your appetite, or comprise ingredients you currently have on hand. You might want to try the "I-Ching" method—opening the menu section at random and just submitting to whatever it may be. Perhaps just stick your toe in and start with some Overnight Oatmeal for breakfast. Whatever your technique, the important thing is to get started nourishing yourself. Along the way (assuming any of these have been lost) you may recover your sense of humor, creativity, adventure, and gratitude as well as your youthful figure and health. Always keep in mind the main goal: to support your recovery. *Bon appétit! ¡Buen apetito!* Enjoy!

Breakfast

Overnight Oatmeal, herbal tea, orange juice

Overnight Oatmeal

4 servings

This hearty and comforting hot cereal is great for sustained energy. Three methods are suggested for shortening the usual cooking time by setting it up at night. Apples and dried fruit provide some natural sweetness, but all are optional and could be replaced with other fruits. For interesting texture and to mix up the taste you can add a handful of chopped walnuts, ground flaxseeds, and/or a dash of cinnamon.

Make plenty to have on hand for even quicker breakfasts later in the week. Leftover steel cut oats also makes a great snack, cold or reheated, with a dollop of vanilla yogurt on top.

1 cup steel cut oats

14 dried apricot halves

1 dried fig

2 tablespoons golden raisins

1 apple, diced

4 cups liquid (skim milk, soy, almond, rice, coconut milk, water, or a mix of your choice)

1. **Method No. 1:** Add all ingredients to slow cooker with a ceramic interior; set to low heat. Cover and cook overnight (8–9 hours).
2. **Method No. 2:** Place all ingredients in a medium saucepan and bring to an almost boil. Turn off the heat and cover saucepan. When cooled, place in covered container and refrigerate overnight. In the morning, the oatmeal will have absorbed all of the water. Scoop one portion of the oatmeal into a bowl; microwave on high for 1½ to 2 minutes and serve.
3. **Method No. 3:** The evening before, mix all ingredients in a sealable plastic container and store in refrigerator overnight. In the morning, transfer oat mixture to a saucepan and cook for 5 minutes until thickened. Heat up refrigerated leftover portions as needed; use within three days. Serve with a dab of molasses, Sucanat, real maple syrup, and/or vanilla yogurt, dairy or soy, to taste.

Lunch

Whole wheat pita with hummus (chickpea dip), sautéed zucchini and yellow squash with onions and garlic, lemonade

Dinner

Tofu and Root Vegetables, green salad

Tofu and Root Vegetables
12 1-cup servings

For a vegan version: Omit the feta cheese. Finely grate fresh ginger over top of vegetables instead.

½ medium rutabaga

1 medium-large beet (root only)

½ turnip

1 pound parsnips

1 medium-large sweet potato

1 pound carrots (cut into sticks or use "baby" carrots)

1 pound firm tofu

1 head fresh garlic cloves (just skin, leave whole)

8 ounces feta cheese, crumbled, or small amount of grated gingerroot

Olive oil

Bragg Liquid Aminos

Fresh ground black pepper to taste

1. Preheat oven to 400°F.
2. Clean, peel, and cut all vegetables and tofu into ½"–1" pieces (keep garlic cloves whole). Evenly distribute these in a large (10" × 15"), ungreased baking dish.
3. Spread feta cheese evenly over the top. Drizzle olive oil, Bragg's, and fresh grated pepper over top.
4. Cover tightly with foil and bake for 40–50 minutes until vegetables are tender and feta has melted.

Gingerroot keeps well in a freezer bag, always at the ready to be easily grated, ideally on a microplane. If kept in the refrigerator it will become mushy, difficult to grate, and rot.

Snack

Fresh fruit

Monday

Breakfast

High fiber cereal, with banana, dried fruit, herbal tea, orange juice

Lunch

Basic Lunch Wrap

Basic Lunch Wrap

1 servings

Simple, quick, and inexpensive, yet nutritious. Ingredients can vary according to taste, time, and what's on hand. Heat and eat at home or make it "to go."

1. Start with 1 burrito-size whole grain wrap on a microwaveable plate or, if "to go," place the wrap skin on a square of aluminum foil.
2. Add one or more of the following: tempeh chunks, cooked black or kidney beans, low-fat refried beans, sliced "soysage." Note: If using a plate you can build the ingredients on one side of the wrap; if "to go," limit the ingredients to a line in the center.
3. Load in any of the following veggies: diced fresh tomato, mushroom slices, grated carrots, a few chunks of avocado.
4. Optional: top with salsa, prepared tomato sauce, and/or dab of low-fat sour cream.
5. Sprinkle some shredded cheese (dairy or soy) over the top.
6. If on a plate, fold the burrito over to form a semi-circle and microwave for 1–2 minutes until cheese melts.
7. If "to go," fold in the bottom and sides of the burrito and then snuggle the foil around tightly to prevent leakage. Remove from foil before "nuking" at work.
8. It's a wrap!

Snack

Yogurt cup

Dinner

Baked Sole Almondine, steamed Green Beans with Garlic (see Week 10, Monday dinner), whole grain dinner rolls

Baked Sole Almondine

4 servings

Almonds contain lots of healthy monoun-saturated fat. Just a few add great flavor and crunch to this classic recipe.

1 egg

¼ cup skim milk, soymilk, or rice/almond milk

½ cup dried whole grain breadcrumbs

¼ cup ground almonds

1 teaspoon dried basil leaves

¼ teaspoon salt

½ teaspoon dried thyme leaves

1 pound sole fillets (organic if possible)

2 tablespoons lemon juice

1 tablespoon water

1 tablespoon butter, melted

¼ cup sliced almonds

3 green onions, chopped

1. Preheat oven to 425°F. Line a baking sheet with parchment paper and set aside.
2. In shallow dish, combine egg and milk; beat until combined.
3. On plate, combine breadcrumbs, ground almonds, basil, salt, and thyme and mix well.
4. Dip the fish into the egg mixture, then in the crumb mixture to coat.
5. Place on prepared baking sheet.
6. In a small bowl, combine lemon juice, water, and melted butter.
7. Sprinkle over the fish. Sprinkle with sliced almonds.
8. Bake for 8 to 10 minutes or until fish flakes easily when tested with fork.
9. Sprinkle with green onions and serve immediately.

Almonds come in several types. Plain whole almonds come with the skin attached. Blanched almonds have had their skins removed. Sliced almonds are thinly sliced unblanched whole almonds. Slivered almonds are blanched almonds cut into little sticks. If a recipe calls for ground almonds, slivered almonds are the best choice; grind them in a food processor.

Tuesday

Breakfast

Overnight Oatmeal (from Sunday breakfast), green tea, grape juice

Lunch

Tofu and Root Vegetables (from Sunday dinner), Green Beans with Garlic (from Monday dinner)

Snack

DIY Trail Mix

DIY Trail Mix

Low cost, with fewer calories and less fat than store-bought. The trick is to use cereal as the major ingredient instead of high-fat nuts. You still end up with tasty, crunchy, sweet, and fun food. Just mix up your favorite ingredients and store in a tightly sealed container or portion out into sandwich bags. Here are some suggested ingredients:

Kashi Heart to Heart Cereal (you may also want to try puffed rice or millet, Cheerios, etc.)

Raisins

Currants

Dried pineapple, apricot, or other dried fruit, diced

Sunflower seeds

Pumpkin seeds

Cashews

Filberts (a.k.a. hazelnuts)

Shredded coconut

Dinner

Marinara Sauce with Italian "Soysage," whole wheat fettuccine pasta, shredded Parmesan, green salad

Marinara Sauce with Italian "Soysage"

8 servings

Marinara sauce is a basic Italian tomato sauce made with onions and herbs.

Adding Italian deli flavor vegetarian "soysage" puts the zip in this quickly prepared sauce.

1 tablespoon olive oil

1 onion, minced

4 cloves garlic, minced

2 large Italian deli type "soysages" (Tofurky makes a good one), sliced

1 14-ounce can diced tomatoes, undrained

1 8-ounce can tomato sauce

1 6-ounce can tomato paste

1 teaspoon dried oregano leaves

⅛ teaspoon salt

1 teaspoon sugar

⅛ teaspoon pepper

¼ cup minced fresh basil

1. In a large saucepan, heat olive oil over medium heat.
2. Add onion and garlic; cook and stir for 3 minutes.
3. Add "soysage" slices and continue sautéing for another 2–3 minutes.
4. Add all remaining ingredients except basil and bring to a simmer.
5. Reduce heat, partially cover pan, and simmer for 10 to 15 minutes or until slightly thickened.
6. Stir in basil and serve with hot cooked pasta.

Breakfast

Whole grain bagel with almond butter, tomato slices, green tea, cranapple juice

Lunch

Fish sandwich and Green Beans with Garlic (from Monday dinner)

Snack

Pistachios

Dinner

Yogurt Chicken Paprika, brown rice, steamed kale

Yogurt Chicken Paprika
6 servings

Yogurt and paprika are a classic combination. Serve this over hot cooked brown rice. The chicken in this recipe can be replaced by tofu or seitan for a low-fat meatless version.

3 boneless, skinless chicken thighs

3 boneless, skinless chicken breasts

⅛ teaspoon pepper

½ teaspoon salt

¼ cup flour

1 tablespoon olive oil

1 onion, diced

½ cup fat-free, low-sodium chicken or vegetable broth

1 tablespoon lemon juice

2 tablespoons cornstarch

2 cups plain low-fat yogurt or soy yogurt

2 teaspoons paprika

1. Season chicken or tofu with salt and pepper. Roll in the flour to coat.
2. In a large skillet, heat oil over medium heat. Add chicken and brown on both sides, about 10 minutes total.
3. Add onion, broth, and lemon juice; bring to a simmer.
4. Cover and simmer until tender and thoroughly cooked, about 12 to 17 minutes. Since the breasts will cook faster than the thighs, keep an eye on them and remove when cooked.
5. Meanwhile, combine cornstarch, yogurt, and paprika in a medium bowl.
6. When chicken is cooked, remove from pan and drain off half of the liquid. Add yogurt mixture to pan drippings and bring to a simmer.
7. Simmer over low heat for 5 minutes, then return chicken to the pan.
8. Simmer for another 3 to 4 minutes until sauce is slightly thickened. Serve immediately.

Thursday

Breakfast

High fiber, whole grain ready to eat cereal, banana, herbal tea, orange juice

Lunch

Marinara Sauce with Italian "Soysage" over whole wheat noodles (from Tuesday dinner) with leftover kale (from Wednesday dinner)

Snack

Fresh pineapple with grated ginger

Dinner

Seitan and Vegetables Stir-Fry over brown rice (from Wednesday dinner)

Seitan and Vegetables Stir-Fry
3 servings

Seitan with veggies cooks up in a matter of minutes, so this is a great weeknight staple for when you want to get a nutritious meal on the table quickly.

2 tablespoons canola oil

½ large onion, sliced

3 cloves garlic, minced

2 carrots, sliced

½ cup chopped cabbage

1 pound seitan, sliced

1 cup broccoli, cut into florets

1 tablespoon low-sodium tamari

½ cup mushrooms

½ red bell pepper, sliced into thin strips

1 tablespoon salt-free curry powder

1 tablespoon arrowroot powder

3 tablespoons fresh ginger, grated

2 tablespoons tahini (sesame paste)

⅔ cup water or vegetable stock

1 teaspoon toasted sesame oil

1. Heat canola oil in wok over high heat. Add onions and garlic, sauté for 3 minutes stirring constantly.
2. Add carrots, cabbage, and seitan, and sauté, stirring for another 3 minutes.
3. Add broccoli, tamari, and about ⅓ cup water to wok, cover immediately and steam for about 3 minutes.
4. In the meantime, mix curry powder, arrowroot, ginger, and tahini with small amount of water until arrowroot mixture dissolves. Then add the rest of liquid and add to wok along with mushrooms and peppers.
5. Continue cooking and stirring until sauce thickens and vegetables are desired tenderness; ideally still bright and not too limp.
6. Serve over reheated brown rice. Drizzle a small amount of sesame oil over each serving to taste.

Breakfast

Multigrain hot cereal, herbal tea, fruit juice

Lunch

Seitan and Vegetables Stir-Fry (from Thursday dinner)

Snack

Rice crackers with apple butter

Dinner

Salmon Cakes with Mango Salsa, Quinoa with Sautéed Garlic

Salmon Cakes with Mango Salsa

4 servings

If you cannot find almond or pecan meal, you can make your own by grinding a cup of raw almonds or pecans in a food processor until a flour consistency is achieved. But be careful not to run it so long that it becomes an oily paste!

1 14-ounce can wild Alaskan salmon
¼ cup minced chives
1 large egg, beaten
1 cup almond or pecan flour
Sea salt to taste
1 ripe mango
½ sweet Vidalia onion
½ red pepper
3" piece gingerroot
Juice of one lemon

1. Preheat oven to 350°F.
2. In a medium bowl, combine salmon, chives, beaten egg, nut flour, and sea salt.
3. Mix well; form into 4 patties.
4. Place on a well-oiled baking sheet; bake 15–20 minutes, or cook in an oiled skillet, browning on both sides.

5. To make the salsa, peel and chop mango into small pieces; place in a medium-size bowl.
6. Mince red pepper and onion; add to bowl.
7. Peel and grate ginger, extracting juice by pressing the fiber against the side of a shallow dish; pour juice into bowl with mango mixture.
8. Juice the lemon, add to mango mixture; mix well.
9. Cover and refrigerate until ready to serve. For a hotter, spicier version, add a fresh, minced jalapeño pepper.

Quinoa with Sautéed Garlic
4–6 servings

This is the type of recipe that can become a staple in your kitchen. Quick, easy, and a very delicious way to prepare any type of grain. Of course, anything tastes great tossed with olive oil and garlic!

1 cup quinoa

2 cups water or vegetable stock

¼ teaspoon sea salt

½ medium onion

6 cloves garlic

¼ cup extra-virgin olive oil

1. Place the quinoa in a metal strainer; rinse well under running water.
2. Drain; add to a heavy saucepan with water or stock and sea salt.
3. Chop onion; add to quinoa.
4. Cover and bring to a boil over medium-high heat; reduce heat and simmer until all water has been absorbed, about 15–20 minutes.
5. Meanwhile, slice the garlic lengthwise along the clove and set aside.
6. Heat oil in a small skillet; sauté garlic until just crisp, but not yet brown. Remove from heat.
7. When quinoa is done, pour garlic and oil over quinoa; toss gently.
8. Serve as a side dish or top with stir-fried beans and vegetables for a main dish.

For gluten-intolerant individuals, quinoa is a good substitute for gluten-based grains such as couscous, a refined wheat product that also cooks quickly and is found in many Middle Eastern recipes. Quinoa is available in grain, flour, bread, cold cereal, and pasta form.

Saturday

Breakfast

Tofu "Egg-less" Scramble, whole wheat bread, herbal chai tea, fruit juice

Tofu "Egg-less" Scramble
4 servings

Turmeric contains potent phytochemicals and is the spice responsible for the yellow color of curry and yellow rice. It also turns this tofu the color of scrambled eggs and more than one of our rehab residents has eaten seconds before the shock of finding out they were eating tofu, not eggs.

1 tablespoon olive oil
½ medium onion, coarsely chopped
8 ounces portabella mushrooms, sliced
1 red bell pepper, sliced
1 pound firm tofu, diced or crumbled
½ teaspoon turmeric
1 teaspoon Bragg Liquid Aminos
½ teaspoon low-sodium Spike or Mrs. Dash

1. Heat olive oil in large cast iron skillet over medium-high heat. (You can also use a large sauté pan.) Add onions and sauté until almost soft. Add mushrooms and peppers, stirring occasionally for 3 minutes.
2. Stir in remaining ingredients. Cover skillet and cook for several minutes.

Lunch

Salmon Cakes with Mango Salsa and Quinoa with Sautéed Garlic (from Friday dinner), spinach salad

Snack

Fresh melon

Dinner

Lima Bean Casserole, barley, steamed broccoli and carrots

Lima Bean Casserole

6 servings

Lima beans are delicious—nutty, soft, and buttery. They're a satisfying meat substitute in this easy casserole.

1 tablespoon olive oil

1 onion, chopped

3 cloves garlic, minced

1 Granny Smith apple, peeled and chopped

¼ cup tomato paste

⅓ cup tomato juice

2 tablespoons mustard

3 tablespoons red wine vinegar

1 teaspoon dried oregano leaves

3 tablespoons honey

⅛ teaspoon pepper

2 10-ounce packages frozen lima beans, thawed

1. Preheat oven to 350°F.
2. Spray a 2-quart baking dish with non-stick cooking spray and set aside.
3. In a large skillet, heat oil over medium heat.
4. Add the onion, garlic, and apple and sauté until the onion is translucent, about 5 minutes.
5. Add tomato paste, juice, mustard, vinegar, oregano, honey, and pepper and remove from heat.
6. Stir gently to combine, then mix in the lima beans.
7. Transfer to prepared dish and cover with foil.
8. Bake until beans are tender, about 30 to 40 minutes.
9. Serve hot with rice or other whole grain.

Breakfast

Buckwheat Pancakes, vanilla yogurt, fresh fruit, real maple syrup, orange juice, herbal tea

Buckwheat Pancakes

4 servings

Eaten in Russia and Poland, energizing and nutritious buckwheat is used in traditional dishes to provide warming energy for cold winter months. Buckwheat is high in magnesium and antioxidants, which can improve cardiovascular health and protect against heart disease.

1 cup buckwheat flour

½ cup spelt flour

1 teaspoon ground cinnamon

⅛ teaspoon salt

3 tablespoons safflower oil

1½ cups dairy, soy, or other plant-based milk

Fruit preserves, maple syrup, or yogurt for garnish (optional)

1. In a large bowl, mix dry ingredients together.
2. Mix wet ingredients together in a separate bowl.
3. Pour wet ingredients into dry ingredients and mix.
4. Cover bowl with moist towel, and let batter sit overnight at room temperature.
5. Brush bottom of skillet with safflower oil and heat over medium heat.
6. Spread batter onto skillet, making a 4" wide pancake.
7. As bottom of pancake becomes browned, flip pancake over.
8. When second side is browned, remove to a plate.
9. Continue with remaining batter.
10. Serve with fruit preserves, maple syrup, and/or nonfat yogurt.

Lunch

Green salad with feta, whole wheat pita bread and hummus

Snack

Fruited yogurt

Dinner

Sweet and Sour Pork or Seitan Skillet, soba noodles

Sweet and Sour Pork or Seitan Skillet

4 servings

Your choice: vegetarian or pork. Seitan, also known as "wheat meat" or "gluten," is an excellent high-protein, unprocessed stand-in for meat with a convincing texture.

12 ounces lean pork tenderloin or seitan, cut into 1" strips

1 tablespoon honey

2 tablespoons rice vinegar or white vinegar

2 teaspoons soy sauce

½ teaspoon grated ginger

½ cup onions, chopped

½ cup carrots, julienne cut

2 cups cauliflower florets

¼ teaspoon Chinese five spice powder

1. In medium bowl, combine pork or seitan, honey, vinegar, soy sauce, and ginger.
2. Coat pork strips or seitan with mixture; allow to marinate for at least 15 minutes.
3. Heat large nonstick skillet or wok. Add pork strips or seitan and onion; quickly stir-fry over high heat for 2–3 minutes.
4. Reserve any leftover marinade to add with vegetables.
5. Add carrots, cauliflower, and leftover marinade.
6. Toss all ingredients and continue to stir-fry over high heat for an additional 3–4 minutes, or until vegetables are crisp-tender.
7. Add five spice powder and mix just before serving.

Aromatic Five Spice Powder

Chinese five spice powder is a blend of cinnamon, anise, fennel (or star anise), ginger, and clove. Five spice powder is an essential base seasoning for many Chinese dishes. A little of this aromatic mix goes a long way, giving dishes a hint of sweet, savory, and sour.

Monday

Breakfast

Multigrain hot cereal (from Friday breakfast), fresh fruit, green tea

Lunch

Polenta triangles, salad with feta (from Sunday lunch)

Snack

Fruit salad

Dinner

Vegetable and Bean Chili, whole grain bread with almond butter

Vegetable and Bean Chili

8 servings

4 teaspoons olive oil

2 cups cooking onions

½ cup green bell pepper, chopped

3 cloves garlic, chopped

1 small jalapeño pepper, finely chopped (include the seeds if you like the chili extra hot)

1 tablespoon chili powder

1 teaspoon ground cumin

1 28-ounce can unsalted tomatoes, chopped and drained, reserve juice

2 zucchinis, peeled and chopped

2 15-ounce cans unsalted kidney beans, rinsed

1 tablespoon chopped semisweet chocolate

3 tablespoons chopped fresh cilantro

1. Heat heavy pot over moderately high heat.
2. Add olive oil, onions, bell pepper, garlic, and jalapeño.
3. Sauté until vegetables are softened, about 5 minutes.
4. Add chili powder and cumin; sauté for 1 minute, stirring frequently to mix well.

5. Add tomatoes with juice and zucchini; bring to a boil.
6. Lower heat and simmer, partially covered, for 15 minutes, stirring occasionally.
7. Stir in beans and chocolate; simmer, stirring occasionally, for additional 5 minutes, or until beans are heated through and chocolate is melted.
8. Stir in cilantro, and serve.

Snack

Spicy Cold Pears

Spicy Cold Pears
4 servings

Fruit, especially when flavored with spices and citrus, makes a wonderful fat-free dessert.

4 pears, peeled and cored
2 cups cranberry juice
3 tablespoons sugar
½ teaspoon cinnamon
¼ teaspoon cloves
1 teaspoon grated orange zest
1 teaspoon grated lemon zest

1. Cut pears in half.
2. In a large saucepan, combine remaining ingredients and mix well.
3. Add pears and bring to a simmer over medium heat.
4. Reduce heat, cover pan, and simmer until pears are tender, about 12 to 17 minutes.
5. Remove from heat and let cool for 30 minutes.
6. Chill pears in liquid until very cold, about 3 to 4 hours.
7. Serve pears with the liquid and low-fat yogurt, soy yogurt, or frozen yogurt.

Tuesday

Breakfast

Homemade Granola, milk of choice, banana, orange juice

Homemade Granola
10 servings

Feel free to experiment with this granola recipe: use different nuts and fruits, add coconut oil, or substitute blackstrap molasses for honey or maple syrup for an added kick of iron. Serve with milk as cereal, sprinkle over salads, or mix into yogurt with fresh fruit.

6 cups rolled oats
¼ cup chopped almonds
¼ cup chopped pecans
2 tablespoons brown sugar
¼ teaspoon sea salt (optional)
⅓ cup maple syrup
¼ cup honey
¼ cup pineapple juice
½ teaspoon almond or vanilla extract
Cooking spray
¼ cup dried cranberries
¼ cup chopped dried apricots

1. Preheat oven to 300°F.
2. Combine first 5 ingredients in a large bowl.
3. Add syrup, honey, juice, and extract; toss well.
4. Spread mixture evenly onto a jelly-roll pan coated with cooking spray (or line the pan with aluminum foil for easy cleanup, but be sure to spray the foil).
5. Bake at 300°F for 45 minutes, stirring every 15 minutes.
6. Stir in cranberries, apricots, and any other fruit you'd like.
7. Cool completely.
8. Store in an airtight container.

Lunch

Sweet and Sour Pork or Seitan Skillet (from Sunday dinner)

Snack

Cup of yogurt

Dinner

A Taste of Italy Baked Fish, whole wheat pasta with olive oil, steamed asparagus with fresh lemon juice

A Taste of Italy Baked Fish

4 servings

This recipe can be "veganized" by using slabs of firm tofu in place of the fish fillets.

1 pound cod fillets
1 14½-ounce can stewed tomatoes
¼ teaspoon dried minced onion
½ teaspoon dried minced garlic
¼ teaspoon dried basil
¼ teaspoon dried parsley
⅛ teaspoon dried oregano
⅛ teaspoon sugar
1 tablespoon grated Parmesan cheese

1. Preheat oven to 375°F.
2. Rinse cod with cold water and pat dry with paper towels.
3. In medium-sized baking pan or casserole treated with nonstick cooking spray, combine all ingredients except fish; mix.
4. Arrange fillets over mixture, folding thin tail ends under; spoon mixture over fillets.
5. For fillets about 1" thick, bake uncovered 20–25 minutes, or until fish is opaque and flaky.

Breakfast

High fiber cold cereal with dates, herbal tea, orange juice

Lunch

Vegetable and Bean Chili (from Monday dinner)

Snack

Fruit Frenzy Sparkler Concentrate

Fruit Frenzy Sparkler Concentrate

8 servings

Refreshing, sugar- and caffeine-free thirst quencher.

1 cup peeled, seeded, and chopped peach or papaya
1 cup peeled and cubed fresh pineapple
1 teaspoon peeled and grated fresh ginger
1 cup orange juice
1 cup frozen banana slices
Seltzer water or carbonated water

1. Place all ingredients except water in food processor; process until smooth.
2. To serve, pour ½ cup concentrate over ice in 12- to 16-ounce glass.
3. Complete filling glass with carbonated water.

Wednesday

Dinner

Broccoli and Arame in Tofu Cream Sauce over quinoa pasta

Broccoli and Arame in Tofu Cream Sauce

8 servings

Miso is fermented soybean paste loaded with beneficial digestive enzymes purported to help rid the body of radiation. Arame is a type of seaweed, one of "nature's mineral pills."

1 pound broccoli

¼ cup dry arame

1 tablespoon olive oil

½ onion, chopped

½ cup fresh basil leaves

2 cloves garlic, minced

1 14-ounce package silken tofu

3 tablespoons mellow white miso

2 green onions, chopped

½ cup fresh parsley

Juice of ½ lemon

1. Cut the florets off broccoli stems; cut into smaller florets and set aside.
2. Soak arame in hot water for 10 minutes; drain and set aside.
3. Steam broccoli florets until tender; rinse under cold water, and set aside.
4. In a large skillet, heat oil; add onion, basil, and garlic; sauté until tender.
5. Add broccoli and arame; stir well. Remove from heat.
6. In a blender or food processor, purée tofu, miso, green onions, parsley, and lemon juice until creamy.
7. Pour tofu mixture over broccoli; mix well. Reheat gently if necessary, but do not boil.
8. Adjust seasonings and serve as a side dish.

> **Simple, Easy Arame**
> Soak arame in hot water until tender, about 10 minutes, then drain and toss with cooked grains, soba noodles, or put into a raw salad. High in calcium and other minerals, it is the most versatile of the sea vegetables and one everyone can enjoy.

Thursday

Breakfast

Whole wheat bagel with almond butter, vegetarian "soysage" and tomato slices, green tea, orange juice

Lunch

Black Bean Burritos, carrot sticks

Black Bean Burritos

4 servings

It's probably no accident that these burritos (which can be made vegan by substituting soy cheese for the Cheddar and Monterey jack) are a source of complete protein, since their origins are hot Mexican lands, where many local residents considered animal protein a luxury.

1 tablespoon oil

1 cup chopped onions

4 large 12" flour or whole wheat tortillas

1 cup shredded cheese, such as a combination of Cheddar and Monterey jack or soy cheese

2 cups cooked brown rice, hot

1 15-ounce can of black beans, heated with some cumin and garlic

½ cup Salsa Fresca or chopped tomatoes and onions

1 ripe Hass avocado, peeled and sliced

½ cup fresh cilantro sprigs

Sour cream (optional)

1. Brown the onions in the oil until soft.
2. Soften a tortilla over a gas burner or in a hot oven; place on a clean work surface. Spoon a quarter of the hot onions into a line, one-third the way up on the tortilla; sprinkle on a quarter of the shredded cheese.
3. Immediately spoon on ½ cup hot rice; this should be hot enough to melt the cheese.
4. Ladle on a quarter of the beans, including some of its sauce; top with the salsa, avocado slices, and cilantro.
5. Fold edge nearest to you up to cover the fillings.
6. Fold side flaps in, to seal ingredients into a pocket.
7. Roll the burrito away from yourself, keeping even tension, and tucking with your fingers as you roll.
8. Repeat with remaining tortillas.

Thursday

Snack

DIY Trail Mix

Dinner

Chicken with Portobello Mushrooms and Roasted Garlic, whole wheat fettuccine, steamed greens

Chicken with Portobello Mushrooms and Roasted Garlic

4 servings

1 tablespoon olive oil

4 boneless, skinless chicken breasts

1 cup reduced-sodium chicken or vegetable broth

1 bulb garlic, dry roasted (see sidebar) and mashed into paste

1 tablespoon butter

2 cups portobello mushrooms

½ teaspoon thyme

2 tablespoons feta cheese, crumbled

1. Heat olive oil in large nonstick skillet; brown chicken breasts on both sides over medium heat, about 5 minutes per side.

2. Add broth and roasted garlic paste to skillet; cover and simmer on low 10 minutes.

3. Meanwhile, sauté mushrooms and thyme in butter in separate, smaller saucepan. Simmer 2 minutes.

4. Add the mushrooms and thyme mixture to the chicken and simmer for an additional 2 minutes.

5. When serving, top each chicken breast with 1½ teaspoons feta cheese and spoon sauce over the top.

> **Dry-Roasting Garlic**
> Preheat oven to 350°F; lightly spray small, covered baking dish with nonstick spray. Slice off ½" from top of each garlic head; rub off any loose skins, being careful not to separate cloves. Place in baking dish, cut-side up (if roasting more than 1 head, arrange in dish so they don't touch). Cover and bake until the garlic cloves are very tender when pierced, about 30–45 minutes. Roasted garlic heads will keep in refrigerator 2–3 days.

Friday

Breakfast

High fiber ready to eat cereal, fresh berries, milk, juice, herbal tea

Lunch

Broccoli and Arame in Tofu Cream Sauce (from Wednesday dinner)

Snack

Gourmet Sorbet

Gourmet Sorbet

4 servings

This is a refreshing, natural alternative to high-fat, high sugar ice creams and frozen desserts as well as an economical use of over-ripe bananas and other perishable fruit (freeze them before they "perish" in sturdy freezer bags or containers). Originally inspired by a bumper crop of fresh figs (cranberries were used here as they seem to be always available and add a tart "kick") this recipe also works very well with peaches, blueberries, strawberries, papaya, or pineapple (and figs, of course) always keeping the bananas as the sweet, smoothly textured base. Chocolate soymilk and other types of juices may be substituted for variety.

2 medium bananas, peeled and frozen

⅓ cup frozen cranberries

¼ cup orange juice

¼ cup unsweetened soymilk

2 tablespoons semisweet chocolate chips (optional)

¼ teaspoon fresh ginger, grated

1. Slice frozen bananas into approximately ½" pieces and place in food processor.
2. Add cranberries, orange juice, and soymilk.
3. Process ingredients for 15 seconds or until fully blended.
4. Add chocolate chips and ginger; process until desired texture is achieved (about 15 seconds).
5. Serve immediately. Enjoy!

Frozen Fruit

With frozen fruit on hand you can go from impulse to ingestion in less than 5 minutes! A time-saving suggestion is to create small bags of the fresh fruits needed for one recipe prior to freezing to obviate the need to hack apart frozen fruit masses.

Dinner

Vegetable Frittata, whole wheat toast

Vegetable Frittata

4 servings

1½ tablespoons olive oil

4 ounces red pepper, chopped

3 large eggs

4 ounces egg substitute (or 2 tablespoons ground flaxseed soaked in 6 tablespoons water for 5 minutes)

4 ounces asparagus, cut diagonally in 1" pieces

¾ cup sweet potatoes, cooked and cubed

⅓ cup feta cheese, crumbled

1 teaspoon oregano

1. Preheat oven to 350°F.
2. Using ovenproof nonstick skillet, heat olive oil over medium heat.
3. Add red peppers; cook until softened.
4. In medium bowl, beat together eggs and egg substitute.
5. Add asparagus, potatoes, feta, and oregano.
6. Pour eggs into skillet; gently stir until eggs on bottom of pan begin to set.
7. Gently pull cooked eggs from side of skillet, allowing liquid uncooked egg on top to come in contact with heated skillet.
8. Repeat, working all around skillet, until most of eggs on top have begun to set.
9. Transfer skillet to oven; bake until top is set and dry to the touch, about 3–5 minutes.
10. Loosen frittata around edges of skillet and invert onto serving plate.

Saturday

Breakfast

Quinoa Berry Breakfast, juice, herbal tea

Quinoa Berry Breakfast
4 servings

Use this basic recipe to make 4 servings at once. Refrigerate any leftover portions; microwave 1 to 1½ minutes on high for single portions as needed. Use cooked quinoa within 3 days. Try a variety of berries, nuts, or spices such as ginger or nutmeg to vary this nutritious breakfast cereal.

1 cup quinoa
2 cups water
¼ cup walnuts
1 teaspoon cinnamon
2 cups berries

1. Rinse quinoa in fine-mesh sieve before cooking.
2. Place quinoa, water, walnuts, and cinnamon in 1½ quart saucepan; bring to a boil.
3. Reduce heat to low; cover and cook for 15 minutes, or until all water has been absorbed.
4. Add berries and serve with milk, soymilk, or sweetener if desired.

Lunch

Grilled Swiss cheese on rye sandwich, green salad

Snack

Almonds and raisins

Dinner

Stir-Fried Ginger Scallops or Tempeh with Vegetables

Stir-Fried Ginger Scallops or Tempeh with Vegetables
4 servings

"Veganize" this recipe with tempeh and vegetable broth.

1 pound scallops or 2 8-ounce packages of tempeh
1 teaspoon peanut or sesame oil
1 tablespoon chopped fresh ginger
2 cloves garlic, minced
4 scallions, thinly sliced
1 teaspoon rice wine vinegar
2 teaspoons Bragg Liquid Aminos
½ cup low-fat reduced-sodium chicken or vegetable broth
2 cups broccoli florets
1 teaspoon cornstarch
¼ teaspoon toasted sesame oil

1. Rinse scallops and pat dry between layers of paper towels. If necessary, slice scallops so they're uniform size. Set aside. If using tempeh, cut into 1" cubes.

2. Add peanut oil to heated nonstick deep skillet or wok; sauté ginger, garlic, and scallions, 1–2 minutes, being careful ginger doesn't burn.

3. Add vinegar, Liquid Aminos, and broth; bring to a boil. Remove from heat.

4. Place broccoli in large, covered microwave-safe dish; pour broth mixture over top. Microwave on high 3–5 minutes, depending on preference. (Keep in mind that vegetables will continue to steam for a minute or so if cover remains on dish.)

5. Heat skillet or wok over medium-high temperature. Add scallops or tempeh; sauté 1 minute on each side. (Do in smaller batches if necessary; be careful not to overcook.)

6. Remove scallops or tempeh from pan when done; set aside.

7. Drain (but do not discard) liquid from broccoli; return liquid to bowl and transfer broccoli to heated skillet or wok.

8. Stir-fry vegetables to bring up to serving temperature.

9. Meanwhile, in small cup or bowl, add enough water to cornstarch to make a slurry or roux.

10. Whisk slurry into reserved broccoli liquid; microwave on high 1 minute.

11. Add toasted sesame oil; whisk again.

12. Pour thickened broth mixture over broccoli; toss to mix.

13. Add scallops or tempeh back to broccoli mixture; stir-fry over medium heat to return to serving temperature.

14. Serve over brown rice or whole grain pasta.

> Tempeh is made by a natural culturing and controlled fermentation process that binds soybeans into a cake form. It has a firm texture and an earthy, nutty flavor which becomes more pronounced as the tempeh ages, but can absorb flavors well from sauces and marinades. It is a good source of protein, dietary fiber, and vitamins, and can be substituted for meat in almost any dish.

Sunday

Breakfast

Tofu "Egg-less" Scramble (see Week 1, Saturday breakfast) with "soysages," whole wheat toast, grape juice, herbal tea

Lunch

Greek salad, pita and hummus

Snack

Fruity Oatmeal Bars

Fruity Oatmeal Bars

18 servings

With five grams of fiber per square, these tasty treats sneak some extra fiber into your afternoon snack.

3 cups quick-cooking oats

1 teaspoon cinnamon

⅓ cup ground flaxseed or wheat germ

¼ teaspoon nutmeg

¾ cup dates or prunes, chopped

¾ cup dried apricots, chopped

1 cup apple butter

1 tablespoon brown sugar

1. Preheat oven to 350°F.
2. Mix the oats, cinnamon, flaxseed or wheat germ, and nutmeg in a large bowl.
3. Add dates and apricots, then apple butter. Ingredients should appear moist and well blended.
4. Spoon into a 8" × 13" nonstick or lightly greased pan.
5. Flatten with spatula to make an even bottom layer.
6. Sprinkle brown sugar over surface.
7. Bake for 20 minutes.
8. Remove from oven and cut into 2" squares, then let cool for 20 minutes.

Dinner

White Chicken Chili, salad with chickpeas and whole wheat croutons

White Chicken Chili

6 servings

This recipe originated with fellow VA dietitian, Sheryl Wehner, MS, RD, for use on her mobile cooking demonstration cart.

2 tablespoons extra-virgin olive oil

2 cloves garlic, minced

1 carrot, peeled and diced

1 medium onion, diced

1 rib celery, diced

½ large red bell pepper, diced

1 cup low sodium chicken stock

2 16-ounce cans reduced-sodium Great Northern beans, undrained

2 cups fresh salsa

6 ounces skinless, boneless chicken breast, roasted and diced

Reduced-fat pepper jack cheese, shredded, optional

Light sour cream, optional

Jalapeños, optional

1. In a stock pot, sauté the garlic, carrot, onion, celery, and bell pepper in the oil on medium-high heat until tender, about 5 minutes.
2. Add chicken stock, beans, salsa, and cooked chicken. Stir until combined.
3. Simmer over low heat for 30 minutes, stirring occasionally.
4. Serve with desired toppings.

Monday

Breakfast

Quinoa Berry Breakfast (from Saturday breakfast)

Lunch

White Chicken Chili (from Sunday dinner)

Snack

Yogurt Fruit Smoothie

Yogurt Fruit Smoothie
2 servings

You can vary this smoothie by substituting other fruits of your choice. Good combinations are strawberry and banana, strawberry and kiwi, or banana and peach. Keep portions of each fruit to no more than ½ cup.

1 cup plain low-fat yogurt of your choice
½ cup sliced strawberries
½ cup orange juice
½ cup nectarines, peeled and sliced
2 tablespoons ground flaxseed

Put all ingredients in blender; process until smooth.

Dinner

Swiss Chard Rolls with Root Vegetables

Swiss Chard Rolls with Root Vegetables

4 servings

This dish is particularly attractive with red Swiss chard, though green is fine.

8 large leaves Swiss chard, thoroughly washed

3 tablespoons olive oil, divided

2 cups roughly chopped red onion

2 carrots, roughly chopped

2 sweet potatoes (about ½ pound), peeled and finely diced

8 cups chopped root vegetables (such as celery root, parsnips, turnips, and white potatoes— try Latino roots, such as yucca, or cassava, malanga, or taro)

¼ cup roughly chopped Italian parsley

2 teaspoons chopped cilantro (optional)

Kosher salt and freshly ground black pepper

Juice of 2 limes (about 4 tablespoons)

1 cup low-sodium stock or water

1. Remove the stems from the chard; chop them finely.
2. Heat 2 tablespoons of the olive oil over a medium flame in a heavy-bottomed Dutch oven or large skillet.
3. Add the chard stems, red onion, carrots, sweet potatoes, root vegetables, parsley, lime juice, and cilantro; season well with salt and pepper.
4. Bring a large pot of salted water to a boil.
5. Blanch the chard leaves for 3 or 4 minutes, then drain and cool.
6. Spoon ¼ cup of filling onto the stem end of a chard leaf.
7. Fold in the sides to envelop the filling; roll away from yourself, keeping even tension so the rolls remain plump.
8. Line the rolls up in a greased skillet; add 1 cup of water or stock, season lightly with salt.
9. Cook 10 minutes; serve garnished with remaining filling.

Breakfast

Whole wheat English muffin with Neufchatel cheese and 100 percent fruit preserves, juice, herbal tea

Lunch

"Soysage" wrap

Snack

Fruity Oatmeal Bar

Dinner

Almond-Encrusted Salmon on Toast Points, Broccoli Pasta Toss

Almond-Encrusted Salmon on Toast Points

6 servings

Serrano peppers have such a thin skin that you don't need to bother removing it.

6 flour or corn tortillas

1 serrano pepper

¼ cup almonds

1 teaspoon chili powder

1 pound salmon fillet

¼ cup milk

1 tablespoon olive oil

1 tablespoon extra-virgin olive oil, plus extra for drizzling

Honey

1. Toast the tortillas under the broiler.
2. Mince the serrano and finely chop the almonds; mix together with chili powder.
3. Clean the salmon in ice water, cut it into 6 portions, then dip it into the milk.
4. Dredge in the almond mix.
5. Heat the olive oil to medium temperature and cook the salmon on each

Tuesday

side for approximately 5 minutes, until thoroughly cooked.
6. Serve on tortillas, drizzled with extra-virgin olive oil and honey.

Herb Gardens

If you enjoy Mediterranean cooking, you may want to consider planting an herb garden. Fresh and inexpensive dish enhancers as well as horticultural therapy.

Broccoli Pasta Toss

4 servings

This easy recipe is good for a last-minute dinner. You can use bell peppers, mushrooms, or carrots instead of the broccoli.

2 cups small broccoli florets
1 12-ounce package whole wheat fettuccine pasta
2 tablespoons olive oil
2 tablespoons lemon juice
½ teaspoon garlic powder
⅛ teaspoon white pepper
3 tablespoons grated Parmesan cheese
1 tablespoon toasted sesame seeds

1. In a large saucepan, cook broccoli and pasta in boiling salted water until the pasta is al dente, stirring once or twice.
2. Drain and place in a bowl.
3. In a small bowl, combine oil, lemon juice, garlic powder, and pepper and mix well.
4. Add to pasta mixture and toss well.
5. Add cheese and sesame seeds and toss to coat. Serve immediately.

Toasting Seeds

Toasting seeds helps increase flavor because it intensifies the oils. Be careful when you toast seeds because they can burn easily. To toast, place seeds in a dry pan and cook over low heat, shaking the pan frequently until seeds are fragrant and turn light golden brown. Cool completely before using in recipes.

Wednesday

Breakfast

High fiber ready to eat cereal, fruit juice, herbal tea

Lunch

Swiss Chard Rolls with Root Vegetables leftovers (from Monday dinner)

Snack

Pumpkin seeds and raisins

Dinner

Portobello Sandwiches, Summer Vegetable Slaw

Portobello Sandwiches

4 servings

Grilled meaty portobello mushrooms are filled with a fragrant tomato mixture, then encased in toasted rolls. Yum!

2 tablespoons low-fat mayonnaise
2 tablespoons mustard
1 teaspoon lemon juice
6 cloves roasted garlic
2 tomatoes, chopped
¼ cup chopped fresh basil leaves
4 large portobello mushrooms
1 tablespoon olive oil
4 kaiser rolls, split and toasted
4 butter lettuce leaves

1. Preheat broiler.
2. In a small bowl, combine mayonnaise, mustard, lemon juice, and garlic; set aside.
3. In another small bowl, combine tomato and basil; set aside.
4. Brush mushrooms with the oil and place on a broiler pan, gill-side up.
5. Broil until tender, about 5 to 7 minutes.
6. Spoon tomato mixture into mushroom caps.
7. Spread mayonnaise mixture over the bottom halves of the rolls and top each

with a mushroom cap, tomato-side up. Top with lettuce.

8. Spread top halves of rolls with remaining mayonnaise mixture and place on lettuce. Serve immediately.

> **Garlic**
>
> Garlic is a member of the lily family, which also includes onions. When fresh, it is quite strong and peppery and has a distinctive aroma. Cooking garlic softens the cloves and reduces the sulfur compounds, making it nutty and sweet.

Summer Vegetable Slaw

8 servings

Bursting with summer's bounty, this slaw is a colorful fiesta. Utilize whatever vegetables are freshest and best at the market—the more the better!

1 small head Napa cabbage or regular green cabbage (about 1 pound)

1 large carrot, or 2 regular carrots, peeled

¼ pound snow peas

1 each red, yellow, and green bell peppers, seeded

12 green beans

1 small red onion

2 ears fresh sweet corn, shucked

½ teaspoon sugar

¼ cup cider vinegar

1 tablespoon vegetable oil (preferably peanut oil)

Pinch of celery seeds

Salt and black pepper to taste

1. Quarter and core the cabbage; slice as thinly as possible.
2. Using a swivel peeler, shave carrot into as many paper-thin curls as you can.
3. Discard or save remaining carrot for another use.
4. Cut carrot curls, snow peas, bell peppers, green beans, and onion into fine julienne.
5. Cut corn kernels from the cob.
6. Combine all vegetables in a large mixing bowl; dress with sugar, vinegar, oil, celery seeds, salt, and pepper.
7. Allow to sit at least 10 minutes before serving.

Thursday

Breakfast

Overnight Oatmeal (see Week 1, Sunday breakfast), fruit juice, herbal tea

Lunch

Sandwich: veggie slices, Muenster cheese, tomato on whole grain bread, Summer Vegetable Slaw (from Wednesday dinner)

Snack

Yogurt Fruit Salad

Yogurt Fruit Salad
1 cup serving

Most commercial flavored yogurts are very heavy on the refined sugar. Mix up your own for real flavor. The basics are plain or vanilla yogurt (dairy, soy, whatever) and fresh and dried fruits, nuts and seeds, plus add-ins such as ground flaxseeds, wheat germ, granola, or whatever you have on hand at the moment. Here's an example of my typical mix.

½ cup mix of plain and vanilla soy yogurt
½ medium banana, sliced
Small handful of fresh blueberries
1 tablespoon ground flaxseeds
1 tablespoon raw hulled sunflower seeds

Stir together and enjoy.

Dinner

Healthy Chicken Nuggets, steamed carrots and asparagus

Healthy Chicken Nuggets

4 servings

The chicken nuggets you buy at the grocery store or fast-food place consist of about 44 percent chicken, are fried in oil, then frozen. These are made from actual chicken, lightly seasoned, then baked—and taste even better!

1¼ cups herb-seasoned crumb stuffing mix or seasoned breadcrumbs

¼ cup grated Parmesan cheese

3 tablespoons non-trans fat margarine, melted

¼ cup low-fat buttermilk or milk

½ teaspoon Mrs. Dash seasoning

4 boneless, skinless chicken breasts (approximately 1 pound)

1. Preheat oven to 350°F.
2. Pour stuffing mix into plastic zip-top bag.
3. Crush crumbs with rolling pin and add Parmesan cheese.
4. Reseal bag and shake to mix thoroughly.
5. Place melted margarine, buttermilk, and seasoning in medium bowl. Stir well with spoon.
6. Rinse chicken breasts and pat dry; cut each breast into 7 to 8 pieces.
7. Dip each chicken chunk into buttermilk mixture, covering all sides. Let extra buttermilk drip off.
8. Place three dipped chunks at a time into the bag of crumbs.
9. Seal bag tightly and shake until chicken pieces are evenly coated with crumbs.
10. Bake coated nuggets on an ungreased baking sheet for 5 minutes.
11. Flip over then bake other side for another 5 minutes or until brown.

Friday

Breakfast

Overnight Oatmeal (from Thursday breakfast) with vanilla yogurt, herbal chai tea

Lunch

Broccoli Pasta Toss (from Tuesday dinner)

Snack

DIY Trail Mix (see Week 1, Tuesday snack)

Dinner

Tuna Panini, Spinach Salad with Apple-Avocado Dressing

Tuna Panini

6 servings

This is like making a marinated sandwich! Make in advance as it needs an hour for the flavors to meld.

1 hard-boiled egg
1 red onion
1 medium apple
¼ teaspoon lemon juice
1 cup water
1 pound cooked or canned tuna or 1 package soft or regular tofu
¼ cup chopped walnuts
2 tablespoons extra-virgin olive oil
1 tablespoon balsamic vinegar
Kosher salt, to taste
Fresh-cracked black pepper
1 small loaf Italian bread
1 head green or red leaf lettuce

1. Medium dice the egg and onion.
2. Dice the apple and toss it in the lemon juice and water; drain.
3. Mix together the tuna/tofu, egg, onion, apple, nuts, oil, and vinegar; season with salt and pepper.
4. Cut the bread in half lengthwise, then layer the lettuce and mound the tuna/tofu mixture on top.

5. Wrap the loaf tightly with plastic wrap and refrigerate for 1 hour.
6. Slice into 6 equal portions and serve.

Spinach Salad with Apple-Avocado Dressing

4 servings

¼ cup unsweetened apple juice

1 teaspoon (or up to 1 tablespoon) cider vinegar

1 clove garlic, minced

1 teaspoon Bragg Liquid Aminos or soy sauce

½ teaspoon Worcestershire sauce* (see sidebar)

2 teaspoons olive oil

1 avocado, peeled and chopped

2½ cups tightly packed spinach and other salad greens

½ cup thinly sliced red onion

½ cup sliced radishes

½ cup bean sprouts

1. In blender or food processor, combine juice, vinegar (the amount of which will depend on how you like your dressing), garlic, Liquid Aminos, Worcestershire, oil, and avocado; process until smooth.
2. In large bowl, toss greens, onions, radishes, and bean sprouts.
3. Pour dressing over salad; toss again.

Worcestershire sauce usually contains anchovies. For a vegetarian adaptation of this dish use a commercially prepared vegetarian version or this DIY Worcestershire Sauce: You will need 1½ cups cider vinegar, ¼ cup plum jam, 1 tablespoon blackstrap molasses, 1 crushed clove garlic, ⅛ teaspoon chili powder, ⅛ teaspoon ground cloves, a pinch of cayenne pepper, ¼ cup chopped onion, ½ teaspoon ground allspice, ⅛ teaspoon dry mustard, and 1 teaspoon Bragg Liquid Aminos. Combine all ingredients in a large saucepan. Cook on medium heat and stir until mixture boils. Lower heat; simmer uncovered for 1 hour, stirring occasionally. This keeps for a long time, if stored in a covered jar in the refrigerator. Makes 1 cup.

Saturday

Breakfast

Omelet, whole grain English muffin with apple butter, grapefruit, herbal tea

Lunch

Sweet Potato Corn Cakes with Wasabi Cream, green salad

Sweet Potato Corn Cakes with Wasabi Cream

6 servings

Silken tofu makes an excellent dairy-cream substitute for both sweet and savory recipes. The lemon juice and sweetener are used to mimic the sweet-sour taste of real cream. Red wine vinegar and a pinch of salt can be substituted for the ume plum vinegar.

1 large sweet potato

4 green onions

1 cup cornmeal

⅔ cup corn kernels

1 egg

Light vegetable oil for frying

1 10-ounce package silken tofu

1 tablespoon plus 1 teaspoon wasabi powder

1 tablespoon ume plum vinegar

Juice of ½ lemon

Pinch of sweetener such as stevia or sugar

1. Preheat oven to 375°F.
2. Pierce sweet potato skin with a fork; bake until tender.
3. Cool, then peel potato.
4. Dice green onions.
5. In a large mixing bowl, combine cornmeal, baked sweet potato, corn kernels, and green onions.
6. In a small bowl, whisk egg; add to cornmeal mixture.
7. Use your hands to form mixture into patties; set on a plate.
8. Heat a small amount of oil; fry patties until brown, turning to do both sides.
9. Place on a platter and keep warm in a low-heat oven while making wasabi cream.
10. Combine tofu, wasabi powder, vinegar, lemon, and sweetener in a blender or food processor; purée until smooth.
11. Divide corn cakes on individual plates; top each cake with a dollop of wasabi cream.

Japanese Horseradish

Wasabi is a member of the cabbage family and is cultivated in Japan. Known as Japanese horseradish, the root has a hot, strong flavor that can get your nose irritated and running if too much is eaten. Wasabi is traditionally served with sushi (raw fish), and was once used medicinally as an antidote for food poisoning.

Snack

Gourmet Sorbet with bananas and blueberries (see Week 2, Friday snack)

Dinner

Cuban Black Beans and Rice, zucchini and yellow crookneck squash sautéed with onions, fruit salad

Cuban Black Beans and Rice

6 to 8 servings

If you like it spicy, add a jalapeño or two to this classic dish of healthy carbohydrates. Serve with a fruit salad for a cooling contrast

1 pound dried black beans
1 tablespoon butter
1 onion, chopped
4 cloves garlic, minced
3 cups water
2 cups low-sodium vegetable broth
2 bay leaves
½ teaspoon dried thyme leaves
½ teaspoon dried oregano leaves
½ teaspoon salt
1 red bell pepper, chopped
1 green bell pepper, chopped
2 tablespoons apple cider vinegar
4 cups hot cooked brown rice

1. Pick over the beans, rinse well, drain, and place in large bowl.
2. Cover with water and let soak overnight.
3. The next day, drain the beans.
4. In a large pot, melt butter over medium heat.
5. Add onion and garlic; cook and stir until translucent, about 6 minutes.
6. Add drained beans, water, broth, bay leaves, thyme, oregano, and salt and mix well.
7. Bring to a boil, then cover pot, reduce heat to low, and simmer until beans are tender, 1 to 1½ hours
8. Add red and green bell pepper to beans along with vinegar; cook for 20 to 30 minutes longer until tender.
9. Serve over hot cooked rice.

Black Beans

Black beans are a wonderful source of soluble fiber, which helps lower cholesterol. The fiber also stabilizes blood sugars, which help keep you feeling full longer. The little beans are also a great source of antioxidants, up to ten times the amount in oranges and equal to the amount in grapes and wine.

Breakfast

Frozen whole grain waffles, vanilla yogurt, sliced bananas, fresh berries, orange juice, herbal tea

Lunch

Divine Carrot-Pumpkin Soup, whole grain bread with SunButter [made from ground sunflower seeds]

Divine Carrot-Pumpkin Soup
14 1-cup servings

This soup recipe has evolved over the years in the kitchens of several cooks: It was originally brought to a potluck by a cook whose husband had just endured cardiac bypass surgery, inspiring them to become low-fat diet groupies. The recipe was borrowed by another cook, and another, and in the process rice milk turned to soy and almond, onions were added, spices upped, and it has become an even more delicious soup.

8 cups sliced carrots

2 cans organic pumpkin

1 sweet potato, mashed (optional)

6 cups vanilla soymilk

2 cups vanilla almond milk

1 tablespoon honey

1 tablespoon cumin

2 teaspoons curry powder

1 teaspoon cinnamon

½ teaspoon salt (optional)

½ teaspoon freshly ground pepper

2 sweet onions, sautéed in olive oil until caramelized

1. Steam carrots until tender.
2. Blend carrots on high speed with vanilla soymilk, in several batches, if necessary.
3. Sauté onions in large pot.
4. Add carrot mixture and pumpkin and heat thoroughly while adding seasonings to taste.
5. Add more soy/almond milk to achieve desired consistency.

Snack

Banana smeared with a dab of tahini (sesame butter)

Dinner

Steak (or Seitan) Stroganoff, whole wheat egg (or eggless) noodles, green salad

Steak (or Seitain) Stroganoff

6 servings

1 pound boneless round steak or 1.5 pounds scitan, sliced in strips

2 tablespoons olive oil

1 onion, chopped

1 8-ounce package sliced mushrooms

3 tablespoons tomato paste

3 tablespoons water

½ teaspoon basil leaves

1 tablespoon cornstarch

1 cup plain low-fat yogurt

¼ cup fat-free beef or vegetable broth

3 cups hot cooked noodles

1. Trim off excess fat from the steak and slice against the grain into ¼" strips.
2. In a large skillet, heat olive oil over medium heat.
3. Add onion and mushrooms; cook and stir until tender, about 5 minutes.
4. Add beef or seitan and cook, stirring frequently, until browned, about 4 minutes longer.
5. Meanwhile, in small bowl combine tomato paste, water, basil, cornstarch, yogurt, and broth and mix with wire whisk until blended.
6. Add to skillet and bring to a simmer.
7. Simmer for 3 to 4 minutes or until sauce thickens.
8. Serve immediately over hot cooked noodles.

Terrific Tomato Paste

Tomato paste is an excellent ingredient to add lots of flavor to a dish without extra fat. If you can find tomato paste in a tube, just store it in the refrigerator and use it as you need it. If you can only find it in a can, remove the paste from the can and freeze it in a small freezer bag. Cut off what you want as needed.

Monday

Breakfast

High fiber ready to eat cereal, raisins, milk, juice, herbal tea

Lunch

Avocado-cheese melt in whole wheat pita, salad (from Sunday dinner)

Snack

Walnuts and raisins

Dinner

Lentil Stuffed Peppers, Coriander Carrots

Lentil Stuffed Peppers
6 servings

Use both red and yellow bell peppers for variety in color and flavor.

2 medium yellow onions
2 stalks celery
2 carrots, peeled
6 sprigs oregano
1 tablespoon olive oil
1 cup plus 3 cups vegetable stock
3 cups red lentils
6 red peppers
3 ounces feta cheese
Fresh-cracked black pepper, to taste

1. Finely dice the onions, celery, and carrots.
2. Reserve the top parts of the oregano sprigs and chop the remaining leaves.
3. Heat the oil to medium temperature in a large saucepot.
4. Add the onions, carrots, and celery; sauté for 5 minutes, then add 1 cup vegetable stock and the lentils.
5. Simmer for 15 to 20 minutes, until the lentils are fully cooked.

6. Cut off the tops of the peppers, leaving the stems attached, and remove the seeds.

7. Place the peppers in a shallow pot with the remaining 3 cups of vegetable stock.

8. Cover and simmer for 10 minutes, then remove from heat.

9. In a bowl, mix together the lentil mixture, the chopped oregano, feta, and black pepper; spoon the mixture into the peppers.

10. Serve the peppers with the stem tops ajar. Garnish with reserved oregano tops.

Coriander Carrots

6 servings

Coriander and bay leaf add a nice spicy touch to tender carrots.

1 tablespoon olive oil

1 onion, chopped

1 cup water

1 bay leaf

½ teaspoon salt

1½ pounds carrots, thickly sliced

¼ cup dried currants

1 tablespoon butter or non-trans fat margarine

2 teaspoons ground coriander

2 tablespoons lemon juice

3 tablespoons minced parsley

1. Heat oil in large saucepan over medium heat.

2. Add onion; cook and stir until crisp-tender, about 4 minutes.

3. Add water, bay leaf, salt, carrots, and currants and bring to a simmer.

4. Cover pan, reduce heat to low, and simmer for 10 to 15 minutes or until carrots are tender when tested with a fork.

5. Drain carrots, removing bay leaf, and return saucepan to heat.

6. Add butter, coriander, lemon juice, and parsley; cook and stir over low heat for 2 to 3 minutes or until carrots are glazed. Serve immediately.

Tuesday

Breakfast

Whole multigrain hot cereal cooked with dates, fruit juice, herbal tea

Lunch

Divine Carrot-Pumpkin Soup (from Sunday lunch)

Snack

Fresh fruit in season

Dinner

Microwave Sole Florentine, Herbed Quinoa with Sun-Dried Tomatoes

Microwave Sole Florentine

4 servings

In the food world, Florentine means served with spinach. This fresh and light dish is easy and quick to make.

1 pound sole fillets
¼ teaspoon salt
⅛ teaspoon white pepper
1 tablespoon lemon juice
1 tablespoon olive oil
2 cups coarsely chopped baby spinach
¼ teaspoon nutmeg

1. In microwave-safe glass baking dish, arrange the fillets.
2. Sprinkle with salt, pepper, lemon juice, and olive oil.
3. Cover with a glass dish and vent 1 corner.
4. Microwave on high, rotating dish once during cooking time, for 4 minutes.
5. Arrange spinach leaves on top; sprinkle with nutmeg.

6. Return to microwave oven and microwave on high for 1 to 2 minutes longer, or until fish flakes easily when tested with fork and spinach wilts slightly.
7. Let stand on solid surface for 3 minutes before serving.

Cooking in the Microwave

Follow recipe directions carefully when cooking in the microwave. Most recipes ask you to turn or rearrange food halfway through cooking time so the food cooks evenly. And if the recipe calls for standing time, let the dish stand on a solid surface (not a wire rack) for the specified time before serving so the food finishes cooking.

Herbed Quinoa with Sun-Dried Tomatoes

6 servings
½ tablespoon olive oil
¼ cup onion, chopped
1 clove garlic, minced
1 cup quinoa
2 cups low-sodium vegetable broth
½ cup fresh mushrooms, sliced
6 sun-dried tomatoes, cut into ¼" pieces
1 teaspoon Italian-blend seasoning

1. In medium saucepan, heat olive oil; sauté onions and garlic.
2. Rinse quinoa in a very fine mesh strainer before cooking.
3. Add quinoa and broth to saucepan; bring to a boil for 2 minutes.
4. Add mushrooms, sun-dried tomatoes, and Italian seasoning.
5. Reduce heat and cover.
6. Cook 15 minutes, or until all water is absorbed.

Quinoa cooks in less than 15 minutes—when grains have turned from white to transparent and the tail-like germ has separated from the seed you know it's done.

Wednesday

Breakfast

Tofu Smoothie

Tofu Smoothie

1 serving

1⅓ cups frozen unsweetened strawberries

½ banana

½ cup (4 ounces) silken tofu

1. In food processor or blender, process all ingredients until smooth.
2. Add a little chilled water for thinner smoothies, if desired.

Lunch

Lentil Stuffed Peppers (from Monday dinner), sliced fresh tomatoes

Snack

Flat rice cakes with fruit preserves

Dinner

Walnut Parsley Pesto over whole wheat pasta

Walnut Parsley Pesto
1 cup

A new twist on an old recipe: Most people are familiar with traditional pesto, which is made with basil and pine nuts, but many prefer this variation with parsley and walnuts.

⅓ cup walnuts
8 cloves garlic
1 bunch parsley, roughly chopped
¼ cup olive oil
Fresh-cracked black pepper, to taste
Kosher salt, to taste

1. Chop the walnuts in a food processor or blender.
2. Add the garlic and process to form a paste.
3. Add the parsley; pulse into the walnut mixture.
4. While the blender is running, drizzle in the oil until the mixture is smooth.
5. Add pepper and salt to taste.

Thursday

Breakfast

Whole multigrain hot cereal topped with fruited yogurt, juice, herbal tea

Lunch

Herbed Quinoa with Sun-Dried Tomatoes (from Tuesday dinner) in salad with fresh greens

Snack

Quick Apple Crisp

Quick Apple Crisp

8 servings

There is nothing like the taste of maple syrup, apples, and cinnamon heated together and baked—an American classic the whole family will enjoy. Serve warm with a scoop of vanilla ice cream or by itself. Delicious!

5 large red apples
½ cup raisins
½ cup apple juice
Juice of 1 lemon
¼ cup maple syrup
1 teaspoon cinnamon powder
2 cups raw oats (not instant)
½ cup walnuts
¼ teaspoon sea salt
1 teaspoon vanilla extract
⅓ cup vegetable oil
⅔ cup maple syrup

1. Preheat oven to 350°F.
2. Peel, core, and slice the apples.
3. Layer in a 9" × 12" baking pan with the raisins.
4. In a small bowl, whisk together the apple juice, lemon juice, ¼ cup maple syrup, and cinnamon; pour over the apples.

5. To make the topping, process the oats in a food processor until they have an almost flour consistency.
6. Add the walnuts and sea salt to the oats; pulse to lightly chop. Pour the mixture into a large bowl.
7. In a medium-size bowl, whisk together the vanilla extract, oil, and ⅔ cup maple syrup.
8. Pour the liquid mixture over the oats; use a wooden spoon to combine. You may need to use your hands to mix well enough to coat the oats and walnuts.
9. When done, spoon the mixture over the top of the apples. Bake 30 minutes, or until apples are tender and topping is a golden brown.
10. Allow to cool slightly before serving.

Maple Syrup

Maple syrup is made from the sap of the sugar, black, or red maple tree. The tree is first tapped (pierced), which allows the sap to run out freely. The clear, tasteless sap is then boiled down to evaporate the water, giving it the characteristic maple flavor and amber color, with a sugar content of 60 percent.

Dinner

Spinach Tofu Pie, Sweet Potato Crisps (see Week 5, Thursday dinner)

Spinach Tofu Pie
8 servings

1 whole wheat or mixed grain pie crust
1 10-ounce package frozen spinach, thawed and juice squeezed out
1 pound reduced-fat tofu, pressed and mashed
¾ tablespoon lemon juice
1 clove garlic, minced
½ teaspoon lemon pepper
1 cup sautéed mushrooms and onions, mixed

1. Preheat oven to 400°F.
2. Mix filling ingredients together in a large bowl.
3. Pile into prebaked crust and bake for about 20 minutes.

Friday

Breakfast

High fiber cereal topped with fresh fruit, fruit juice, green tea

Lunch

Black bean wrap with sprouts, mushrooms, and salsa

Snack

Yogurt Fruit Salad (see Week 3, Thursday snack)

Dinner

Traditional Stovetop Tuna (or Tofu) Noodle Casserole, salad with Tangy Lemon-Garlic Tomato Dressing

Traditional Stovetop Tuna (or Tofu) Noodle Casserole

4 servings

This recipe uses homemade cream of mushroom soup for a much lower sodium content than canned.

1⅓ cups whole wheat egg (or eggless) noodles (yields 2 cups when cooked)

1 recipe Condensed Cream of Mushroom Soup (see Week 12, Saturday dinner)

1 teaspoon steamed chopped onion

1 tablespoon steamed chopped celery

½ cup skim milk

1 ounce American, Cheddar, or Colby cheese, shredded (to yield ¼ cup)

1 cup frozen mixed peas and carrots

1 cup steamed sliced fresh mushrooms

1 5-ounce can water-packed tuna, drained, or ½ 16-ounce package soft or regular tofu, drained and crumbled

1. Cook egg noodles according to package directions. Drain and return to pan.
2. Add all remaining ingredients to pan; stir to blend.
3. Cook over medium heat, stirring occasionally, until cheese is melted.

Tangy Lemon-Garlic Tomato Dressing

¾ cup (suggested serving size: 1 tablespoon)

1 tablespoon ground flaxseeds

2 cloves garlic

⅛ cup cider vinegar

⅛ teaspoon freshly ground pepper

1 small tomato, chopped

¼ teaspoon celery seed

1 tablespoon lemon juice

¼ cup water

Place all ingredients in blender; blend until smooth.

Friendly Fat and Fiber

In addition to providing fiber, ground flaxseeds are rich sources of omega-3 and -6 essential fatty acids.

Saturday

Breakfast

Country-Style Omelet, whole grain toast, melon, herbal tea

Country-Style Omelet

2 servings

2 teaspoons olive oil

1 cup zucchini, diced

¼ cup red pepper, diced

1 cup plum tomatoes, skinned and cubed

⅛ teaspoon pepper

4 eggs

1 tablespoon Parmesan cheese

1 teaspoon fresh basil, minced

1. Heat oil in nonstick skillet.
2. Add zucchini and red pepper; sauté for 5 minutes.
3. Add tomatoes and pepper; cook uncovered for another 10 minutes, allowing fluid from tomatoes to cook down.
4. In small bowl, whisk together eggs, Parmesan cheese, and fresh basil; pour over vegetables in skillet.
5. Cook over low heat until browned, approximately 10 minutes on each side.

Lunch

Traditional Stovetop Tuna (or Tofu) Noodle Casserole (from Friday dinner)

Snack

Quick Apple Crisp with vanilla yogurt (from Thursday snack)

Dinner

Chickpea Stew, brown rice

Chickpea Stew

6 servings

You'll need to set up the beans to soak the night before. Serve on a bed of rice or pasta. Also, don't forget to serve a hearty bread for dipping!

1 large eggplant

1 medium yellow onion

3 cloves garlic

4 medium tomatoes

1 large potato

1 large zucchini

1 teaspoon fennel seeds

3 tablespoons olive oil

1 cup dried chickpeas

1 cup low-sodium vegetable stock

Fresh-cracked black pepper, to taste

1. Soak the beans overnight in water; rinse and drain.
2. Cube the eggplant and sprinkle it with salt.
3. Place eggplant in a colander and cover with a paper towel; let sit for about 30 minutes, then rinse and pat dry.
4. Meanwhile, chop the onion and mince the garlic.
5. Peel and chop the tomatoes.
6. Cube the potato and zucchini.
7. Crush and chop the fennel seeds.
8. Heat the oil in a sauté pan over medium heat.
9. Add the onion and garlic, and sauté for 2 to 3 minutes or until the onion is translucent. Be sure not to let the garlic brown.
10. Add the eggplant and sauté lightly until it becomes golden.
11. Add the tomatoes, potatoes, zucchini, fennel seeds, chickpeas, and stock.
12. Season with salt and pepper to taste.
13. Bring to a boil, cover, and simmer for 30 minutes or until the chickpeas are tender.

> **A Quick Tip on Peeling Tomatoes**
> Heat a pot of water to boiling on the stove. Cut an X on the bottom of each tomato with the tip of a sharp knife (this facilitates the peeling). Place the tomatoes in the boiling water for 10 to 15 seconds, then immediately submerge the tomatoes in ice water. The skin will easily peel off.

Breakfast

Ginger Pear Wheat Pancakes, vanilla yogurt and real maple syrup for toppings, orange juice, herbal tea

Ginger Pear Wheat Pancakes

3 servings

Variation: Add ¼ cup of chopped walnuts to the chopped pears for more texture.

1½ cups whole wheat flour
2 tablespoons applesauce
1 tablespoon brown sugar
1 cup water
1½ teaspoons baking powder
1½ teaspoons ground ginger
1 teaspoon ground cinnamon
2 chopped pears

1. Combine the whole wheat flour, applesauce, brown sugar, water, and baking powder in a medium bowl.
2. Add the ginger and ground cinnamon.
3. Fold in the chopped pears.
4. Pour the batter onto a hot griddle or skillet, ¼ cup for each pancake, and cook until golden.

What's the Deal with Ginger?

Ginger is a fibrous root that adds a warm, spicy flavor to dishes. It's also often used as a remedy for a cold or upset stomach, and has anti-inflammatory properties that can help with conditions such as arthritis. You'll find ginger in many forms: fresh, ground, candied, and even pickled.

Lunch

Spinach Tofu Pie (from Thursday dinner)

Snack

Fruity Oatmeal Bar (see Week 3, Sunday snack)

Dinner

Zesty Pecan Chicken and Grapes, Herbed Quinoa with Sun-Dried Tomatoes (see Week 4, Tuesday dinner)

Zesty Pecan Chicken and Grapes

6 servings

Coating your chicken with nuts adds a crispy skin to keep the breast inside moist and tender.

¼ cup chopped pecans

12 ounces white grapes

1 teaspoon chili powder

6 cups salad greens

¼ cup olive oil

1½ pounds boneless, skinless chicken breasts

1. Preheat oven to 400°F.
2. In a blender, mix the chopped nuts and chili powder.
3. Pour in the oil while the blender is running.
4. When the mixture is thoroughly combined, pour it into a shallow bowl.
5. Coat the chicken with the pecan mixture and place on racked baking dish; roast for 40 to 50 minutes, until the chicken is thoroughly cooked.
6. Remove from oven and thinly slice.
7. Slice the grapes and tear the greens into bite-size pieces.
8. To serve, fan the chicken over the greens and sprinkle with sliced grapes.

Toasting Nuts for Fresher Flavor and Crispness

Nuts aren't truly "ready to eat" right out of the bag or can. They're asleep. To wake up their natural flavor, and to ensure that they're crisp and delicious—not chewy and flat—heat them on the stovetop or in the oven for a few minutes. It improves the quality of very fresh nuts, and it's the way to liven up nuts that may not be completely fresh.

For the stovetop, spread the nuts in a dry skillet, and heat over a medium flame until their natural oils come to the surface, giving them a sheen. For the oven, spread the nuts in a single layer on a baking sheet, and toast for 5 to 10 minutes at 350°F, until the oils are visible. Cool nuts to just above room temperature before serving.

Monday

Breakfast

High fiber ready to eat cereal, bananas and raisins, juice, herbal tea

Lunch

Chickpea Stew (from Saturday dinner)

Snack

Orange-Pineapple Froth

Orange-Pineapple Froth

1 serving

1 tablespoon frozen orange juice concentrate

1 tablespoon frozen pineapple juice concentrate

1 cup skim milk, soymilk, rice or almond milk

½ cup chilled water

½ teaspoon vanilla

1. Combine all ingredients in blender; process until mixed.
2. Serve in a chilled glass.

Dinner

Sweet Potato Pancakes, steamed Brussels sprouts sprinkled with Parmesan cheese

Sweet Potato Pancakes

4 servings

1½ cups sweet potatoes, cooked

¼ cup onions, grated

1 egg

3 tablespoons whole wheat pastry flour

½ teaspoon cinnamon

½ teaspoon baking powder

½ cup egg whites

2 tablespoons canola oil

8-12 tablespoons unsweetened applesauce

1. Scrub 2 medium sweet potatoes; pierce skins with fork and microwave on high for 4–5 minutes.
2. When sweet potatoes have cooled enough to handle, scoop sweet potatoes out of skins and lightly mash with a fork.
3. In a medium bowl, mix together sweet potatoes, grated onion, and egg.
4. Add in flour, cinnamon, and baking powder.
5. In separate small bowl, beat egg whites until rounded peaks form.
6. Gently fold egg whites into potato mixture.
7. Heat oil in skillet (nonstick preferably) until hot.
8. Spoon batter onto skillet to form pancakes approximately 4" in diameter.
9. Brown on both sides.
10. Serve hot with unsweetened applesauce.

Tuesday

Breakfast

Whole grain English muffin with almond butter, Yogurt Fruit Salad (see Week 3, Thursday snack) with ground flaxseeds, fruit juice, green tea

Lunch

Zesty Pecan Chicken and Grapes (from Sunday dinner)

Snack

Pumpkin seeds and currants

Dinner

Salmon with Fettuccine, Lemon Asparagus and Carrots

Salmon with Fettuccine

6 servings

Salmon is a rich, nutritious fish that is easy to cook. It's tossed in a light tomato sauce in this simple main dish recipe. Alternatively, use firm tofu in place of the salmon.

1½ cups low-sodium, fat-free vegetable broth
1 pound salmon fillets, cubed
⅛ teaspoon white pepper
¼ cup fresh dill, minced
1 tablespoon olive oil
3 shallots, minced
3 cloves garlic, minced
1 14-ounce can diced tomatoes, undrained
3 tablespoons tomato paste
½ cup nonfat evaporated milk
1 12-ounce package whole wheat fettuccine
⅓ cup grated Parmesan cheese

1. Bring a large pot of water to a boil.
2. Meanwhile, in large skillet bring broth to a boil.
3. Reduce heat to low so the mixture simmers.
4. Add salmon, sprinkle with pepper and dill, cover, and simmer until the fish is opaque, about 5 to 6 minutes.
5. Remove fish from skillet with slotted spoon and set aside.

6. Turn heat to high and reduce liquid to ½ cup.
7. In another large skillet, heat oil over medium heat.
8. Add the shallots and garlic; cook and stir until tender, about 5 minutes.
9. Add tomatoes, tomato paste, milk, reduced liquid, and the pepper and bring to a boil.
10. Simmer until the sauce thickens slightly, about 10 minutes.
11. Meanwhile, cook pasta until al dente.
12. Add the salmon to the tomato sauce and heat through.
13. Drain pasta and add to the salmon mixture; toss gently over low heat.
14. Serve sprinkled with Parmesan cheese.

Lemon Asparagus and Carrots
6 servings

Steaming is one of the best ways to cook vegetables. It retains nutrients and keeps the bright color you want.

1 pound baby carrots
1 pound fresh asparagus
2 tablespoons lemon juice
1 tablespoon olive oil
1 tablespoon mustard
½ teaspoon lemon pepper
½ teaspoon salt

1. Steam the carrots and asparagus until crisp-tender, then plunge them into cold water to cool.
2. Drain and place in a bowl.
3. In a small bowl, combine lemon juice, oil, mustard, lemon pepper, and salt and mix well.
4. Arrange carrots and asparagus on a platter and drizzle with lemon mixture and lemon pepper.

Steaming Vegetables

To steam vegetables, place water in a large saucepan and bring to a simmer. Cover with a steamer insert or a metal colander, making sure that the insert or colander sits above the water. Add the vegetables to the insert, cover, and simmer until tender, checking with a fork for tenderness every few minutes.

Wednesday

Breakfast

Overnight Oatmeal (see Week 1, Sunday breakfast) cooked with apples and dates, juice, herbal tea

Lunch

Basic Lunch Wrap (see Week 1, Monday lunch) with tomatoes and Swiss cheese, green salad with Lemon Asparagus and Carrots (from Tuesday dinner)

Snack

Pineapple-Banana Blast

Pineapple-Banana Blast

1 serving

¼ frozen banana, sliced

1 tablespoon frozen pineapple juice concentrate

3 tablespoons water

½ cup milk, soymilk, rice or almond milk

1. Combine all ingredients in blender; process until mixed.
2. Serve in chilled glass.

Dinner

Split Pea Soup with Herbes de Provence,
focaccia bread with goat cheese

Split Pea Soup with Herbes de Provence
4-6 servings

This is adapted from Great Vegetarian Cooking Under Pressure *by Lorna Sass (my heroine!). Split peas will also cook conventionally, in about 45 minutes. Presoaking will shorten the cooking time. Pressure cooking melds the flavors beautifully.*

1 tablespoon olive oil

1 tablespoon minced fresh garlic

2 cups coarsely chopped onions

1 tablespoon herbes de Provence (blended dried basil, oregano, rosemary leaves, and lavender)

1 teaspoon whole fennel seeds

1 large bay leaf

2 large carrots, halved lengthwise and cut into ¼" slices

2 large celery ribs

6 cups boiling water (or saved vegetable stock)

2 cups dried green split peas, picked over and rinsed

¼ cup minced fresh parsley

Salt to taste

1. Heat oil in cooker. Cook the garlic over medium heat, stirring constantly until it begins to brown.
2. Immediately add onions and continue to cook for another minute.
3. Stir in herbs, vegetables, and boiling water (stand back to avoid sputtering oil) and split peas.
4. Lock lid in place. Over high heat, bring to high pressure.
5. Lower the heat just enough to maintain high pressure and cook for 12 minutes.
6. Allow the pressure to come down naturally.
7. Remove the lid, tilting it away from you to allow any excess steam to escape.
8. Remove the bay leaf.
9. Stir the soup well as you add the parsley and salt to taste.

Thursday

Breakfast

High fiber ready to eat cereal, milk, juice, herbal tea

Lunch

Avocado, Italian veggie slice, tomato sandwich on whole grain bread, carrot and red pepper sticks

Snack

Yogurt Fruit Salad

Dinner

Kale Stuffed with Basmati Rice, Sweet Potato Crisps

Kale Stuffed with Basmati Rice

6 servings

1 head kale, tough lower stems removed

1 red pepper

1 leek

1 tablespoon olive oil

1½ cups basmati rice

¼ cup sunflower seeds

3 cups vegetable stock

3 sprigs thyme, leaves only

¼ teaspoon ground cardamom seeds

½ teaspoon ground cumin

Fresh-cracked black pepper, to taste

1. Steam the kale.
2. Finely dice the red pepper.
3. Thinly slice the whole leek.
4. Heat the oil in a large saucepan and sauté the peppers and leeks for approximately 1 minute.
5. Add the rice and seeds; toss for 1 minute.
6. Add the stock, thyme, and spices; cover and simmer for 10 to 15 minutes, until the rice is cooked.

7. Lay out the kale leaves, spoon on the rice mixture, and fold into rolls.
8. Serve either at room temperature or heated slightly in a 375°F oven.

What Is Kale?

Kale is a hearty peppery, five-star green that is a member of the cabbage family. It is a good source of vitamins A and C, iron, calcium, and folic acid.

Sweet Potato Crisps

2 servings

1 small sweet potato or yam
1 teaspoon olive oil
Sea salt and freshly ground black pepper, to taste (optional)

1. Preheat oven to 400°F.
2. Scrub sweet potato and pierce flesh several times with fork.
3. Place on microwave-safe plate; microwave 5 minutes on high.
4. Remove from microwave; wrap in aluminum foil.
5. Set aside 5 minutes.
6. Remove foil; peel and cut into French fries.
7. Spread on baking sheet treated with nonstick spray; spritz with olive oil.
8. Bake 10–15 minutes, or until crisp.
9. There's a risk that sweet potato strips will caramelize and burn; check often while cooking to ensure this doesn't occur. Lower oven temperature, if necessary.
10. Season with a little salt and pepper, if desired.

Friday

Breakfast

Overnight Oatmeal (from Wednesday breakfast) with vanilla yogurt, orange juice, herbal tea

Lunch

Split Pea Soup with Herbes de Provence (from Wednesday dinner), hearty whole grain bread

Snack

Chocolate/Carob Chip Cookies

Chocolate/Carob Chip Cookies
24 cookies (depends on size of cookie)

This is an eggless batter—you can safely eat it raw!

½ cup whole wheat flour

¼ cup rolled oats

1 teaspoon baking powder

¼ cup (or more) carob or chocolate chips

½ cup brown sugar

3 tablespoon non-trans fat margarine, melted (such as Earth Balance)

¼ cup orange juice

1 teaspoon vanilla extract

Dried fruit and crystallized ginger, optional

1. Preheat oven to 375°F.
2. Lightly oil a baking sheet.
3. Combine well: flour, oats, and baking powder. Add in chips (optional: currants, dried sweetened cranberries, crystallized ginger cut into small pieces, etc.).
4. In a small bowl, combine remaining ingredients, mixing well.
5. Add to dry mixture, mixing until all ingredients are moistened.
6. Shape into balls (1½" wide) and flatten onto baking sheet.
7. Bake 12-15 minutes, until bottoms begin to brown.
8. Remove to wire rack to cool.

Dinner

Curried Shrimp (or Tofu) and Vegetables, steamed "grain" (millet, quinoa, or brown rice)

Curried Shrimp (or Tofu) and Vegetables

6 servings

1 tablespoon olive oil

1 onion, chopped

3 cloves garlic, minced

1 tablespoon salt-free curry powder

½ teaspoon cinnamon

1½ cups water

2 carrots, sliced

2 sweet potatoes, peeled and cubed

1 zucchini, sliced

1 14½-ounce can diced tomatoes

1 pound raw shrimp or 1 16-ounce package of firm tofu, diced into 1" cubes

4 cups hot cooked whole grain (brown rice, millet, quinoa)

1. In a large skillet, heat oil over medium heat.
2. Add onion and garlic; cook and stir until crisp-tender, about 4 minutes.
3. Add curry powder and cinnamon; cook and stir for 1 minute longer.
4. Add water, carrots, and potatoes; bring to a simmer.
5. Reduce the heat to low, cover, and cook for 8 to 10 minutes or until carrots are crisp-tender.
6. Add zucchini, tomatoes, and shrimp or tofu, cover again, and simmer for 5 to 8 minutes longer or until shrimp are pink.
7. Spoon rice onto individual plates and top with shrimp and vegetables; serve immediately.

Cooking with Curry

The flavors in curry powder are enhanced when they are heated, which is why the powder is often cooked in the first step of many Indian recipes. It's still good when uncooked. You can buy curry powder in many blends, from hot to mild, as well as salt-free versions. Curry powder is a blend of spices, and each blend is usually unique to a particular area of India.

Saturday

Breakfast

Whole Wheat Biscuits, Tofu "Egg-less" Scramble (see Week 1, Saturday breakfast)

Whole Wheat Biscuits

8 servings

Biscuits can be "recycled" into sandwiches, mini-pizzas, etc.

1½ cups all-purpose flour

1½ cups whole wheat flour

4½ teaspoons baking powder

1½ teaspoons salt

1 tablespoon sugar

6 tablespoons cold butter or non-trans fat margarine

1¼ cups buttermilk (or plant-based milk with 2 tablespoons of vinegar)

1. Preheat oven to 400°F.
2. Combine flours, baking powder, salt, and sugar in a mixing bowl.
3. Cut butter into small pieces and mix into dry ingredients with a pastry cutter or your fingers.
4. Add buttermilk and mix with a wooden spoon.
5. Roll dough on a floured board to 1" thickness.
6. Cut circles with a 2" to 3" round cookie cutter.
7. Place rounds on a baking sheet and bake for 12 minutes.

Lunch

Kale Stuffed with Basmati Rice (from Thursday dinner)

Snack

Chocolate/Carob Chip Cookies (from Friday snack)

Dinner

Tuscan Pasta Fagioli (pronounced "fah-zool"), salad with Tangy Lemon-Garlic Tomato Dressing (see Week 4, Friday dinner)

Tuscan Pasta Fagioli

6 servings

2 tablespoons olive oil

⅓ cup onion, chopped

3 cloves garlic, minced

½ pound tomatoes, peeled and chopped

5 cups low-sodium vegetable stock

¼ teaspoon freshly ground pepper

3 cups canned cannellini beans, rinsed and drained

2½ cups whole grain pasta shells

2 tablespoons Parmesan cheese

1. Heat olive oil in large pot; gently cook onions and garlic until soft but not browned.
2. Add tomatoes, vegetable stock, and pepper.
3. Purée 1½ cups of cannellini beans in food processor or blender; add to stock.
4. Cover and simmer 20–30 minutes.
5. While stock is simmering, cook pasta until al dente; drain.
6. Add remaining beans and pasta to stock; heat through.
7. Serve with Parmesan cheese.

Cannellini Beans

Cannellini beans are large white beans, about ½" long, with a firm texture and skin and a nut-like flavor. Very popular in Italy, and especially Tuscany, cannellini beans are mild in flavor and hold their shape well. A variety of the "common bean," cannellini are related to kidney beans, Great Northern, navy, and green beans, among others. As such they share the common bean's many health benefits: low in fat, high in protein, high in fiber, and high in minerals and B vitamins.

Sunday

Breakfast

Biscuit, Neufchatel cheese, fruit preserves, orange juice, herbal tea

Lunch

Portobello Sandwich (see Week 3, Wednesday dinner), spinach salad

Snack

Quick Apple Crisp (see Week 4, Thursday snack) with vanilla yogurt

Dinner

Edamame Salad, Passion Beet Borscht

Edamame Salad

4 servings

If you can't find shelled edamame, try this recipe with lima beans instead.

2 cups frozen shelled edamame, thawed and drained

1 red or yellow bell pepper, diced

¾ cup corn kernels

3 tablespoons chopped fresh cilantro (optional)

3 tablespoons olive oil

2 tablespoons red wine vinegar

1 teaspoon low-sodium soy sauce

1 teaspoon salt-free chili powder

2 teaspoons lemon or lime juice

Salt and pepper to taste

1. Combine edamame, bell pepper, corn, and cilantro in a large bowl.
2. Whisk together the olive oil, vinegar, soy sauce, chili powder, and lemon or lime juice and combine with the edamame. Add salt and pepper to taste.
3. Chill for at least 1 hour before serving.

Passion Beet Borscht

4 servings

This is a creamy version of the classic Russian-style soup. Beets are nutrition-packed elixirs of life, chock full of anti-aging, immune-boosting nutrient compounds.

2 cups beets, diced
5 cups water
1 medium carrot, diced
1 medium parsnip, diced
1 medium onion, diced
1½ teaspoons caraway seeds
½ cup red cabbage, chopped
1 teaspoon sesame oil
4 teaspoons sweet white miso paste
Lemon juice, to taste
¼ cup fresh dill, chopped

1. In a saucepan, add beets in water.
2. Bring to boil, cover, and simmer for about 15 minutes.
3. Add carrot and parsnip and continue to cook over medium heat until vegetables are tender, about 15 minutes.
4. In a skillet, sauté onions with caraway seeds and cabbage in oil until soft.
5. Add onions and cabbage to the soup.
6. Purée miso in a little cooking liquid.
7. Add miso purée to soup and simmer for 3 more minutes.
8. Purée soup in a blender until creamy.
9. Add lemon juice to taste.
10. Garnish with freshly chopped dill.

Monday

Breakfast

High fiber, whole grain cold cereal, low-fat milk, juice, herbal tea

Lunch

Tuscan Pasta Fagioli (from Saturday dinner)

Snack

Chocolate/Carob Chip Cookies (from Friday snack)

Dinner

Cajun Chicken/Tofu Strips, Squash and Bulgur Pilaf

Cajun Chicken/Tofu Strips
6 servings

Serve these tender little strips of chicken or tofu with a variety of sauces, including barbecue sauce, Dijon vinaigrette, Tangy Lemon-Garlic Tomato Dressing (see Week 4, Friday dinner), and Cashew-Garlic Ranch Dressing (see Week 12, Tuesday dinner).

2 cloves garlic, minced

¾ cup dried whole grain breadcrumbs

¼ cup grated Parmesan cheese

1 tablespoon dried parsley flakes

½ teaspoon paprika

½ teaspoon dried oregano leaves

⅛ teaspoon pepper

1½ pounds boneless, skinless chicken breasts or 2 16-ounce packages of extra firm tofu

1 cup buttermilk

1. Preheat oven to 425°F.
2. Spray a cookie sheet with nonstick baking spray containing flour; set aside.
3. In shallow dish, combine garlic, breadcrumbs, cheese, parsley, paprika, oregano, and pepper and mix well.

4. Cut chicken or tofu into ½" × 3" strips.
5. Combine with buttermilk on plate, toss to coat, and let stand for 10 minutes.
6. Dip chicken or tofu into breadcrumb mixture, then place in single layer on prepared cookie sheet.
7. Bake for 5 minutes, then carefully turn with a spatula and bake for 5 to 6 minutes longer until chicken or tofu is thoroughly cooked. Serve immediately.

Squash and Bulgur Pilaf

6 servings

½ cup onions, chopped

1 teaspoon garlic, minced

1½ cups yellow summer squash, cut into ½" pieces

1 cup bulgur wheat

2 cups low-sodium vegetable or chicken broth

½ teaspoon cinnamon

¼ cup dried currants

¼ cup walnuts, chopped

1. In large nonstick skillet, sauté onions, garlic, yellow squash, and bulgur wheat in olive oil until onions are tender, about 5 minutes.

2. Stir in chicken or vegetable broth and cinnamon; heat to boiling. Reduce heat and simmer, covered, for 10 minutes.
3. Stir in currants; continue to simmer an additional 15 minutes.
4. Add walnuts just before serving.

Bulgur
This cereal grain is a Middle Eastern staple that is created by steaming, drying, and crushing wheat kernels. It is low in fat and high in protein, as well as having twice the fiber of brown rice, which will keep you feeling full with fewer calories.

Tuesday

Breakfast

Yogurt Fruit Smoothie (see Week 3, Monday snack)

Lunch

Edamame Salad and Passion Beet Borscht (from Sunday dinner)

Snack

Quick Apple Crisp (see Week 4, Thursday snack) with vanilla yogurt

Dinner

Rice with Black Beans and Ginger, Hot Vinaigrette for Greens

Rice with Black Beans and Ginger

4 servings

1 tablespoon olive oil

2 cloves garlic, minced

1 onion, chopped

1 tablespoon minced fresh gingerroot

1 cup brown rice

2 cups fat-free vegetable broth

1 15-ounce can black beans

⅛ teaspoon pepper

1. In a large skillet, heat oil over medium heat.
2. Add garlic, onion, and ginger; cook and stir for 4 minutes.
3. Add rice; cook and stir for 3 minutes.
4. Stir in broth and bring to a boil.
5. Lower heat, cover pan, and simmer for 30 to 40 minutes or until rice is tender and liquid is absorbed.
6. Drain black beans, rinse well, and drain again. Add along with pepper to the rice mixture; cook and stir over medium heat for 5 to 6 minutes until hot. Serve immediately.

Cooking Rice

Some people have a hard time cooking rice so it ends up fluffy and separate. If you have this problem, try these tips. Rinse the rice before cooking to remove surface starch. Use double the amount of liquid than rice when cooking, and don't lift the lid or stir the pot while the rice is cooking. Finally, let it stand, off heat, for 5 minutes, covered, then fluff and serve.

Hot Vinaigrette for Greens
6 servings

Colorful blanched vegetables or bitter greens seasoned with hot vinaigrette makes a delicious warming side dish in cold weather. You can also use hot vinaigrette for marinating vegetables or tempeh.

2 medium scallions, sliced

1 clove garlic, minced

3 tablespoons sesame oil

¼ cup balsamic vinegar

¼ teaspoon shoyu (low-sodium tamari or soy sauce)

¼ teaspoon dried tarragon

1. In a skillet, sauté scallions and garlic in oil for 2 minutes.
2. Add balsamic vinegar, shoyu, and tarragon. Mix until blended.
3. Heat over low flame.
4. Serve over cooked bitter greens or blanched vegetables.

Wednesday

Breakfast

High fiber, whole grain cereal, fresh fruit, juice, herbal tea

Lunch

Cajun Chicken/Tofu Strips (from Monday dinner)

Snack

DIY Trail Mix (see Week 1, Tuesday snack)

Dinner

Blackened and Bleu Tilapia, Whole Grain Noodles with Caraway Cabbage

Blackened and Bleu Tilapia
6 servings

Use thicker fillets of fish for this dish to keep the full-flavored bleu cheese from overpowering the flavor of the tilapia.

1½ pounds fresh tilapia
1 tablespoon olive oil
¼ teaspoon cayenne pepper
3 ounces bleu cheese
¼ teaspoon salt-free chili powder
Fresh cracked black pepper, to taste

1. Rinse the fish in ice water and pat dry.
2. Sift together the cayenne, chili powder, and black pepper; season the fish with the mixture.
3. Heat the oil to medium temperature in a medium-size skillet; sauté the fish on each side until crispy, golden brown, and flaky.
4. Drain on paper-toweled rack.
5. To serve, plate the drained fish and sprinkle with bleu cheese.

Wednesday

Whole Grain Noodles with Caraway Cabbage

6 servings

2 tablespoons olive oil

½ cup onion, chopped

2 cups cabbage, coarsely chopped

1½ cups Brussels sprouts, sliced, trimmed, and halved

2 teaspoons caraway seed

1½ cups low-sodium vegetable broth

¼ teaspoon fresh ground pepper

¼ teaspoon salt

6 ounces whole grain noodles

1. Heat olive oil in large saucepan; sauté onions for about 5 minutes until translucent.
2. Add cabbage and Brussels sprouts; cook over medium heat 3 minutes.
3. Stir in caraway seed, broth, pepper, and salt; cover and simmer 5–8 minutes, until vegetables are crisp-tender.
4. Cook noodles in boiling water until tender; drain.
5. Mix noodles and vegetables together in a large bowl; serve.

Breakfast

Hot rice cereal cooked with raisins, topped with ground flaxseeds, maple syrup, cranberry-apple juice, green tea

Lunch

Rice with Black Beans and Ginger (from Tuesday dinner)

Snack

Ginger Lime Iced Tea

Ginger Lime Iced Tea
6 servings

Very refreshing! Ginger is a natural remedy for tummy aches, nausea, as well as pain relief.

6 cups boiling water

4 green tea bags

2 tablespoons honey

1 tablespoon lime juice

1 tablespoon coarsely chopped crystallized ginger

1. In ceramic or glass container, pour boiling water over tea bags, honey, lime juice, and ginger; cover and allow to steep for 5 minutes.
2. Stir until honey is dissolved.
3. Remove teabags and ginger.
4. Chill in refrigerator and serve over ice. (May also be served hot.)

Dinner

Pasta and Spinach Casserole, green salad

Pasta and Spinach Casserole
6 servings

If you enjoy macaroni and cheese, you'll likely love this fancier, lower-fat version. The good ol' mac and cheese just won't ever be the same. The casserole can be assembled in advance to save time.

3 heads fresh spinach

1 shallot

3 cloves garlic

3 ounces goat cheese

3 ounces firm tofu

2 tablespoons olive oil, plus extra for greasing

2½ tablespoons all-purpose unbleached flour

2 cups skim or plant-based milk

3 cups cooked pasta

¼ cup chopped Spanish olives

Fresh-cracked black pepper, to taste

1. Preheat oven to 350°F.
2. Steam the spinach.
3. Mince the shallot and garlic.
4. Crumble the goat cheese and cut the tofu into small cubes.
5. Heat the 2 tablespoons oil to medium temperature in a medium-size saucepan, then add the flour to form a roux.
6. Whisk in the milk, and cook until thickened to make white sauce.
7. Grease a casserole pan and ladle in the white sauce. Layer the pasta, spinach, cheese, tofu, olives, shallots, garlic, pepper, and more white sauce (in that order).
8. Continue to layer until all ingredients are used.
9. Bake, covered, for approximately 15 to 20 minutes until heated through.
10. Uncover and brown for 5 to 10 minutes longer.

Friday

Breakfast

Whole wheat bagel with almond butter, red onion, orange juice, green tea

Lunch

Pasta and Spinach Casserole (from Thursday dinner)

Snack

Yogurt Fruit Salad (see Week 3, Thursday snack)

Textured Vegetable Protein (TVP)

A food product made from soybeans, TVP has a long shelf life if stored properly and is an excellent source of protein and fiber. Plain TVP has zero cholesterol. It is very high in potassium, a good source of the essential amino acids, and also contributes calcium and magnesium to your diet. It can be found in most health food stores, often in bulk, and has been notoriously used as an inexpensive "meat extender" especially in institutional foods. In keeping with Michael Pollan's rule to "eat food," I recommend TVP and other processed soy products be used rarely. Instead, focus on eating traditional whole soy foods such as edamame and tempeh.

Dinner

Turkey or TVP Chili, Multigrain Corn Bread, green salad

Turkey or TVP Chili

6 servings

This delicious chili can be made with turkey or TVP (textured vegetable protein). If using TVP, add an extra 2 cups of water because it will absorb liquid.

1 pound ground turkey or 2 cups dried TVP
1 cup onions, chopped
½ cup green pepper, chopped
2 teaspoons garlic, finely chopped
2 28-ounce cans crushed canned tomatoes
1 cup canned black beans, drained
1 cup canned red kidney beans, drained
3 tablespoons chili powder
1 tablespoon ground cumin
1 teaspoon crushed red pepper
Dash Tabasco

1. Brown ground turkey in large nonstick pot over medium-high heat. If substituting TVP, skip this step and just sauté the vegetables; add the TVP with the remaining ingredients later.
2. Drain off any fat; add chopped onion, green pepper, and garlic. Continue

cooking until onion is translucent, about 5 minutes.

3. Add remaining ingredients; bring to a slow boil.

4. Reduce heat, cover, and let simmer at least 2–3 hours before serving.

Multigrain Corn Bread

16 servings

Nonstick cooking spray

1 egg

2 tablespoons egg whites

3 tablespoons butter, melted

1½ cups low-fat buttermilk

1 teaspoon imitation vanilla

1¾ cups cornmeal

¾ cup whole wheat pastry flour

1 tablespoon ground flaxseed

4 tablespoons brown sugar or Sucanat

4 teaspoons baking powder

½ teaspoon baking soda

Pinch salt

1. Preheat oven to 375°F.

2. Spray 8" × 8" square baking pan with nonstick cooking spray.

3. In medium bowl, whisk together egg, egg whites, butter, buttermilk, and vanilla. Set aside.

4. In larger bowl, combine cornmeal, flour, flaxseed, sugar, baking powder, baking soda, and salt; mix well.

5. Make well in center of dry ingredients; pour in buttermilk mixture.

6. Mix gently with spoon until all dry ingredients are moistened; do not overmix.

7. Spoon batter into prepared pan.

8. Bake for 25–30 minutes, or until center springs back when lightly touched.

9. Cool on wire rack before slicing into 16 pieces.

> **Don't Have Buttermilk?**
> When baking, soured milk is a good substitution for buttermilk. To replace 1 cup of buttermilk in a recipe, stir 1 tablespoon of white vinegar or fresh lemon juice into 1 cup of dairy or plant-based milk. Let the milk stand for 5 minutes, or until milk thickens.

Saturday

Breakfast

Hot rice cereal (from Thursday breakfast), vanilla yogurt, juice, herbal tea

Lunch

My Favorite Grilled Cheese Sandwich, steamed green beans

My Favorite Grilled Cheese Sandwich

1 sandwich

A re-creation of a memorable sandwich with an unusual juxtaposition of tastes, bought from a truck behind the New York City public library.

2 slices whole grain raisin-nut-cranberry bread (if not available, add in as suggested below)

1 slice medium Cheddar cheese

½ fresh pear, sliced thin

2 teaspoons coarse brown mustard, prepared

1 small handful raisins, dried sweetened cranberries, and walnuts if available bread does not already contain these

1 tablespoon olive oil

1. Spread ½ of mustard on each slice of bread.
2. Layer cheese, pear slices, dried fruits, and coarsely chopped walnuts on one side of bread.
3. Cover with second piece of bread.
4. Heat olive oil in heavy skillet over medium heat; carefully transfer sandwich to skillet, press down with spatula.
5. When first side is browned, flip over, cover skillet.
6. Check often. When cheese is melted, remove sandwich to plate and cut in two diagonally.

Saturday

Snack

Fresh melon

Dinner

Tofu and Root Vegetables (see Week 1, Sunday dinner), salad with Lemon-Almond Dressing

Lemon-Almond Dressing
⅔ cup (suggested serving: 1 tablespoon)

¼ cup raw almonds

1 tablespoon lemon juice

¼ cup water

1½ teaspoons honey

¼ teaspoon lemon pepper

½ slice (1" diameter) peeled ginger

¼ clove garlic

1½ teaspoons chopped fresh chives, or ½ teaspoon dried chives

1½ teaspoons chopped fresh sweet basil, or ½ teaspoon dried basil

Put all ingredients in food processor or blender; process until smooth.

Breakfast

Egg White Pancakes, orange juice, herbal tea

Egg White Pancakes

2 servings

4 egg whites

½ cup oatmeal

4 teaspoons reduced-calorie or low-sugar strawberry jam

1 teaspoon powdered sugar

1. Put all ingredients in blender; process until smooth.
2. Preheat nonstick pan treated with cooking spray over medium heat.
3. Pour half of mixture into pan; cook for 4–5 minutes.
4. Flip pancake and cook until inside is cooked.
5. Repeat using remaining batter for second pancake.
6. Dust each pancake with powdered sugar, if using.

Creative Toppings

Experiment with toast and pancake toppings. Try a tablespoon of raisins, almonds, apples, bananas, berries, nut butters (limit these to 1 teaspoon per serving), peanuts, pears, walnuts, or wheat germ.

Lunch

Turkey or TVP Chili (from Friday dinner), salad, Multigrain Corn Bread

Snack

Gourmet Sorbet (see Week 2, Friday snack)

Sunday

Dinner

Pasta and Trout or Tempeh with Lemon Pesto

Pasta and Trout or Tempeh with Lemon Pesto

4 servings

For a slightly different taste, substitute the basil for fresh parsley. Add dried basil to supplement flavour.

2 cloves garlic

2 cups fresh basil leaves, tightly packed

⅛ cup pine nuts, toasted

2 teaspoons fresh lemon juice

2 teaspoons water

4 teaspoons extra-virgin olive oil

4 tablespoons grated Parmesan cheese, divided

1⅓ cups uncooked linguine or other whole grain pasta (to yield 2 cups cooked pasta)

2 ounces whole boneless smoked trout or 2 ounces "crispy" tempeh (see sidebar)

Freshly ground black pepper, to taste

1. Put garlic in food processor; pulse until finely chopped.
2. Add basil, pine nuts, lemon juice, and water; process until just puréed.
3. Add olive oil and 3 tablespoons of Parmesan cheese; pulse until pesto is

smooth, occasionally scraping down side of bowl, if necessary. Set aside.

4. Cook pasta according to package directions.
5. While it is cooking, flake trout.
6. When pasta is done, quickly pulse pesto again to ensure it has remained blended.
7. Toss pesto and trout or tempeh with pasta.
8. Sprinkle remaining Parmesan and some pepper on top of each serving.

Crispy Tempeh

A quick and tasty way to use tempeh is to marinate bite-size pieces in a blend of 2 parts soy sauce to one part sesame oil, plus a touch of honey to taste. Sauté the tempeh in olive oil over low heat, stirring often for 10 to 15 minutes. The result will be crispy mouthfuls of flavor that you can add to salads and any grain dishes you enjoy.

Monday

Breakfast

Fruit and Cheese Quesadillas, iced green tea

Fruit and Cheese Quesadillas

4 servings

Mild mozzarella is a perfect backdrop for fruit, and you can vary the fruit and jam according to what's seasonally available. These are knife-and-fork quesadillas, too gooey for finger food.

4 tablespoons "just fruit" strawberry jam

4 (6"–8") whole wheat flour tortillas

2 cups shredded part skim mozzarella cheese

1 cup diced fresh strawberries plus extra for sprinkling

4 tablespoons strawberry yogurt for garnish

Confectioners' sugar for dusting

1. Spread 1 tablespoon jam on a tortilla and sprinkle it with ½ cup mozzarella cheese and ¼ cup diced strawberries.
2. Fold over the tortilla to enclose the filling.
3. Repeat with the remaining tortillas, mozzarella, jam, and strawberries.
4. Spray the skillet with nonstick cooking spray and heat it over medium heat.
5. Cook the quesadillas, one or two at a time, until golden on the bottom, about 3 minutes.
6. Flip over and cook the second side until golden and the cheese has melted.
7. Top each quesadilla with a dollop of yogurt, a sprinkling of strawberries, and a dusting of confectioners' sugar. Serve hot.

Marvelous Quesadillas

Much like omelets, quesadillas are one of those foods that can be made in a wide variety of flavors. This breakfast quesadilla includes fruit and cheese, and you can swap out the mozzarella cheese and strawberry jam for any other types that you prefer. A great lunch quesadilla might have sautéed vegetables and hummus, and you can also make a dinner quesadilla with Tex-Mex fillings such as grilled chicken, black beans, salsa, and Cheddar cheese. When quesadillas are on the menu, let your imagination run wild!

Lunch

Tofu and Root Vegetables to-go (from Saturday dinner)

Snack

Pumpkin seeds and dried apricots

Dinner

Zucchini Parmesan, Pasta and Trout or Tempeh with Lemon Pesto (from Sunday dinner)

Zucchini Parmesan

6 servings

Try adding thin-sliced fresh basil or chopped oregano for flair and extra flavour.

3 medium zucchini

2 egg whites

1 cup skim or soymilk

½ cup whole grain breadcrumbs

1 teaspoon olive oil

2 cups tomato sauce

6 ounces part-skim mozzarella cheese, shredded

Fresh-cracked black pepper, to taste

1. Preheat oven to 375°F.
2. Slice the zucchini into ½" thick coins.
3. Beat the egg whites and mix with the milk.
4. Brush a baking sheet with oil.
5. Dip the zucchini into the egg mixture, then into the breadcrumbs, and shake off excess; place on baking sheet and bake for 10 to 15 minutes, until the zucchini is just fork tender.
6. Ladle the sauce into a large casserole or baking dish.
7. Cover the bottom of the dish with a single layer of zucchini, then top with the cheese, then sauce. Repeat the process until you have used all the ingredients.
8. Bake for 5 to 10 minutes, until the cheese has melted and begins to brown on top.

Tuesday

Breakfast

High fiber, whole grain ready to eat cereal, bananas, juice, herbal tea

Lunch

Turkey/avocado wrap with spicy sprouts, shredded carrots

Snack

Yogurt Fruit Salad (see Week 3, Thursday snack)

Dinner

Southwest Black Bean Burgers on whole grain hamburger buns, Orange Guacamole with tortilla chips, carrots, celery, and red peppers for scooping

Southwest Black Bean Burgers
5 servings

For a vegetarian version, use 3 cups of black beans instead of adding beef.

1 cup black beans, cooked

¼ cup onion, chopped

1 teaspoon salt-free chili powder

1 teaspoon ground cumin

1 tablespoon fresh parsley, minced

1 tablespoon fresh cilantro, minced

¾ pound lean ground beef

1. Place beans, onion, chili powder, cumin, parsley, and cilantro in food processor.
2. Combine ingredients using pulse setting until beans are partially puréed and all ingredients are mixed. (If using canned beans, drain and rinse first.)
3. In a separate bowl, combine ground beef and bean mixture. Shape into 5 patties.

4. Meat mixture will be quite soft after mixing and should be chilled or partially frozen prior to cooking.
5. Grill or broil on oiled surface.

Swapping Fresh Herbs for Dried

If you do not have fresh herbs such as parsley or cilantro available, 1 teaspoon dried can be used in place of 1 tablespoon fresh.

Orange Guacamole
4 ⅓-cup servings

Serving Suggestion: Place Orange Guacamole in a hollowed out orange half. Serve with blue and yellow corn tortilla chips, and a selection of fresh vegetables such as carrot, celery, and jicama sticks, and red and yellow bell pepper strips.

½ cup fresh orange segments, diced
2 tablespoons fresh orange juice
1 cup avocado, ripe, mashed
1 tablespoon red onion, grated
⅛ teaspoon salt
Pinch of pepper

1. Add fresh-squeezed orange juice and diced orange segments to mashed avocado; blend together until avocado is smooth.
2. Stir in grated onion and season with salt and pepper.
3. Cover and refrigerate until ready to serve.

Wednesday

Breakfast

Green Tea Smoothie, English muffin with almond butter and jam

Green Tea Smoothie

2 servings

To kick this smoothie up a notch, add fruit or grate in some fresh ginger.

1 cup brewed green tea, chilled
½ cup skim or soymilk
1 frozen banana or ½ cup ice cubes
1–3 tablespoons honey, to taste

1. Combine all ingredients in a blender until smooth.
2. Pour into a tall glass and enjoy at home or take with you on the go.

Green Means Good

This smoothie is packed with benefits. Green tea is chock full of antioxidants, which protect living cells from damage and deterioration. Researchers think antioxidants can help prevent cancer and some of the side effects of arthritis.

Lunch

Zucchini Parmesan (from Monday dinner)

Snack

Berrylicious Yogurt Granola Parfait

Berrylicious Yogurt Granola Parfait

1 serving

A healthy snack recipe, courtesy of my colleague Linda Rocufort, MPH, RD.

½ cup fresh or partially thawed berries (strawberry, blueberry, raspberry)
¾ cup low-fat vanilla yogurt
2 tablespoons low-fat granola

1. Into a parfait glass, layer berries, yogurt, and granola.
2. Repeat layering until all the ingredients have been used.

Dinner

Sweet and Sour Pork or Seitan Skillet (see Week 2, Sunday dinner), steamed brown rice

Thursday

Breakfast

Quinoa Berry Breakfast (see Week 2, Saturday breakfast)

Lunch

Southwest Black Bean Burgers (from Tuesday dinner) with tomato slices on whole grain bun

Snack

Summer Fruit Cobbler

Summer Fruit Cobbler

8 servings

Any combination of fresh fruit will work well with this recipe. You will need a total of 4 cups of fruit. Fruit suggestions include blueberries, blackberries, peaches, mangoes, or plums.

Nonstick cooking spray

1½ cups raspberries

1½ cups peaches, peeled and sliced

1 cup strawberries, sliced

5 tablespoons brown sugar or Sucanat

2 tablespoons whole wheat pastry flour

1 teaspoon cinnamon

¾ cup whole wheat pastry flour

1 tablespoon sugar

1½ teaspoons baking powder

2½ tablespoons canola oil

2 tablespoons milk

2 tablespoons egg whites

1. Preheat oven to 350°F.
2. Spray 9" × 9" square baking pan with nonstick cooking spray.
3. Put fruit in bottom of baking dish.
4. In small bowl, mix sugar, 2 tablespoons flour, and cinnamon; sprinkle evenly over fruit.
5. In another small bowl, sift together ¾ cup flour, 1 tablespoon sugar, and

baking powder. Add oil, milk, and egg whites; stir quickly until just mixed.

6. Spoon dough over fruit.
7. Bake for 25–30 minutes, until dough is golden brown.

Dinner

Easy Miso Noodle Soup

Easy Miso Noodle Soup
4 servings

This is a delicious soup made to relax and nourish the body after a long day. A white-colored miso will give a lighter taste than a dark red or brown miso. The darker the miso, the longer it has been fermented and the more live enzymes it will provide. Feel free to add other vegetables to the soup. Wakame is a mineral-rich sea vegetable.

½ onion

2 medium carrots

2 green onions

4–6 cups vegetable broth or water

1 tablespoon dried wakame

1-pound package firm tofu

4 teaspoons mellow white miso

1 8-ounce package cooked soba noodles

4 tablespoons pumpkin seeds, toasted

1. Cut the onion in thin half-moon slices; julienne carrots into matchstick shapes; slice green onions on the diagonal into pieces.
2. Heat broth and add onion, carrot, wakame, and tofu. Simmer until onion is just tender.
3. Ladle broth into individual bowls; dissolve 1 teaspoon of miso into each.
4. Add ½ cup of noodles to each bowl; ladle in soup with vegetables and tofu.
5. Top with pumpkin seeds and sliced green onions before serving.

Soba Noodles

Soba noodles are a traditional Japanese noodle made of buckwheat and wheat and sometimes yam flour. They are a round, thin noodle that can be served either hot or cold.

Friday

Breakfast

High fiber, whole grain ready to eat cereal, juice, herbal tea

Lunch

Sweet and Sour Pork or Seitan Skillet with brown rice (from Wednesday dinner)

Snack

Kiwi Banana Smoothie

Kiwi Banana Smoothie
2 servings

High daily levels of vitamin B6 may reduce the risk of getting colon cancer by 58 percent, claims a study from Harvard Medical School. Reductions in cancer risk started showing up at levels of just 3.3 milligrams a day. Bananas and kiwi are both good sources of B6.

2 kiwi fruit, peeled and sliced
1 ripe banana, peeled
¼ cup plain low-fat yogurt
3 ice cubes
1 teaspoon vanilla
½ teaspoon nutmeg

1. Place the kiwi, banana, yogurt, and ice cubes in a blender.
2. Process until smooth, adding vanilla and nutmeg to taste.
3. Divide into 2 glasses.

Friday

Dinner

Lemon Sole with Capers, Herbed Quinoa with Sun-Dried Tomatoes (see Week 4, Tuesday dinner), green salad with dressing of your choice

Lemon Sole with Capers

6 servings

3 cloves garlic

3 sprigs fresh dill, leaves only

1½ pounds sole

Fresh-cracked black pepper, to taste

1 teaspoon fresh-grated lemon zest

1 teaspoon olive oil

½ teaspoon capers

1. Preheat oven broiler.
2. Mince the garlic and chop the dill.
3. Place the sole on a broiler pan; sprinkle with pepper, zest, garlic, and drizzle with the oil.
4. Place under broiler for 3 minutes, then turn carefully and broil for 1 minute longer.
5. Remove from broiler and top with dill and capers.

Saturday

Breakfast

Stuffed French Toast, juice, herbal green tea

Stuffed French Toast

4 servings

For this recipe, be sure to cut thick slices of bread. This will make stuffing easier, and you'll get great big slices of Stuffed French Toast.

Butter-flavored cooking spray
4 (1" thick) slices whole grain French bread
4 teaspoons Neufchatel (reduced-fat cream cheese)
4 teaspoons favorite all-fruit preserves
1 cup skim or low-fat soy milk
1 teaspoon vanilla
1 teaspoon cinnamon or to taste
½ teaspoon nutmeg or to taste

1. Prepare a skillet with the butter-flavored spray.
2. Cut a pocket through the top of each slice of bread, ¾ of the way through the bread.
3. Insert cream cheese and preserves.
4. Combine milk, vanilla, cinnamon, and nutmeg to make the batter.
5. Dip the bread in the batter and cook on the skillet.

A New Life for Stale Bread

Don't know what to do with that bread that's going stale? It's perfect for French toast! The fresher your bread, the more it will fall apart in the batter. Use bread that is nearing the end of its shelf life. It will be a little tougher and will hold together better when soaked in batter.

Lunch

Fresh Mint Spring Rolls with Easy Asian Dipping Sauce, Easy Miso Noodle Soup (from Thursday dinner)

Fresh Mint Spring Rolls

3–4 servings

Wrapping spring rolls is a balance between getting them tight enough to hold together, but not so tight that the thin wrappers break! It's like riding a bike: Once you've got it, you've got it, and then spring rolls can be very quick and fun to make.

1 3-ounce package clear bean thread noodles
1 cup hot water
1 tablespoon soy sauce
½ teaspoon powdered ginger
1 teaspoon sesame oil
½ cup shiitake mushrooms, diced

1 carrot, grated
10–12 spring roll wrappers
Warm water
½ head green leaf lettuce, chopped
1 cucumber, sliced thin
1 bunch fresh mint

1. Break noodles in half to make smaller pieces, then submerge in 1 cup hot water until soft, about 6-7 minutes. Drain
2. In a large bowl, toss together the hot noodles with the soy sauce, ginger, sesame oil, mushrooms, and carrots, tossing well to combine.
3. In a large shallow pan, carefully submerge spring roll wrappers, one at a time, in warm water until just barely soft.
4. Remove from water and place a bit of lettuce in the center of the wrapper.
5. Add about 2 tablespoons of noodle mixture, a few slices of cucumber, and 2–3 mint leaves on top.
6. Fold the bottom of the wrapper over the filling, fold in each side, then roll.

Easy Asian Dipping Sauce
⅓ cup

Tangy, salty, spicy, and a bit sour—this easy dipping sauce has it all! Use it for dipping spring rolls. It would also make an excellent marinade for a baked tofu dish.

¼ cup low-sodium soy sauce
2 tablespoons rice vinegar
2 teaspoons sesame oil
1 teaspoon sugar
1 teaspoon fresh ginger, minced
2 cloves garlic, minced and crushed
¼ teaspoon crushed red pepper flakes, or to taste

Whisk together all ingredients.

Snack

Summer Fruit Cobbler (from Thursday snack)

Dinner

Marinara Sauce (see Week 1, Tuesday dinner) with added sautéed vegetarian Italian sausage, over whole wheat fettuccine noodles, green salad

Breakfast

Whole wheat bagel with "fixings," orange juice, herbal tea

Lunch

Fresh corn on the cob with low-sodium seasoning, vegetable medley with tofu, nutritional yeast, and Italian seasoning

Snack

Chocolate Candy Substitute

Chocolate Candy Substitute
15–20 servings

This dessert is intended to be used as a way to curb a candy craving. (You grab a chunk from the freezer and eat it like candy.)

1 tablespoon cocoa
1 tablespoon sugar
¾ cup fresh pineapple chunks
1-3 teaspoons nonfat dry milk (optional)

1. In small bowl, mix cocoa and sugar.
2. Place waxed paper on baking sheet.
3. Dip each piece of pineapple in cocoa-sugar mixture. (The choice whether to coat only 1 side of the pineapple or all sides depends on whether you prefer a dark, bittersweet chocolate taste or a milder one.)
4. Add dry milk powder to mixture if you prefer milk chocolate.
5. Place each piece of pineapple on waxed paper–covered baking sheet.
6. Place baking sheet in freezer for several hours.
7. Once pineapple is frozen, layer "candies" on waxed paper in airtight freezer container.
8. Place a piece of aluminum foil over top layer before putting on lid, to prevent freezer burn.

Dinner

Creamy Chickpea and Rosemary Soup, whole wheat pita veggie melt

Creamy Chickpea and Rosemary Soup

6 servings

Another winning recipe from another winning dietitian friend: Maria Soler, MS, RD, who also worked in the field of substance abuse for many years. To prepare this via pressure cooker, soak dry chickpeas overnight, use salt-free broth, and cook on high pressure for 15–20 minutes.

3 tablespoons olive oil
5 garlic cloves, finely chopped
1 tablespoon fresh rosemary leaf, minced
½ teaspoon crushed red pepper flakes
3 16-ounce cans chickpeas, rinsed and drained
4 cups low-sodium vegetable broth
2 tablespoons fresh lemon juice
Sea salt to taste

1. In a large saucepan, heat the oil over medium heat and add garlic, rosemary, and red pepper flakes.
2. Cook, stirring constantly, until the garlic starts to brown, about 1 minute.
3. Add chickpeas and cook 2 minutes, stirring constantly.
4. Add vegetable broth and bring to a boil.
5. Reduce heat and simmer 30 minutes; let cool slightly.
6. Transfer soup to a blender; cover loosely, and purée until just smooth.
7. Return to the saucepan and stir in lemon juice and sea salt to taste.
8. Serve, garnished with a fresh rosemary sprig, or an additional drizzling of olive oil.

Monday

Breakfast

Homemade Granola (see Week 2, Tuesday breakfast), fresh berries, juice, herbal tea

Lunch

Veggie slice sandwich with avocado and tomato

Snack

Gourmet Sorbet (see Week 2, Friday snack)

Dinner

Classic Chicken (or Tofu) Parmesan, whole wheat pasta, French Tarragon Green Beans (see Week 10, Wednesday dinner)

Classic Chicken (or Tofu) Parmesan

6 servings

Tofu can easily replace the bird in this healthier version of the restaurant fave.

6 boneless, skinless chicken breast halves

1 egg

½ cup breadcrumbs

½ teaspoon dried basil

½ teaspoon dried oregano

2 teaspoons minced garlic

2 tablespoons olive oil

1¾ cups tomato sauce

½ cup shredded mozzarella cheese

2 tablespoons grated Parmesan cheese

¼ cup chopped fresh parsley

1. Pound the chicken to desired thickness.
2. Beat the egg slightly.
3. Combine the breadcrumbs, basil, oregano, and garlic.
4. Dip the chicken in the egg, then into the breadcrumb mixture to coat.
5. Sauté in an oven-safe pan with the oil until brown on both sides.

6. Add the tomato sauce, and reduce heat. Cover and simmer for 10 minutes.
7. Preheat broiler.
8. Sprinkle cheeses and parsley over the chicken, then place under broiler until cheese is melted.

Tuesday

Breakfast

Overnight Oatmeal (see Week 1, Sunday breakfast) with chopped walnuts and currants, juice, herbal tea

Lunch

Creamy Chickpea and Rosemary Soup (from Sunday dinner)

Snack

Asian Popcorn

Asian Popcorn

1 serving

Tastier and healthier than artificially flavored microwave popcorn.

Cooking spray

4 cups air-popped popcorn

1 teaspoon Bragg Liquid Aminos, or low-sodium soy sauce

2 teaspoons fresh lemon juice

1 teaspoon five spice powder

¼ teaspoon ground coriander

¼ teaspoon garlic powder

1. Preheat oven to 250°F.
2. Spread popcorn on nonstick cookie sheet; lightly coat with nonstick or butter-flavored cooking spray.
3. Mix together all remaining ingredients and drizzle over popcorn; lightly toss to coat evenly.
4. Bake for 5 minutes; toss popcorn and rotate pan; bake for an additional 5 minutes.
5. Serve warm.

Popcorn Cooking Methods

Air-poppers are inexpensive and a great way to save money and calories on your high fiber popcorn. Another easy, tasty version is to toss popcorn with melted non-trans fat buttery tasting margarine, nutritional yeast, and a low-sodium seasoning.

Dinner

Gingered Tofu and Bok Choy Stir-Fry, steamed quinoa

Gingered Tofu and Bok Choy Stir-Fry

3 servings

Dark leafy bok choy is a highly nutritious vegetable that can be found in well-stocked groceries. Keep an eye out for light green baby bok choy, which is a bit more tender but carries a similar flavor.

3 tablespoons low-sodium soy sauce

2 tablespoons lemon or lime juice

1 tablespoon fresh ginger, minced

1 block firm or extra-firm tofu, well pressed

2 tablespoons olive oil

1 head bok choy or 3–4 small baby bok choys

½ teaspoon sugar

½ teaspoon sesame oil

1. Whisk together soy sauce, lemon or lime juice, and ginger in a shallow pan.
2. Cut tofu into cubes, and marinate for at least 1 hour. Drain, reserving marinade.
3. In a large skillet or wok, sauté tofu in olive oil for 3 to 4 minutes.
4. Carefully add reserved marinade, bok choy, and sugar, stirring well to combine.
5. Cook, stirring, for 3 to 4 more minutes, or until bok choy is done.
6. Drizzle with sesame oil and serve over whole grains.

It's Easy Being Green

Learn to love your leafy greens! Pound for pound and calorie for calorie, dark, leafy green vegetables are the most nutritious food on the planet. Try a variety of greens: bok choy, collard greens, spinach, kale, mustard greens, Swiss chard, or watercress. When you find one or two that you like, sneak it in as many meals as you can!

Wednesday

Breakfast

High fiber, whole grain cereal, banana, juice, herbal tea

Lunch

Classic Chicken (or Tofu) Parmesan with French Tarragon Green Beans (from Monday dinner), green salad with Creamy Feta Vinaigrette

Creamy Feta Vinaigrette

⅔ cup (suggested serving size: 1 tablespoon)

½ cup plain low-fat yogurt

1 tablespoon lemon juice

1 tablespoon olive oil

1½ ounces feta cheese

2 teaspoons mint

½ tablespoon honey (optional)

Fresh-ground pepper, to taste

Process all ingredients in food processor or blender. Chill before serving.

Snack

Pumpkin seeds and raisins

Dinner

Cuban Black Beans and Sweet Potatoes, brown rice, steamed kale with lemon juice

Cuban Black Beans and Sweet Potatoes

4 servings

Stir some plain steamed brown rice right into the pot, or serve it alongside these well-seasoned beans.

3 cloves garlic, minced

2 large sweet potatoes, chopped small

2 tablespoons olive oil

2 15-ounce cans black beans, drained

¾ cup low-sodium vegetable broth

1 tablespoon salt-free chili powder

1 teaspoon paprika

1 teaspoon cumin

1 tablespoon lime juice

Hot sauce, to taste

2 cups cooked brown rice

1. In a large skillet or soup pot, sauté garlic and sweet potatoes in olive oil for 2 to 3 minutes.
2. Reduce heat to medium-low and add beans, vegetable broth, chili powder, paprika, and cumin.
3. Bring to a simmer, cover, and cook for 25 to 30 minutes, until sweet potatoes are soft.
4. Stir in lime juice and hot sauce, to taste. Serve hot over rice.

Thursday

Breakfast

Yogurt Fruit Smoothie (see Week 3, Monday snack)

Lunch

Cuban Black Beans Wrap (use leftovers from Wednesday dinner in a wrap with feta, heat to melt)

Snack

Fruity Oatmeal Bar (see Week 3, Sunday snack)

Dinner

Baked Halibut with Lemon, Apricot Rice, steamed broccoli

Baked Halibut with Lemon

6 servings

2 large lemons

¼ cup dried whole grain breadcrumbs

1½ pounds halibut fillets

Sea or kosher salt and freshly ground white or black pepper, to taste (optional)

1. Preheat oven to 375°F.
2. Wash 1 lemon; cut into thin slices.
3. Grate 1 tablespoon of zest from the second lemon, then juice it.
4. Combine grated zest and breadcrumbs in small bowl; stir to mix. Set aside.
5. Put lemon juice in shallow dish; arrange lemon slices in bottom of baking dish treated with nonstick spray.
6. Dip fish pieces in lemon juice; set on lemon slices in baking dish.
7. Sprinkle breadcrumb mixture evenly over fish pieces along with salt and pepper, if using.
8. Bake until crumbs are lightly browned and fish is just opaque, 10–15 minutes. (Baking time will depend on thickness of fish.)
9. Serve immediately, using lemon slices as garnish.

Lemon Infusion

Mildly flavored fish such as catfish, cod, halibut, orange roughy, rockfish, and snapper benefit from the distinctive flavor of lemon. Adding slices of lemon to the top of fish allows the flavor to infuse into fish.

Apricot Rice
4 servings

Apricot nectar and dried apricots add flavor to plain white rice in this easy pilaf recipe. Serve it with grilled chicken breasts or grilled tempeh and a spinach salad for a delicious meal.

1 tablespoon olive oil
2 shallots, finely chopped
3 cloves garlic, minced
1½ cups long-grain white rice
½ cup finely chopped dried apricots
2 cups apricot nectar
1 cup water
¼ teaspoon salt
⅛ teaspoon cayenne pepper
2 tablespoons butter or non-trans fat
  margarine

1. In heavy saucepan, combine olive oil, shallots, and garlic.
2. Cook and stir over medium heat until vegetables are tender, about 4 minutes.
3. Stir in rice; cook and stir for 2 minutes longer.
4. Add apricots along with remaining ingredients except butter.
5. Bring to a boil, then reduce heat, cover, and simmer for 20 to 25 minutes or until rice is tender and liquid is absorbed.
6. Add butter, cover, and remove from heat. Let stand for 5 minutes.
7. Stir until butter is combined and serve.

Friday

Breakfast

Multigrain hot cereal cooked with dried fruit, apples, juice, herbal tea

Lunch

Tempeh "Chicken" Salad on bed of leaf lettuce, fresh tomato slices, whole grain bread, steamed broccoli (from Thursday dinner)

Tempeh "Chicken" Salad
3-4 servings

Turn this great dish into a sandwich, or slice up some tomatoes and serve on a bed of lettuce. For a curried version, omit the dill and add half a teaspoon of salt-free curry powder and a dash cayenne and black pepper.

1 pound tempeh, diced small

3 tablespoons vegan mayonnaise

2 teaspoons lemon juice

½ teaspoon garlic powder

1 teaspoon Dijon mustard

2 tablespoons sweet pickle relish

½ cup green peas

2 stalks celery, diced small

1 tablespoon chopped fresh dill (optional)

1. Cover tempeh with water and simmer for 10 minutes, until tempeh is soft. Drain and allow to cool completely.
2. Whisk together mayonnaise, lemon juice, garlic powder, mustard, and relish.
3. Combine tempeh, mayonnaise mixture, peas, celery, and dill and gently toss to combine.
4. Chill for at least 1 hour before serving to allow flavors to combine.

Snack

Fresh pineapple with grated fresh ginger

Dinner

Pasta Shells with Zucchini, mozzarella layered with fresh tomato and basil with olive oil drizzle

Pasta Shells with Zucchini

4 servings

Rosemary adds a rich depth of flavor to this simple summer pasta recipe, and the Parmesan cheese topping adds just the right texture and taste.

1 tablespoon butter or non-trans fat margarine

2 cloves garlic, minced

3 zucchini, sliced

2 teaspoons fresh rosemary leaves, minced

¼ teaspoon salt

⅛ teaspoon white pepper

1 12-ounce package medium whole wheat pasta shells

3 tablespoons chopped parsley

¼ cup grated Parmesan cheese

1. Bring a large pot of water to a boil.
2. In a large skillet, melt butter over medium heat.
3. Add garlic and zucchini and cook until crisp-tender, about 5 to 6 minutes.
4. Add rosemary and season with salt and pepper.
5. Cook for 2 to 3 minutes to blend flavors. Remove from heat.
6. Meanwhile, cook pasta in boiling salted water until al dente.
7. Drain and add to zucchini mixture.
8. Return to the heat and toss until the shells are coated with sauce, 2 to 3 minutes.
9. Add the parsley and cheese and toss again. Serve immediately.

Saturday

Breakfast

Whole wheat bagel topped with tempeh salad, cucumbers, herbal tea, fruit juice

Lunch

Baked Halibut with Lemon with salad greens in whole grain wrap (from Thursday dinner)

Snack

Sneaky Apple Cookies

Sneaky Apple Cookies
24 servings

These cookies are of the "stealth" genre. You may know of others who are resistant to eating healthy foods. There are taste-good, look-like-normal versions of foods that contain beans, vegetables, and other nutrient-dense food items where least expected. For more dishes in this genre check out dietitian Evelyn Tribole's book, Stealth Health.

1 tablespoon ground flaxseed

¼ cup water

¼ cup firmly packed brown sugar

⅛ cup granulated sugar

¾ cup cooked pinto beans, drained

⅓ cup unsweetened applesauce

2 teaspoons baking powder

⅛ teaspoon sea salt

1 teaspoon ground cinnamon

½ teaspoon ground nutmeg

¼ teaspoon ground cloves

¼ teaspoon ground allspice

1 cup Vita-Spelt white spelt flour

1 medium-sized Golden Delicious apple

1 cup dried sunflower seed kernels (unroasted, unsalted)

1. Preheat oven to 350°F.
2. Put flaxseed and water in microwave-safe container; microwave on high for 15 seconds, or until mixture thickens and has consistency of egg whites.
3. Add flaxseed mixture, sugars, beans, and applesauce to mixing bowl; mix well.
4. Sift dry ingredients together; fold into bean mixture. (Do not overmix; this will cause cookies to become tough.)
5. Peel and chop apple; fold into batter with sunflower seeds.
6. Drop by teaspoonful onto baking sheet treated with nonstick spray; bake for 12–18 minutes.

Dinner

Risotto with Winter Squash, steamed greens

Risotto with Winter Squash
6 servings

Sweet and tender squash combines wonderfully with sage, onion, and leek in this creamy risotto. This could be the main dish for a vegetarian dinner.

4 cups fat-free vegetable broth

1 tablespoon olive oil

3 cups cubed butternut squash

1 onion, chopped

3 cloves garlic, minced

1 cup chopped leek

1 teaspoon dried sage leaves

½ teaspoon salt

⅛ teaspoon white pepper

1½ cups Arborio rice

¼ cup grated Parmesan cheese

1 tablespoon butter or non-trans fat margarine

¼ cup chopped flat-leaf parsley

1. Place broth in medium saucepan; place over low heat.
2. In a large saucepan, heat oil over medium heat.
3. Add squash to large saucepan; cook and stir until squash begins to brown, about 6 to 7 minutes.
4. Add onion, garlic, and leek; cook and stir for 4 to 5 minutes longer until onion is translucent.
5. Stir in sage, salt, pepper, and rice; cook and stir for 3 minutes longer.
6. Slowly add warm broth, ½ cup at a time, stirring frequently.
7. When rice is al dente (slightly firm to the bite) and squash is tender, add the cheese, butter, and parsley, cover, and remove from heat.
8. Let stand for 5 minutes, then stir and serve immediately.

Sunday

Breakfast

Tofu "Egg-less" Scramble (see Week 1, Saturday breakfast), whole grain toast, "soysages," orange juice, herbal tea

Lunch

Frozen bean burritos with peach salsa and avocado

Snack

Sneaky Apple Cookies (see Week 8, Saturday snack)

Dinner

Sweet and Sour Turkey Burgers on whole grain buns, Mustard Greens and Lemon Sauté

Sweet and Sour Turkey Burgers
4 servings

Sweet and sour is an excellent flavor combination to use in low-fat cooking because the main ingredients are fat-free. These tender and juicy burgers are really delicious.

1 tablespoon low-sodium soy sauce

1 tablespoon honey

1 tablespoon apple cider vinegar

¼ cup dried whole grain breadcrumbs

1 pound ground turkey breast

¼ cup chopped green onions

6 slices canned pineapple, drained

6 hamburger buns, split

¼ cup chili sauce

6 butter lettuce leaves

1. In a medium bowl, combine soy sauce, honey, vinegar, and breadcrumbs until blended.
2. Add ground turkey and green onions and mix well. Shape into four patties.

3. In a nonstick skillet over medium heat, fry patties, turning once, until done, about 8 to 10 minutes.
4. To serve, spread chili sauce on hamburger buns and top with a patty, pineapple ring, and lettuce.
5. Top with half of the bun.

Ground Turkey

When you buy ground turkey, look for an evenly colored product that has very little liquid in the package. If there is a lot of liquid, the meat will be dry when cooked. Ground turkey freezes very well, so purchase a lot when there's a sale.

Mustard Greens and Lemon Sauté

4 servings

1 bunch mustard greens, chopped
2 teaspoons untoasted sesame oil
2 tablespoons water
Lemon juice, to taste
¼ cup walnuts, toasted

1. In a skillet, sauté greens in oil for 2 minutes.
2. Add water.
3. Bring to boil, lower heat, and simmer, covered, 2 minutes.
4. Season with lemon juice.
5. Chop walnuts and garnish over greens.

Monday

Breakfast

Multigrain hot cereal (from Friday breakfast) with vanilla yogurt, juice, herbal tea

Lunch

Risotto with Winter Squash and greens (from Saturday dinner)

Snack

Homemade Fruit Pops

Homemade Fruit Pops
6 servings

If you do not have an ice crusher, place the ice in a plastic bag and smash it with a hammer or other hard object to crush it before adding it to a blender. The ice is important for bulking up the mixture.

1 12-ounce bag frozen strawberries
3 cups 100 percent fruit strawberry juice
1 cup crushed ice

1. Place fruit, juice, and ice in a blender, in that order. Blend on high.
2. Pour mixture into ice pop molds.
3. Freeze for 1 hour.
4. Remove ice pops from the freezer and insert a stick into the center of each treat.
5. Return to the freezer and let solidify for another 7 to 9 hours before eating.

Ice Pop Tools

If you don't have an ice pop mold, don't fret. Just use paper cups! Allow the pops to freeze about 1 hour, then insert sticks just as you would in the original recipe. If you don't have official ice pop sticks, try plastic spoons. Anything clean that stays in the center of the ice pop and makes a decent handle will work.

Dinner

White Bean Pistachio Salad, focaccia bread with fresh tomato and low-fat mozzarella

White Bean Pistachio Salad

4 servings

Pistachios actually lower cholesterol levels, so don't worry about including them in a low-fat diet.

1 15-ounce can small white beans, rinsed and drained

2 cups sliced celery

½ cup diced red onion

⅓ cup pistachios, chopped

2 tablespoons fresh thyme leaves

1 teaspoon dried tarragon leaves

¼ cup apple cider vinegar

2 tablespoons extra-virgin olive oil

2 tablespoons sugar or Sucanat

¼ teaspoon salt

½ teaspoon pepper

4 cups mixed salad greens

1. In a large bowl, combine all ingredients except vinegar, olive oil, sugar, salt, pepper, and salad greens; toss to blend.
2. In a small bowl, combine vinegar, oil, sugar, salt, and pepper and mix well to blend.
3. Pour over other ingredients in bowl and stir gently.
4. Cover and chill for 2 to 3 hours.
5. To serve, arrange salad greens on plates and top with bean mixture.

Tuesday

Breakfast

High fiber, whole grain cereal, banana, orange juice, herbal tea

Lunch

Tofu "Egg-less" Scramble wrap (from Sunday breakfast)

Snack

Carrot Fruit Cup

Carrot Fruit Cup

4 servings

1 tablespoon raisins

2 carrots, grated

1 apple, grated

1 tablespoon frozen apple juice concentrate

1 teaspoon cinnamon

Pinch of ginger

1 frozen banana, sliced

1. Soak raisins overnight in little more than enough water to cover.
2. When ready to prepare dessert, drain water from raisins and pour into bowl.
3. Add carrots and apple.
4. Stir in frozen apple juice concentrate and spices until blended.
5. Add banana slices; stir again.
6. Chill until ready to serve.

Dinner

Red Snapper with Peppers and Vinegar, Herbed Quinoa with Sun-Dried Tomatoes (see Week 4, Tuesday dinner), steamed asparagus with lemon juice

Red Snapper with Peppers and Vinegar

6 servings

Red snapper has a unique flavor of its own. The tartness of the vinegar and the sweetness of the peppers create a perfect medley.

¼ cup all-purpose flour

1 tablespoon curry powder

Fresh-cracked black pepper, to taste

1 red pepper

1 green pepper

3 sprigs cilantro, leaves only, chopped

1½ pounds red snapper

1 tablespoon cider vinegar

1 tablespoon olive oil

1. Mix together the flour, curry powder, and black pepper.
2. Stem, seed, and finely slice the red and green peppers.
3. Dust the snapper with the flour mixture.
4. Heat the oil to medium-high temperature in a large sauté pan; cook the snapper on each side for approximately 5 minutes.
5. Add the peppers and vinegar; let reduce by half. (The cooking liquid will reduce into a nice thickened sauce.)
6. Serve with the cooking liquid and sprinkle with cilantro.

Curry Powder

Since curry powder is a blend of several spices and herbs, the flavor varies quite a bit. Use your favorite Caribbean or Indian curry powder, or venture to make your own mixture.

Wednesday

Breakfast

Quinoa flake hot cereal with flaxseeds and chopped figs, herbal tea, juice

Lunch

Sweet and Sour Turkey Burgers on whole grain buns (from Sunday dinner) with steamed asparagus (from Tuesday dinner)

Snack

Almond-Stuffed Dates

Almond-Stuffed Dates
6 servings

Combining almonds and dates is a delicious way to create candy–like sweets that are fiber-rich. If you roast or toast the almonds, they will be crunchier and even more satisfying.

¼ cup powdered sugar
12 Medjool dates
½ cup whole almonds

1. Place the powdered sugar in a bowl.
2. Cut a slit on one side of each date and remove the pit. Replace it with an almond.
3. Roll the dates in the powdered sugar.

Dinner

Barbecue tempeh, Multigrain Corn Bread
(see Week 6, Friday dinner), greens

Barbecue Sauce

**10 servings (this would be more than
enough for 2 pounds of tempeh)**

*This is a quick to make barbecue sauce that
starts with low-sodium ketchup. Tomatoey,
relatively sweet, with the spices having a basic
chili flavor. In other words, not too different
from most bottled sauces.*

½ cup low-sodium ketchup

½ cup vinegar

½ cup honey

¼ cup molasses

1 tablespoon chili powder

1 tablespoon onion powder

½ teaspoon garlic powder

1 tablespoon dry mustard

¼ teaspoon cayenne

1. Combine all ingredients and mix well.
2. Store in a covered jar in the
   refrigerator.
3. Dredge tempeh (that has been cut into
   ½" strips) in sauce, place on baking
   sheet, and bake at 350°F for 15–20
   minutes until slightly dry.

Thursday

Breakfast

Overnight Oatmeal (see Week 1, Tuesday breakfast) with add-ins of your choice, fruit juice, herbal tea

Lunch

White Bean Pistachio Salad (from Monday dinner) with fresh diced tomato in a whole grain wrap

Snack

Carrot Fruit Cup (from Tuesday snack)

Dinner

Lentil Soup with Herbs and Lemon, open-face cheese melt with sprouts

Lentil Soup with Herbs and Lemon

4 servings

1 cup lentils, soaked overnight in 1 cup water

6 cups low-fat, reduced-sodium chicken or vegetable broth

1 carrot, sliced

1 stalk celery, sliced

1 yellow onion, thinly sliced

2 teaspoons olive oil

1 tablespoon dried tarragon

½ teaspoon dried oregano

Sea salt and black pepper, to taste (optional)

1 tablespoon lemon juice

4 thin slices of lemon

1. Drain and rinse lentils.
2. Add lentils and broth to pot over medium heat; bring to a boil.
3. Reduce heat and simmer until tender, approximately 15 minutes. (If you did not presoak the lentils, increase cooking time by about 15 more minutes.)

4. While lentils are cooking, sauté carrot, celery, and onion in oil for 8 minutes, or until onion is golden brown. Remove from heat and set aside.
5. When lentils are tender, add vegetables, tarragon, oregano, and salt and pepper, if using; cook for 2 minutes.
6. Stir in lemon juice.
7. Ladle into 4 serving bowls; garnish with lemon slices.

Friday

Breakfast

English muffin with SunButter and fruit preserves, juice, herbal tea

Lunch

Barbecue tempeh and greens (from Wednesday dinner)

Snack

Fruited yogurt

Dinner

Chicken Thighs Cacciatore, Herbed Rice Pilaf, steamed broccoli and carrots

Chicken Thighs Cacciatore

4 servings

2 teaspoons olive oil

½ cup chopped onion

2 cloves garlic, minced

4 chicken thighs, skin removed

½ cup white grape juice

1 14½-ounce can unsalted diced tomatoes, undrained

1 teaspoon dried parsley

½ teaspoon dried oregano

¼ teaspoon pepper

⅛ teaspoon sugar

¼ cup grated Parmesan cheese

4 cups cooked spaghetti

2 teaspoons extra-virgin olive oil

1. Heat deep, nonstick skillet over medium-high heat; add 2 teaspoons olive oil.
2. Add onion; sauté until transparent.
3. Add garlic and chicken thighs; sauté 3 minutes on each side, or until lightly browned.
4. Remove thighs from pan; add grape juice and undrained tomatoes, parsley,

oregano, pepper, and sugar. Stir well, bring to a boil.

5. Return chicken to pan; sprinkle Parmesan cheese over top.

6. Cover, reduce heat, and simmer 10 minutes.

7. Uncover and simmer 10 more minutes.

8. To serve, put 1 cup of cooked pasta on each of 4 plates.

9. Top each serving with a chicken thigh; divide sauce between dishes.

10. Drizzle ½ teaspoon extra-virgin olive oil over top of each dish and serve.

Herbed Rice Pilaf
4 servings

The tiny thyme leaves will drop off the stem as the pilaf cooks, adding a lemony-mint flavor to this easy recipe.

1 tablespoon olive oil

1 onion, chopped

2 stalks celery, chopped

2 cloves garlic, minced

1 fresh thyme sprig

¼ teaspoon salt

⅛ teaspoon pepper

1 bay leaf

2½ cups water

1 cup long-grain brown rice

1. In a large saucepan, heat oil over medium heat.

2. Add onion, celery, garlic, and thyme and sauté until onion is translucent, about 5 minutes.

3. Add salt, pepper, bay leaf, and water, and bring to a boil.

4. Add rice, bring to a simmer, then cover, reduce heat to low, and simmer until all the water is absorbed and rice is tender, about 20 minutes.

5. Remove and discard the bay leaf and the thyme stem; stir gently. Serve immediately.

Breakfast

Vegetable Frittata (see Week 2, Friday dinner), whole wheat toast

Lunch

Lentil Soup with Herbs and Lemon (from Thursday dinner)

Snack

Gourmet Sorbet (see Week 2, Friday snack)

Dinner

Kale Pesto with whole wheat pasta, Sweet Red Salad with Strawberries and Beets

Kale Pesto

Makes 1 cup

Another dietitian favorite contributed by co-worker Mariel Hensley, MSH, RD.

1 bunch kale
2 small shallots
2 cloves garlic
1 jalapeño (or other mildly spicy pepper)
½ cup goat cheese or feta
½ cup of pine nuts or walnuts
2–3 tablespoons fresh lemon juice
¼ cup olive oil
Fresh-ground black pepper and salt, to taste

1. Bring a large pot of salted water to a boil, cook peeled garlic, shallot, and jalapeño for 2 minutes in boiling water.
2. Drop cleaned, roughly chopped kale into boiling water for 30 seconds.
3. Pour out all of the boiling water and drop kale, shallots, garlic, and jalapeño in an ice bath for 30–60 seconds to stop the cooking, then drain well.

4. Put all of the ingredients except for oil into a food processor, start the processor and slowly drizzle olive oil into the processor while it is running.
5. Process all ingredients until combined and a medium-fine texture is achieved.

Sweet Red Salad with Strawberries and Beets
4 servings

Colorful and nutritious, this vibrant red salad can be made with roasted or canned beets, or even raw grated beets, if you prefer.

3–4 small beets, chopped
Spinach or other green lettuce
1 cup sliced strawberries
½ cup chopped pecans
¼ cup olive oil
2 tablespoons red wine vinegar
2 tablespoons agave nectar
2 tablespoons orange juice
Salt and pepper to taste

1. Boil beets until soft, about 20 minutes. Allow to cool completely.
2. In a large bowl, combine spinach, strawberries, pecans, and cooled beets.

3. In a separate small bowl, whisk together the olive oil, vinegar, agave nectar, and orange juice, and pour over salad, tossing well to coat.
4. Season lightly with salt and pepper, to taste.

Sunday

Breakfast

Stuffed French Toast (see Week 7, Saturday breakfast), orange juice, herbal tea

Lunch

Quinoa and Pumpkin Seed Pilaf, Sweet Red Salad with Strawberries and Beets (from Saturday dinner)

Quinoa and Pumpkin Seed Pilaf

4 servings

Heart healthy and nutritious quinoa is a gluten-free grain. Any seasonal blanched vegetables can be used, including corn, broccoli, beets, green beans, and peas. You can also add sautéed mushrooms or marinated tempeh.

1 teaspoon olive oil
½ cup onion, diced
½ cup carrot, diced
¼ cup celery, diced
1 cup quinoa, rinsed
2 cups water or low-sodium vegetable broth
⅛ teaspoon salt
¼ cup fresh parsley, finely chopped
¼ cup pumpkin seeds, toasted
1 teaspoon tahini
½ teaspoon low-sodium shoyu (or soy sauce)
Lemon juice, to taste

1. In a skillet, heat oil and sauté onion, carrot, and celery until onion is translucent.
2. In a saucepan, dry roast quinoa over low flame for 5 minutes until fragrant.
3. Add water or broth, onion, carrot, celery, and salt.

4. Bring to boil, lower heat, and simmer, covered, 20 minutes.
5. Mix in remaining ingredients except lemon juice.
6. Add lemon juice, to taste.

Snack

Fruit salad

Dinner

Tuna Panini (see Week 3, Friday dinner), sautéed onion and chard

Monday

Breakfast

Overnight Oatmeal (from Thursday breakfast), fruit juice, herbal tea

Lunch

Lentil Soup with Herbs and Lemon (from Thursday dinner), whole grain bread with spread of choice

Snack

DIY Trail Mix (see Week 1, Tuesday snack)

Dinner

Mock Macaroni and Cheese (cook extra noodles to use for Wednesday dinner), Green Beans with Garlic

Mock Macaroni and Cheese

5 servings

Grated mochi melted into hot butternut squash sauce brings a cheesy consistency to vegan "mac and cheese."

4 cups water

8 ounces quinoa macaroni

Pinch sea salt

1 cup fresh peas, blanched

1 batch Butternut Squash Tahini Sauce (see sidebar)

1. Bring 4 cups water to boil, add macaroni, and a pinch of sea salt.
2. Cook until done, about 10 minutes, depending on macaroni shape.
3. Add blanched peas.
4. Mix Butternut Squash Tahini Sauce with macaroni. Serve.

Butternut Squash Tahini Sauce

This vegan cheese sauce adds a nutritious cheesy flavor to pasta. Cook 1 peeled and chopped medium butternut squash in 2 cups water for 20 minutes. Blend squash and cooking water with ¼ cup tahini, ¼ cup sweet white miso, 1 cup grated mochi, and 2 tablespoons red wine vinegar. Slowly add more water if desired.

Green Beans with Garlic

4 servings

Green beans, garlic, and tomatoes combine in a delicious side dish that's perfect with grilled chicken or tempeh.

1 pound green beans
1 tablespoon olive oil
1 onion, chopped
3 cloves garlic, minced
1 tablespoon flour
¼ teaspoon salt
⅛ teaspoon pepper
1 14-ounce can diced tomatoes

1. Assemble a steamer and place water in bottom section. Bring to a simmer over high heat.
2. Trim beans and add to top of steamer.
3. Cook until beans are tender, about 5 to 7 minutes.
4. Remove from steamer and set aside.
5. In a medium saucepan, heat oil over medium heat.
6. Add onion and garlic; cook and stir until tender, about 6 minutes.
7. Sprinkle flour, salt, and pepper over onions; cook and stir until bubbly.
8. Drain tomatoes, reserving liquid.
9. Add liquid to saucepan; cook and stir until thickened.
10. Add green beans and drained tomatoes; cook and stir over medium heat for 2 to 3 minutes until blended. Serve immediately.

Don't overcook the beans; they're best cooked until crisp-tender. They'll also retain more color cooked that way.

Tuesday

Breakfast

Green Tea Smoothie (see Week 7, Wednesday breakfast), English muffin with tahini and fruit preserves

Lunch

Tuna Panini and chard (from Sunday dinner)

Snack

Fruity Oatmeal Bars (see Week 3, Sunday snack)

Dinner

Guava Cheddar Appetizer, Red Beans and Rice, green salad

Guava Cheddar Appetizer
About 20 pieces

Guava fruit, grown in the tropics and subtropics, is a rich source of vitamin C and fiber. Guava paste contains lots of sugar, hardly a health food, but a small amount goes a long way in this tantalizing appetizer with an odd juxtaposition of flavors and textures.

1 box guava paste
8-ounce block of medium sharp Cheddar
  cheese

Cut cheddar cheese into mini slabs (approximately 1" × ½" × ⅜") and place similarly sized pieces of guava paste atop the cheese.

Red Beans and Rice

4 servings

Another marriage of legume and grain this is a Caribbean favorite that will fill up a family without leaving anyone hungry.

¼ cup diced celery

¼ cup diced onion

¼ cup diced green bell pepper

1 clove garlic, minced

1 tablespoon olive oil

2 cups cooked red beans

½ teaspoon dried thyme

¼ teaspoon cayenne pepper

¾ cup water

Salt to taste

2 cups cooked brown rice

1–4 drops liquid smoke (optional)

1. Sauté celery, onion, green bell pepper, and garlic in olive oil.
2. Add beans, thyme, cayenne pepper, water, and salt.
3. Simmer for 45 minutes.
4. Adjust seasoning and serve over rice.

Wednesday

Breakfast

Overnight Oatmeal (leftover from Monday breakfast), orange juice, herbal tea

Lunch

Basic Lunch Wrap (see Week 1, Monday lunch) with raw vegetable sticks

Snack

Fruit salad

Dinner

Quick Chicken/Tofu Mozzarella, whole wheat noodles, French Tarragon Green Beans

Quick Chicken/Tofu Mozzarella

2 servings

When it's just the two of you, this super quick recipe is easy and delicious. It also works for a laid-back lunch with guests. Feel free to use dredged and baked slabs of tofu in place of the chicken breasts.

2 boneless, skinless chicken breast halves

2 tablespoons low-fat buttermilk

3 tablespoons seasoned dry whole grain breadcrumbs

1 tablespoon olive oil

⅓ cup shredded low-fat mozzarella cheese

2 tomato slices (½" thick)

1 tablespoon chopped fresh basil

1. Place chicken, smooth-side down, between waxed paper.
2. Working from the center to the edges, pound gently with a meat mallet or rolling pin until meat is ⅛ inch thick.
3. Brush chicken with buttermilk and dip into breadcrumbs to coat both sides.

4. In a medium skillet, heat olive oil over medium heat.
5. Add chicken and sauté, turning once, until golden brown and cooked through, about 7 to 8 minutes total.
6. Reduce heat to low.
7. Top chicken with cheese, tomato, and basil.
8. Cover pan and cook for 1 minute, then serve immediately.

French Tarragon Green Beans

4 servings

1½ tablespoons butter or non-trans fat margarine
¼ cup red onion, chopped
½ pound fresh green beans
1 tablespoon tarragon, finely chopped

1. Melt butter in nonstick pan.
2. Add onions; sauté until translucent.
3. Add green beans. Cover and steam 2–3 minutes.
4. Add tarragon; combine well. Steam an additional 2–3 minutes.

Breakfast

Protein and Berry Pita, herbal tea, fruit juice

Protein and Berry Pita

1 serving

Why not pack your naturally sweet and creamy breakfast into a pita for easy transport?

3 tablespoons fat-free ricotta

½ teaspoon imitation vanilla extract

½ teaspoon honey

3 tablespoons of your favorite in-season berries

½ whole wheat pita

1. In a small bowl, mix ricotta, vanilla, and honey.
2. Add berries to ricotta mix.
3. Open pita and scoop ricotta mix into middle.
4. Wrap pita in foil or put in a container and take with you.

Lunch

Red Beans and Rice (from Tuesday dinner)

Snack

Apple Bread Pudding

Apple Bread Pudding

8 servings

Bread pudding is such a comforting dessert. Serve it on a cold winter day when the kids come home from school. It makes good use of bread ends.

4 cups crumbled whole grain bread

2 apples, peeled and grated

½ cup raisins

½ cup chopped pecans

1½ cups 1 percent milk or soymilk

3 eggs

2 teaspoons vanilla

¾ cup brown sugar

3 tablespoons honey

1 teaspoon cinnamon

½ teaspoon nutmeg

2 tablespoons lemon juice

1. Preheat oven to 350°F.
2. Spray a 9" square baking pan with nonstick baking spray containing flour.
3. Combine breadcrumbs, apples, raisins, and pecans in the prepared pan and spread evenly.
4. Combine remaining ingredients in a medium bowl and mix until well blended. Be sure the bread is saturated; push it down into the liquid mixture if necessary. Let stand for 10 minutes.
5. Bake the pudding until top is golden brown, about 35 to 45 minutes.
6. Serve warm with warmed honey or maple syrup.

Bread Pudding Toppings

Bread pudding can be topped with low-fat vanilla ice cream or yogurt (dairy, soy, or coconut).

Dinner

Stir-fry vegetables and tofu (using rice from Tuesday dinner)

Friday

Breakfast

High fiber, whole grain ready to eat cereal, banana, chopped dates, fruit juice, herbal tea

Lunch

Veggie slices/avocado sandwich, Simple Green Salad with Vinaigrette

Simple Green Salad with Vinaigrette

4–6 servings

Another recipe from a dietitian friend; this time, a tangy vinaigrette courtesy of Jennifer Stavig, MS, RD.

2 tablespoons minced red onion

1½ tablespoons balsamic vinegar

2 teaspoons olive oil

¼ teaspoon salt

¼ teaspoon fresh ground pepper

¼ teaspoon coarse dark brown mustard

¼ cup thinly sliced red onion

1 bag mixed salad greens

1 pint cherry tomatoes, halved

1. Combine minced onion and vinegar in a small bowl and let stand 5 minutes.
2. Add oil, salt, pepper, and mustard; stir well with a whisk.
3. Toss with salad greens, sliced onion, and tomatoes and serve.

Snack

Pumpkin seeds and dried, sweetened cranberries

Dinner

Blackened and Bleu Tilapia (see Week 6, Wednesday dinner), Orange Pilaf

Orange Pilaf

4 servings

Orange and raisins add flavor and wonderful aroma to this simple pilaf.

⅓ cup slivered almonds

⅓ cup orange juice

1 teaspoon grated orange zest

1 teaspoon Asian sesame oil

1 tablespoon olive oil

1 cup long-grain brown rice

1 onion, chopped

2 cups water

¼ teaspoon salt

½ teaspoon dried tarragon leaves

⅛ teaspoon white pepper

½ cup raisins

1. Combine almonds, orange juice, zest, and sesame oil in a blender or food processor.
2. Blend or process until smooth, about 10 to 15 seconds.
3. In a large saucepan, heat olive oil over medium heat.
4. Add rice and onion and sauté for 3 minutes.
5. Add salt, tarragon, pepper, and raisins and stir.
6. Add orange mixture and water.
7. Bring to a simmer, then reduce heat to low, cover, and cook until rice is tender, about 18 to 23 minutes.
8. Fluff with a fork before serving.

Breakfast

Ginger Pear Wheat Pancakes (see Week 5, Sunday breakfast), herbal tea, fresh fruit

Lunch

Cashew Cream of Asparagus Soup, Twisted Tabbouleh

Cashew Cream of Asparagus Soup

4 servings

A dairy-free and soy-free asparagus soup with a rich cashew base brings out the natural flavors of the asparagus without relying on other enhancers.

1 onion, chopped

4 cloves garlic, minced

2 tablespoons olive oil

2 pounds asparagus, trimmed and chopped

4 cups low-sodium vegetable broth

¾ cup raw cashews

¾ cup water

¼ teaspoon sage

¼ teaspoon salt

¼ teaspoon black pepper

2 teaspoons lemon juice

2 tablespoons nutritional yeast (optional)

1. In a large soup or stockpot, sauté onion and garlic in olive oil for 2 to 3 minutes, until onion is soft.
2. Reduce heat and carefully add asparagus and vegetable broth.
3. Bring to a simmer, cover, and cook for 20 minutes.
4. Cool slightly, then purée in a blender, working in batches as needed, until almost smooth.
5. Return to pot over low heat.
6. Purée together cashews and water until smooth and add to soup.
7. Add sage, salt, and pepper, and heat for a few more minutes, stirring to combine.
8. Stir in lemon juice and nutritional yeast just before serving, and adjust seasonings to taste.

Twisted Tabbouleh

4 1-cup servings

This dish, a favorite of Mariel Hensley, MSH, RD, is a great source of fiber (from the veggies and quinoa), vegetarian protein (from the soybeans and quinoa), and vitamin C (from the parsley).

1 cup of quinoa uncooked, or 2 cups cooked

1 cup of shelled edamame

½ cup chopped green onions

1 cup chopped fresh tomatoes

⅔ cup crumbled low-fat feta cheese

1 cup chopped parsley

2–3 tablespoons fresh lemon juice

¼ cup olive oil

1 garlic clove, minced

Fresh-ground black pepper, to taste

1. Cook quinoa if needed and chill in refrigerator while prepping other ingredients.
2. Combine edamame, green onions, tomatoes, feta, and parsley in a bowl and gently mix.
3. Combine lemon juice, olive oil, garlic, and black pepper, stir/shake until emulsified.
4. Add chilled quinoa and dressing to other ingredients and toss to coat and mix. Serve chilled.

Snack

Apple Bread Pudding (from Thursday snack)

Dinner

Spaghetti Squash and Vegetables, salad with feta cheese, chickpeas, spring mix lettuce

Spaghetti Squash and Vegetables
6 servings

Dinner doesn't get much easier or more delicious than this.

2 pounds spaghetti squash

Cooking spray

1 cup peas, fresh or frozen

2 tablespoons butter or non-trans fat margarine

8 ounces cherry tomatoes, cut in half

1 ounce grated Romano cheese

¼ teaspoon fresh-ground pepper

1. Cut spaghetti squash in half and scoop out seeds.
2. Spray 9" × 13" baking dish with cooking spray; place squash halves face down.
3. Bake at 400°F for 45 minutes, or until squash is soft-cooked.
4. When squash is cool enough to handle, use a fork to scoop out cooked squash from the outer shell into a medium-sized microwaveable bowl.
5. In separate small saucepan, lightly steam peas 2–3 minutes. Add to squash, along with butter, and mix well.
6. Place covered bowl in microwave; cook on high 2–3 minutes.
7. Add cherry tomato halves and top with Romano cheese and pepper. Serve.

Breakfast

Tofu "Egg-less" Scramble (see Week 1, Saturday breakfast), orange juice, herbal tea

Lunch

Cashew Cream of Asparagus Soup (from Saturday lunch), Orange Pilaf (from Friday dinner)

Snack

Hot Artichoke Spinach Dip with crudités and French bread

Hot Artichoke Spinach Dip
6–8 servings

Serve this creamy dip hot with some baguette slices, crackers, pita bread, or sliced bell peppers and jicama. If you want to get fancy, you can carve out a bread bowl for an edible serving dish.

1 12-ounce package frozen spinach, thawed
1 14-ounce can artichoke hearts, drained
¼ cup non-trans fat margarine
2 cups soymilk
¼ cup flour
½ cup nutritional yeast
1 teaspoon garlic powder
1½ teaspoons onion powder
¼ teaspoon salt

1. Preheat oven to 350°F.
2. Purée spinach and artichokes together until almost smooth and set aside.
3. In a small saucepan, melt the non-trans fat margarine over low heat.
4. Slowly whisk in flour, 1 tablespoon at a time, stirring constantly to avoid lumps, until thick.

5. Remove from heat and add spinach and artichoke mixture, stirring to combine.
6. Add remaining ingredients.
7. Transfer to an ovenproof casserole dish or bowl and bake for 20 minutes. Serve hot.

Dinner

Spicy Beef or Seitan and Cabbage, brown rice

Spicy Beef or Seitan and Cabbage

4 servings

Cabbage is delicious when lightly cooked. It adds color, crunch, and fiber to this simple dish.

¾ pound top round beef steak or seitan

½ cup orange juice

2 tablespoons hoisin sauce

2 tablespoons rice vinegar

1 tablespoon cornstarch or arrowroot powder

⅛ teaspoon cayenne pepper

1 tablespoon vegetable oil

1 tablespoon minced gingerroot

1 onion, chopped

1 10-ounce package shredded cabbage

1½ cups shredded carrots

3 green onions, julienned

1. Trim excess fat from steak and cut into ⅛" × 3" strips against the grain. If using seitan, cut into strips or chunks as desired.
2. In a small bowl, combine orange juice, hoisin sauce, rice vinegar, cornstarch, and pepper and mix well; set aside.
3. In a large skillet, heat vegetable oil over medium-high heat.
4. Add gingerroot and onion; cook and stir for 3 to 4 minutes until onion is crisp-tender.
5. Add beef/seitan and cook for 2 to 3 minutes or until browned.
6. Remove beef/seitan and onion from skillet with slotted spoon and set aside.
7. Add cabbage, carrots, and green onion to skillet; stir fry for 3 minutes.
8. Stir orange juice mixture and add to skillet along with beef/seitan.
9. Stir-fry until sauce thickens slightly and beef/seitan and vegetables are tender.
10. Serve immediately over hot cooked brown rice.

Monday

Breakfast

Hot multigrain cereal, herbal tea, fruit juice

Lunch

Spaghetti Squash and Vegetables (from Saturday dinner)

Snack

Raspberry Almond Milk Frappe

Raspberry Almond Milk Frappe
2 servings

You can substitute maple syrup for the honey in this recipe for a different flavor, or throw in more frozen fruits to add variety. For a protein and calorie boost, add a tablespoon or two of your favorite nut butter.

1 cup frozen raspberries

1 frozen banana or ¾ cup ice cubes

½ cup almond milk (your choice: vanilla or chocolate)

1 teaspoon honey

1. Place all ingredients in a blender and blend until smooth.
2. Pour into two glasses and serve as a quick breakfast.

Dinner

Polenta, steamed kale, tofu, and sweet potatoes

Polenta

4–6 servings

Polenta is Italian comfort food. You can serve it in a bowl in its more porridgy form or pour it into a pie plate or loaf pan, let it cool, and use later cut into triangles or slabs. Vary your polenta by using different herbs and add-ins— sun-dried tomatoes, mushrooms, and black olives work well. The following instructions assume use of a pressure cooker; cooking time in a regular saucepan is about 45 minutes.

1 tablespoon olive oil

1 cup chopped onion

2 cloves garlic, minced

½ cup chopped red pepper (if you have it)

1 cup polenta (coarse cornmeal or true corn grits)

4 cups low-sodium vegetable broth

¼ teaspoon salt

½ teaspoon dried rosemary leaves

1 large bay leaf

Chopped Italian parsley, for garnish

1. Add the oil to the cooker over medium heat.
2. Sauté the onion for 2 minutes. Then add the garlic and red pepper and sauté another minute.
3. Add the polenta, broth, salt, rosemary leaves, and bay leaf, stirring well.
4. Lock on the lid and bring to high pressure.
5. Reduce the heat to maintain high pressure for 5 minutes.
6. Let the pressure come down naturally.
7. Carefully remove the lid, stir.
8. Remove bay leaf, add salt and pepper to taste, and garnish with parsley.

Tuesday

Breakfast

Whole wheat bagel with almond butter, "soysage," red onion

Lunch

Greek salad, whole wheat pita with Hummus

Hummus

6 servings

For a tasty variation of traditional hummus, sprinkle toasted sesame seeds over the top; they provide a nice little crunch and a slight tahini flavor.

1 lemon

¼ bunch fresh parsley

1 cup chickpeas (or other type of white bean), cooked

½ bulb roasted garlic

2 teaspoons extra-virgin olive oil

Fresh-cracked black pepper

Kosher salt or sea salt (optional)

1. Zest and juice the lemon.
2. Chop the parsley.
3. In a blender, purée the cooked chickpeas, then add the garlic, lemon zest, and juice.
4. Continue to purée until the mixture is thoroughly combined.
5. Drizzle in the olive oil in a stream while continuing to purée until all the oil is incorporated and the mixture is smooth.
6. Remove the mixture from the blender and season with salt and pepper. Adjust seasonings to taste.
7. Before serving, sprinkle with chopped parsley.

Traditional Hummus

Traditional hummus is made with chickpeas, which are also known as "garbanzo beans," but this appetizer can be prepared with many different kinds of beans. Hummus can be used as a dip, spread, sauce, or topping.

Snack

Asian Gingered Almonds

Asian Gingered Almonds

1 cup

2 teaspoons unsalted butter

1 tablespoon Bragg Liquid Aminos

1 teaspoon ground ginger

1 cup slivered almonds

1. Preheat oven to 350°F.
2. In microwave-safe bowl, mix butter, Bragg Liquid Aminos, and ginger.
3. Microwave on high 30 seconds, or until butter is melted; blend well.
4. Spread almonds on shallow baking sheet treated with nonstick spray.
5. Bake for 12–15 minutes, or until light gold, stirring occasionally.
6. Pour seasoned butter over almonds; stir to mix.
7. Bake for an additional 5 minutes.
8. Store in an airtight container in a cool place.

Dinner

Stir-Fry Ginger Scallops or Tempeh with Vegetables (see Week 2, Saturday dinner), brown rice (from Sunday dinner)

Wednesday

Breakfast

Hot multigrain cereal, fruit juice, herbal tea

Lunch

Polenta and kale leftovers (from Monday dinner)

Snack

No-Bake Oatmeal Love Cookies

No-Bake Oatmeal Love Cookies
6 servings

These were brought into my life by my incredible daughter, Meira. She says: "You can add slivered almonds, chocolate chips, dried fruit, honey, mashed banana, or whatever suits you." The calorie content is going to depend on how much nut butter you use to hold it together. Nut butter is super healthy, but it is calorific, so if you are watching your weight you can use less. Note: these require time to chill.

⅓ cup oats

1½ teaspoons nut butter (peanut, almond, cashew, SunButter, or any combination)

⅛ cup milk (soymilk, almond milk, etc.)

1 teaspoon raisins

1 teaspoon maple syrup

1. Mix all ingredients in a small bowl with your (sterile) hands (kids will love this!).
2. Form into 6 cookies, place on a plate, wrap with plastic wrap, and place in refrigerator for 2 hours or overnight.

Wednesday

Dinner

Ratatouille over whole wheat pasta with shredded Parmesan

Ratatouille

6 servings

There are no limits to the types of vegetables that can be added to ratatouille. Get creative and experiment!

1 small eggplant
1 small zucchini squash
1 small yellow squash
½ leek
1 plum tomato
1 shallot
2 cloves garlic
2 sprigs marjoram
¼ cup kalamata olives
½ teaspoon olive oil
1 cup low-sodium vegetable stock
Fresh-cracked black pepper, to taste

1. Large-dice the eggplant, zucchini, yellow squash, leek, and tomato.
2. Finely dice the shallot and garlic.
3. Mince the marjoram and chop the olives.
4. Place all the ingredients in a saucepot and cook at low temperature for 1½ hours.

Summer and Winter Squash

You will often hear yellow squash referred to as "summer squash." Squash is normally divided into 2 groups: summer squash and winter squash. Summer squashes have thin skins and soft seeds. Winter squashes have tough skins and hard seeds.

Thursday

Breakfast

High fiber, whole grain ready to eat cereal, banana, fruit juice, herbal tea

Lunch

Stir-Fry Gingered Scallops or Tempeh with Vegetables (from Tuesday dinner)

Snack

"Gee Whiz" Spread on rice crackers

"Gee Whiz" Spread

2 cups

Vegan version of the infamous goo—another use of high in B-vitamins nutritional yeast flakes.

1 15-ounce can Great Northern beans, rinsed and well drained

½ cup pimiento pieces, drained

6 tablespoons nutritional yeast flakes

3 tablespoons lemon juice

2–3 tablespoons tahini

½ teaspoon onion granules

½ teaspoon mustard

¼ teaspoon salt

1. Mix all ingredients in blender or food processor until smooth.
2. Chill and serve.

Dinner

Turkish Lentil Soup

Turkish Lentil Soup

4 servings

Lentils by another color—this time red (although actually orange).

¼ cup onion, diced

1 clove garlic, crushed

1 teaspoon sesame oil

½ teaspoon dried sage

½ teaspoon cumin powder

½ teaspoon dried thyme

1 piece wakame, 3" long, soaked

4 cups water

1 medium carrot, diced

1 cup red lentils

Low-sodium tamari, to taste

Lemon juice, to taste

¼ cup scallions, chopped

1. In a soup pan, sauté onion and garlic in oil with sage, cumin, and thyme until tender.
2. Slice wakame into thin strips.
3. Add water, wakame, carrot, and lentils.
4. Bring to a boil, remove foam, lower heat, and simmer until lentils are tender, about 40 minutes.
5. Add tamari to taste, and simmer for 5 more minutes.
6. Place all but 1 cup soup in a food processor or blender and blend briefly.
7. Return blended soup to the pot with the reserved cup of soup.
8. Season to taste with more tamari and lemon juice.
9. Garnish with scallions.

Friday

Breakfast

Hot brown rice cereal with walnuts and chopped figs, fruit juice, herbal tea

Lunch

Ratatouille (from Wednesday dinner)

Snack

Basic Banana Smoothie

Basic Banana Smoothie

A good reason to buy those overripe bananas on special. Peel and freeze in a sturdy freezer bag so you're always ready for smoothies, sorbet, banana breads . . .

1 frozen banana
1 cup chocolate soymilk
½ cup fruit juice
grated ginger, to taste

Add all ingredients to blender and process until smooth. Enjoy!

Dinner

Salmon Cakes with Mango Salsa (see Week 1, Friday dinner), Onion Rings, roasted Brussels sprouts and apple, whole wheat dinner rolls

Onion Rings

4 servings

Baked not fried—what a treat!

1 cup yellow onion slices (¼" thick)

½ cup flour

½ cup nonfat plain yogurt

½ cup breadcrumbs

Sea salt and freshly ground black pepper, to taste (optional)

1. Preheat oven to 350°F.
2. Dredge onion slices in flour; shake off any excess.
3. Dip onions in yogurt; dredge through breadcrumbs.
4. Prepare baking sheet with nonstick cooking spray.
5. Arrange onion rings on pan; bake 15–20 minutes.
6. Place under broiler additional 2 minutes to brown.
7. Season with salt and pepper, if desired.

Breakfast

Banana Bread, Yogurt Fruit Salad (see Week 3, Thursday snack), herbal tea

Banana Bread
About 14 slices (½" thick)

Another delicious use for those overripe bananas. This recipe features applesauce instead of oil, which greatly reduces the calories and increases the taste and moistness.

3 very ripe bananas

3 tablespoons orange juice

⅓ cup unsweetened applesauce

½ cup Sucanat

1½ cups whole wheat flour

½ teaspoon baking powder

½ teaspoon baking soda

½ cup wheat germ (can use ground flaxseeds for part of this, too)

1 cup chopped dates

1 cup chopped walnuts (or chocolate chips)

1. Preheat oven to 375°F.
2. Mash bananas and mix them with orange juice until smooth.
3. Mix applesauce and Sucanat together and add to banana mixture.
4. Sift together flour, baking powder, and baking soda.
5. Mix in wheat germ and ground flax-seeds, if using, into dry ingredients and add to bananas.
6. Fold in dates, nuts, and/or chocolate chips, if desired.
7. Pour into a greased loaf pan and bake for about 45 minutes (or alternatively, use an 8" square pan or muffin tins for 30 minutes) or until done.

Lunch

Orange Ginger Mixed Vegetable Stir-Fry with edamame, Cold Sesame Noodles

Orange Ginger Mixed Vegetable Stir-Fry
4 servings

Rice vinegar can be substituted for the apple cider vinegar, if you prefer. As with most stir-fry recipes, the vegetables are merely a suggestion; use your favorites or whatever looks like it's been sitting too long in your crisper.

3 tablespoons orange juice

1 tablespoon apple cider vinegar

2 tablespoons low-sodium soy sauce

2 tablespoons water

1 tablespoon maple syrup

1 teaspoon powdered ginger

2 cloves garlic, minced

2 tablespoons oil

1 bunch broccoli, chopped

½ cup sliced mushrooms

½ cup snap peas, chopped

1 carrot, sliced

1 cup chopped cabbage or bok choy

1 cup edamame

1. Whisk together the orange juice, vinegar, soy sauce, water, maple syrup, and ginger.
2. Heat garlic in oil and add veggies and edamame.
3. Allow to cook, stirring frequently, over high heat for 2 to 3 minutes, until just starting to get tender.
4. Add sauce and reduce heat. Simmer, stirring frequently, for another 3 to 4 minutes, or until veggies are cooked.

Cold Sesame Noodles

6 servings

The sauce is very highly seasoned because the noodles are so bland. You can make this dish ahead of time; add more soy sauce and tea if needed to moisten.

10 cloves garlic, minced

2" piece gingerroot, minced

3 tablespoons water

⅓ cup tahini

3 tablespoons low-sodium soy sauce

⅓ cup strong brewed tea

1 tablespoon Asian sesame oil

1 tablespoon white wine vinegar

1 tablespoon sugar

½ teaspoon five spice powder

½ teaspoon chili oil

1 pound thin buckwheat noodles

6 green onions, thinly sliced

1. Bring a large pot of water to a boil.
2. Meanwhile, combine garlic, ginger-root, and water in a food processor.
3. Add tahini, soy sauce, tea, sesame oil, vinegar, sugar, five spice powder, and chili oil; process to blend.
4. Cook noodles in boiling water until al dente according to package directions.
5. Drain and place in large bowl; immediately pour garlic mixture over and toss to coat.
6. Sprinkle with green onions and serve, or cover and chill to blend flavors.

Snack

Homemade Ice Pop (see Week 9, Monday snack)

Dinner

Chickpea Stew (see Week 4, Saturday dinner), green salad

Sunday

Breakfast

Omelet/Tofu "Egg-less" Scramble (see Week 1, Saturday breakfast) with onions, portobellos, and red peppers, whole wheat toast, orange juice, herbal tea

Lunch

Greek salad, whole wheat pita with "Gee Whiz" Spread (from Thursday snack)

Snack

No-Bake Oatmeal Love Cookies, Version "B"

No-Bake Oatmeal Love Cookies, Version "B"

24 servings

This one requires some cooking—but still no baking.

⅔ cup maple syrup

¼ cup vegetable oil

5 tablespoons unsweetened cocoa powder

1 teaspoon ground cinnamon

½ cup nut butter

1 cup rolled oats

1 teaspoon imitation vanilla extract

1. In a saucepan over medium heat combine the maple syrup, oil, cocoa, and cinnamon.
2. Boil for three minutes, stirring constantly.
3. Remove from heat and stir in the nut butter, rolled oats, and vanilla until well blended.
4. Drop by heaping spoonfuls onto waxed paper and chill to set, about 30 minutes.

Dinner

Sole Florentine (see Week 4, Tuesday dinner), Steamed Millet, steamed vegetable medley

Steamed Millet

4 1-cup servings

This recipe can be varied by adding a handful of chopped fresh mushrooms and Italian herbs or using orange juice for part of the cooking liquid and tossing in some currants or raisins.

1 cup millet
2¼ cups water or low-sodium vegetable broth
1 teaspoon olive oil
¼ teaspoon salt

1. Rinse millet and drain in a strainer.
2. Place in saucepan, then add liquid, oil, and salt and bring to a boil.
3. Reduce heat, cover, and simmer for 20 minutes until water has been absorbed.
4. Remove from heat and let stand (covered) for five minutes.
5. Fluff with a fork and serve.

Millet is a nutritious, round, yellow grain, a mainstay in Asian diets, yet considered by Americans as mere birdseed. Rich in B vitamins, it has a pleasant taste and works well in a variety of ethnic cuisines.

Monday

Breakfast

High fiber, whole grain ready to eat cereal with banana and raisins

Lunch

Wrap with Omelet/Tofu "Egg-less" Scramble (from Sunday breakfast), carrot and broccoli crudités

Snack

Banana Bread (from Saturday breakfast)

Dinner

Lovely Lentil Soup with Greens, My Favorite Grilled Cheese Sandwich (see Week 6, Saturday lunch)

Lovely Lentil Soup with Greens
5 servings

Beauty is a reflection of what goes in your body as well as what goes on it. Rich in fiber and folate, lentils stabilize blood sugar levels, lower cholesterol, and improve cardiovascular health. These health benefits create radiant beauty from the inside out.

1 cup lentils, soaked
1 cup onion, diced
1 teaspoon sesame oil
2 cloves garlic, crushed
1 teaspoon cumin
4–5 cups water or low-sodium vegetable broth
½ cup winter squash
1 piece wakame, 3" long, soaked
1 medium bay leaf
¼ cup celery, diced
½ cup carrot, diced
1½ tablespoons sweet white miso
1 cup kale or collards, chopped into bite-sized
  pieces
Lemon juice, to taste

1. Soak lentils overnight and drain.
2. In a stockpot, sauté onion in oil until translucent.
3. Add garlic and cumin and cook for 1 minute.
4. Add lentils and water, bring to a boil, and skim off the foam.
5. Peel squash and cut into ½" chunks.
6. Slice wakame into thin strips.
7. Add squash, wakame, bay leaf, and remaining vegetables except greens to pot.
8. Bring to boil, lower heat, and simmer until lentils are soft, about 45 minutes.
9. Purée miso with a little cooking liquid. Add miso purée to soup.
10. Add greens and simmer, covered, for 5 minutes.
11. Season with lemon juice.

Breakfast

Overnight Oatmeal (see Week 1, Sunday breakfast), orange juice, herbal tea

Lunch

Chickpea Stew (from Saturday dinner)

Snack

Pistachios

Dinner

Healthy "Fried" Chicken, green salad with Cashew-Garlic Ranch Dressing

Healthy "Fried" Chicken

4 servings

10 ounces raw boneless, skinless chicken breasts (fat trimmed off)

½ cup nonfat plain yogurt

½ cup whole grain breadcrumbs

1 teaspoon garlic powder

1 teaspoon paprika

¼ teaspoon dried thyme

1. Preheat oven to 350°F.
2. Prepare baking pan with nonstick cooking spray.
3. Cut chicken breasts into 4 equal pieces; marinate in yogurt for several minutes.
4. Mix together breadcrumbs, garlic powder, paprika, and thyme; dredge chicken in crumb mixture.
5. Arrange on prepared pan; bake 20 minutes.
6. To give chicken a deep golden color, place pan under broiler last 5 minutes of cooking, but watch closely to ensure chicken "crust" doesn't burn.

Chicken Fat Facts

When faced with the decision of whether to have chicken with or without the skin, consider that ½ pound of skinless chicken breast has 9 grams of fat; ½ pound with the skin on has 19 grams!

Cashew-Garlic Ranch Dressing

¾ cup (suggested serving size: 1 tablespoon)

¼ cup raw cashews, or ⅛ cup cashew butter without salt

½ cup water

½ teaspoon stone-ground mustard

1½ tablespoons chili sauce

½ teaspoon horseradish

1 teaspoon Bragg Liquid Aminos, or low-sodium tamari sauce

1 clove garlic

1½ teaspoons honey

⅛ teaspoon pepper

1. Process cashews and water in blender or food processor until creamy.
2. Add remaining ingredients; mix well.
3. Refrigerate for 30 minutes.

Wednesday

Breakfast

Whole wheat bagel with Neufchatel cheese, tomato, green tea, fruit juice

Lunch

Lovely Lentil Soup with Greens (from Monday dinner), Carrot Salad with Raisins

Carrot Salad with Raisins

1 serving

Carrots are high in beta-carotene, which supports good vision and protects against macular degeneration. Enjoy with optional ingredients such as apple, celery, coconut, cranberries, lemon, parsley, red cabbage, or ginger.

1 cup carrots, grated
¼ cup raisins
⅛ teaspoon mild curry powder, optional
¼ cup toasted walnuts, chopped
Sweet brown rice vinegar, to taste

1. In a mixing bowl, toss all ingredients together.
2. Season with sweet brown rice vinegar, to taste.
3. Marinate for 2 hours before serving.

Snack

Yogurt Fruit Salad (see Week 3, Thursday snack)

Dinner

Pasta and Spinach Casserole (see Week 6, Thursday dinner), Winter Squash and Parsnip Purée

Winter Squash and Parsnip Purée

4 servings

Enjoy this sweet, creamy, warming soup when late summer weather becomes cool. Different versions of this soup can be made using various winter squash: butternut, buttercup, acorn, kabocha, or carnival. Peel squash skins if they are tough.

1 medium onion, diced
1 clove garlic, crushed
1 teaspoon sesame oil
4 cups water
3 cups winter squash, cubed
1 cup parsnips, diced
1 piece wakame, 3" long, soaked
4 teaspoons sweet white miso
Low-sodium tamari, to taste
Lemon juice, to taste
¼ cup fresh dill, chopped

1. In a soup pot, sauté onion and garlic in oil over medium heat.
2. Add water, squash, parsnips, and wakame.
3. Bring to boil, and simmer, covered, for 30 minutes.
4. Season with sweet white miso.
5. Purée in a food mill or blender. Return soup to pot.
6. Season with tamari, to taste, and simmer, covered, 3 minutes.
7. Add lemon juice, to taste. Garnish with chopped dill.

Other possible garnishes: scallions, parsley, watercress, chives, arugula, grated carrots, grated ginger, lemon zest, dill, cilantro, and nori.

Thursday

Breakfast

Overnight Oatmeal (from Tuesday breakfast), fruit juice, herbal tea

Lunch

Steamed Millet (from Sunday dinner) and steamed vegetables, open face mozzarella melt

Snack

Baked Pears

Baked Pears

6 servings

Make this dessert special by serving it in a parfait dish, topped with some fresh mint sprigs.

2 tablespoons lemon juice

6 pears, peeled

4 tablespoons sugar

3 cups nonfat frozen yogurt or vanilla soy or dairy yogurt (optional)

1. Preheat oven to 375°F.
2. Place lemon juice in a 2-quart baking dish and add just enough water to cover the bottom.
3. Cut pears in half, remove cores, and place pears in baking dish, cut-side down.
4. Cover and bake until pears are tender when pierced with a knife, 20 to 25 minutes.
5. Remove from oven and sprinkle each pear with 2 teaspoons sugar.
6. Bake, uncovered, for 10 minutes longer to glaze.
7. Serve warm or chilled with frozen yogurt or cottage cheese.

Baked Fruit

Baked fruit is a simple and nutritious low-fat dessert. You can also make it with fruits like peaches or apples. The peaches would bake for about 15 minutes, and apples for about 40 to 50 minutes. Also think about adding some spices to the sugar glaze; cinnamon, cardamom, and nutmeg are delicious.

Dinner

Southwest Black Bean Burgers (see Week 7, Tuesday dinner) on whole wheat buns, Orange Guacamole (see Week 7, Tuesday dinner), Pan-Fried Green Beans

Pan-Fried Green Beans
6 servings

Allowing the pan to come up to temperature before adding the beans enables the outside of the bean to be crispy while keeping the inside crunchy.

2 pounds fresh green beans
1 tablespoon olive oil
⅓ cup shelled walnuts
½ teaspoon salt-free chili powder
½ teaspoon fresh-cracked black pepper
Coarse sea salt or kosher salt, to taste

1. Toss the green beans in half the oil.
2. Finely chop the walnuts in a food processor or blender.
3. Add the pepper and chili powder, and blend.
4. Toss the oiled beans in the nut mixture to coat.
5. Heat the remaining oil to medium-high temperature in a large sauté pan; quickly brown the beans on all sides.
6. Remove from pan and drain on paper towels, then transfer to a platter.
7. Sprinkle with salt, and serve.

Friday

Breakfast

High fiber, whole grain ready to eat cereal, fresh berries, herbal tea

Lunch

Pasta and Spinach Casserole (from Wednesday dinner)

Snack

Pineapple-Banana Blast (see Week 5, Wednesday snack)

Dinner

Pizza night! Spinach Salad with Apple-Avocado Dressing (see Week 3, Friday dinner)

Quick Whole Wheat Pizza Dough
2 (12") pizza crusts

After making this delicious dough, cover it with pizza sauce (see recipe following), cheese, and any toppings you desire (e.g., broccoli, pineapple, tomatoes, spinach, feta). Pizza decorating is a fun and therapeutic outlet for your creativity!

1 tablespoon yeast

1 cup warm water

3 cups whole wheat flour

1 teaspoon honey

1½ teaspoons salt

¼ cup cooking oil

1. Dissolve yeast in water—let sit for 5 minutes.
2. Mix the remaining ingredients with the dissolved yeast.
3. Turn onto a floured surface and knead for 5 minutes.
4. Press onto a greased cookie sheet or use 2 12-inch pizza pans. Brush dough with oil.

5. Cover with your favorite pizza sauce and toppings.
6. Bake for 10 to 20 minutes at 400°F. The pizza is ready when the cheese has melted and the crust is lightly browned.

Pizza Sauce

1½ cups (enough for 2 pizzas)

1 clove garlic, mashed and minced
1 6-ounce can tomato paste
1 8-ounce can tomato sauce
½ teaspoon sugar
⅛ teaspoon pepper
½ teaspoon oregano
1 tablespoon olive oil
Dash red pepper, optional

1. Combine all ingredients.
2. Spread thinly on pizza crust or cover and store in refrigerator for up to 3 days.

Breakfast

Ginger Pear Wheat Pancakes (see Week 5, Sunday breakfast) with vanilla yogurt

Lunch

Southwest Black Bean Burgers on whole grain buns (see Week 7, Tuesday dinner), sliced tomato, salad (from Friday dinner)

Snack

Baked Pears (from Thursday snack)

Dinner

Condensed Cream of Mushroom Soup, Whole Wheat Couscous Salad

Condensed Cream of Mushroom Soup

2 servings, or equivalent of 1 10¾-ounce can

You can use this concentrated soup to make regular soup by adding water until it reaches your preferred consistency, or as a sauce for other recipes.

½ cup water
⅛ cup potato flour
¾ cup finely chopped fresh mushrooms
1 teaspoon chopped onion, optional
1 tablespoon chopped celery, optional

1. In a microwave-safe covered container, microwave mushrooms (and onion and celery, if using) in water for 2 minutes, or until tender.
2. Drain and save any resulting liquid; add enough water to equal 1 cup.
3. Place all ingredients in a blender; process.
4. The thickness of soup concentrate will vary according to how much moisture remains in the mushrooms. If necessary, add 1–2 tablespoons of water to achieve a paste.

Condensed Cream of Mushroom Soup can be used in a variety of other recipes: tossed with pasta or rice, over green beans, as a superb gravy, or baked in casseroles.

Whole Wheat Couscous Salad

8 servings

Traditionally from North Africa and steamed over fragrant stews, couscous is a very tiny pasta and about the quickest route to a cooked whole grain.

1 cup low-sodium vegetable broth

¼ cup dried currants

½ teaspoon cumin

¾ cup whole wheat couscous

¼ cup olive oil

2 tablespoons lemon juice

1 cup broccoli, chopped and steamed until crisp-tender

3 tablespoons pine nuts

1 tablespoon fresh parsley, chopped

1. Combine broth, currants, and cumin; bring to a boil.
2. Remove from heat; stir in couscous. Cover and let sit until cool.
3. Fluff couscous with fork 2–3 times during the cooling process.
4. Whisk together olive oil and lemon juice.
5. Add steamed broccoli and pine nuts to the couscous.
6. Pour oil and lemon juice over couscous; toss lightly.
7. Garnish with chopped parsley.

Aren't Currants Just Small Raisins?

Dried currants may look like miniature raisins, but they are actually quite different. Currants are berries from a shrub, not a vine, and there are red and black varieties. Black currants are rich in phytonutrients and antioxidants. They have twice the potassium of bananas and four times the vitamin C of oranges!

APPENDIX

Resources for Recovery

Gaines, Fabiola Demps, and Roneice Weaver. *The New Soul Food Cookbook for People with Diabetes.* 2nd ed. (Alexandria, VA: American Diabetes Association, 2006).

Kano, Susan. *Making Peace With Food: Freeing Yourself from the Diet/Weight Obsession.* (New York: Harper and Row, 1989).

Katz, Lawrence, and Manning Rubin. *Keep Your Brain Alive.* (New York: Workman Publishing Company, 1999).

Kessler, David. *The End of Overeating: Taking Control of the Insatiable American Appetite.* (New York: Rodale Books, 2009).

Kesten, Deborah. *Feeding the Body Nourishing the Soul: Essentials of Eating for Physical, Emotional, and Spiritual Well-Being.* (Berkeley: Connari Press, 1997).

Kingsolver, Barbara. *Animal, Vegetable, Miracle: A Year of Food Life.* (New York: Harper-Collins Publishers, 2007).

Nestle, Marion. *What to Eat.* (New York: North Point Press, 2006).

Pennington, Jean A. T., and Judith Spungen. *Bowes and Church's Food Values of Portions Commonly Used.* 19th ed. (Philadelphia: Lippincott Williams & Wilkins, 2010).

Pollan, Michael. *In Defense of Food: An Eater's Manifesto.* (New York: Penguin Press, 2008).

Pollan, Michael. *Food Rules: An Eater's Manual.* (New York: Penguin Books, 2009).

Scott, Liz. *The Sober Kitchen: Recipes and Advice for a Lifetime of Sobriety.* (Boston: Harvard Common Press, 2003).

Wansink, Brian. *Mindless Eating: Why We Eat More Than We Think*. (New York: Bantam Dell, 2006).

If you wanted to buy one general nutrition textbook, this is an excellent one; understandable, even if you lack a heavy science background. It includes a terrific section on alcohol and nutrition:
Whitney, Ellie, and Sharon Rady Rolfes. *Understanding Nutrition*. 12th ed. (Belmont, CA: Wadsworth, 2010).

Useful Websites

Information and statistics on alcohol and health, from the Centers for Disease Control and Prevention: *www.cdc.gov/alcohol/index.htm*

National Institute on Drug Abuse (part of the National Institutes of Health) does scientific research to bear on the problem of addictions: *www.nida.nih.gov/nidahome.html*

The Centre for Addiction and Mental Health, a Canadian institute that provides treatment, does research, and helps guide policy, has lots of good free information on its website: *www.camh.net/About_Addiction_Mental_Health/index.html*

Link to an article from Nutrition Action Healthletter that rates vegetables:
www.cspinet.org/nah/01_09/ratings.pdf

Fish advisory card: *www.montereybayaquarium.org/cr/cr_seafoodwatch/download.aspx*

Good online sources for recipes:
www.lowsodiumcooking.com
www.fatfreevegan.com/beans/beans.shtml
www.pressurecooking.blogspot.com

The website of the American Dietetic Association offers oodles of useful information for consumers on a wide variety of diet-related topics: *www.eatright.org*

Excellent information for everything vegetarian, mostly written by registered dietitians: *www.vrg.org*

About the Author

Renée Hoffinger, MHSE, RD, has worked at the North Florida/South Georgia Veterans Health System on the substance abuse treatment team for the past eighteen years. As a strong proponent of hands-on nutrition education, she teaches, shops, and cooks with residents in recovery. Renée is the Substance Abuse Resource Professional for the Behavioral Health Nutrition Practice group of the American Dietetic Association. She lives in Gainesville, Florida, with her husband, has two incredible young adult children, and enjoys kayaking, biking, photography, hanging out at farmers' markets, and, of course, cooking.

Index

Alcohol
    depleting B vitamins, 9
    diet benefit and abstaining
        from, 5–6
    malabsorption from, 3, 11
    maldigestion from, 2–3
    malnutrition from, 1–3, 4
    medical issues and. *See*
        Medical concerns and diet
    not burning off in cooking, 57
    poor food intake and, 2
    road to recovery, 4–5
    toll of, 1
Almonds. *See* Nuts and seeds
Apples
    Apple-Avocado Dressing, 101
    Apple Bread Pudding, 196–97
    Carrot Fruit Cup, 178
    Quick Apple Crisp, 112–13
    Sneaky Apple Cookies, 172
Apricot Rice, 169
Arame
    about: sea vegetables, 59
    Broccoli and Arame in Tofu
        Cream Sauce, 83
    Simple, Easy Arame, 83
Arrowroot, 57
Artichokes, in Hot Artichoke
    Spinach Dip, 202–3
Asian Dipping Sauce, 159
Asian Gingered Almonds, 207
Asian Popcorn, 164–65

Asparagus
    Cashew Cream of Asparagus
        Soup, 200
    Lemon Asparagus and
        Carrots, 123
    Vegetable Frittata, 87
Avocado
    Apple-Avocado Dressing, 101
    Orange Guacamole, 151

Bananas
    Banana Bread, 214
    Basic Banana Smoothie, 212
    Carrot Fruit Cup, 178
    Fruit Frenzy Sparkler
        Concentrate, 82
    Gourmet Sorbet, 86
    Green Tea Smoothie, 152
    Kiwi Banana Smoothie, 156
    Pineapple-Banana Blast, 124
    Tofu Smoothie, 110
    Yogurt Fruit Salad, 98
    Yogurt Fruit Smoothie, 92
Barbecue Sauce, 181
Basic Lunch Wrap, 64
Beans and legumes. *See also*
    Edamame; Green beans
    about: black beans, 103;
        cannellini beans, 131;
        chickpeas, 54; protein from,
        60; as superfood, 54
    Black Bean Burritos, 84
    Chickpea Stew, 116–17

Creamy Chickpea and
    Rosemary Soup, 161
Cuban Black Beans and Rice,
    103
Cuban Black Beans and Sweet
    Potatoes, 167
"Gee Whiz" Spread, 210
Hummus, 206
Lentil Soup with Herbs and
    Lemon, 182–83
Lentil Stuffed Peppers, 106–7
Lima Bean Casserole, 75
Lovely Lentil Soup with
    Greens, 218–19
Red Beans and Rice, 193
Rice with Black Beans and
    Ginger, 136
Southwest Black Bean
    Burgers, 150–51
Split Pea Soup with Herbes de
    Provence, 125
Turkish Lentil Soup, 211
Tuscan Pasta Fagioli, 131
Vegetable and Bean Chili,
    78–79
White Bean Pistachio Salad,
    177
White Chicken Chili, 91
Beef
    about: safe cooking
        temperatures, 50; thawing,
        49

Beef—*continued*
    Spicy Beef or Seitan and
      Cabbage, 203
    Steak (or Seitan) Stroganoff,
      105
Beets
    Passion Beet Borscht, 133
    Sweet Red Salad with
      Strawberries and Beets, 187
    Tofu and Root Vegetables, 63
Benefits of diet, 5–6
Berries
    about: frozen, 86; as
      superfoods, 54
    Berrylicious Yogurt Granola
      Parfait, 153
    Gourmet Sorbet, 86
    Homemade Fruit Pops,
      176–77
    Protein and Berry Pita, 196
    Quinoa Berry Breakfast, 88
    Raspberry Almond Milk
      Frappe, 204
    Summer Fruit Cobbler,
      154–55
    Sweet Red Salad with
      Strawberries and Beets, 187
    Tofu Smoothie, 110
    Yogurt Fruit Salad, 98
    Yogurt Fruit Smoothie, 92
Beverages
    about: avoiding caffeine, 16;
      best, 16; green tea, 152;
      hydration and, 16; soda
      alternative, 16; sports drinks,
      16
    Basic Banana Smoothie, 212
    Fruit Frenzy Sparkler
      Concentrate, 82
    Ginger Lime Iced Tea, 140
    Green Tea Smoothie, 152
    Kiwi Banana Smoothie, 156
    Orange-Pineapple Froth, 120
    Pineapple-Banana Blast, 124
    Raspberry Almond Milk
      Frappe, 204
    Tofu Smoothie, 110
    Yogurt Fruit Smoothie, 92

Black beans. *See* Beans and
  legumes
Blackened and Bleu Tilapia, 138
Blood lipids. *See* Cholesterol
Blood sugar levels, 12–14
Body mass index (BMI), 34
Bok choy, in Gingered Tofu and
  Bok Choy Stir-Fry, 165
Book overview and use, vii–viii,
  6–7
Bragg Liquid Aminos, 57
Breads. *See also* Pancakes;
  Sandwiches and wraps
    about: crispbread as superfood,
      54
    Banana Bread, 214
    Multigrain Cornbread, 143
    Quick Whole Wheat Pizza
      Dough, 226–27
    Stuffed French Toast, 158
    Whole Wheat Biscuits, 130
Breakfast
    about, 54–55; daily diet and
      nutrition, 54–55; eating
      regularly, 15; importance of,
      15, 54–55; making it easy, 15
    Banana Bread, 214
    Buckwheat Pancakes, 76
    Country-Style Omelet, 116
    Egg White Pancakes, 146
    Fruit and Cheese Quesadillas,
      148
    Ginger Pear Wheat Pancakes,
      118
    Green Tea Smoothie, 152
    Homemade Granola, 80
    Overnight Oatmeal, 62
    Protein and Berry Pita, 196
    Quinoa Berry Breakfast, 88
    Stuffed French Toast, 158
    Tofu "Egg-less" Scramble, 74
    Tofu Smoothie, 110
    Whole Wheat Biscuits, 130
Breakfast menus. *See specific Week*
  menus (Week 1 through 12)
Broccoli
    about: as superfood, 54

Broccoli and Arame in Tofu
  Cream Sauce, 83
Broccoli Pasta Toss, 95
Orange Ginger Mixed
  Vegetable Stir-Fry, 214–15
Seitan and Vegetables Stir-Fry,
  70–71
Brown bagging, 56
Buckwheat Pancakes, 76
Bulgur, in Squash and Bulgur
  Pilaf, 135
Burritos, Black Bean, 84
Buttermilk substitute, 143
B vitamins and, 3, 9, 11–12, 17,
  58

Cabbage
    Seitan and Vegetables Stir-Fry,
      70–71
    Spicy Beef or Seitan and
      Cabbage, 203
    Summer Vegetable Slaw, 97
    Whole Grain Noodles with
      Caraway Cabbage, 139
Caffeine, avoiding, 16
Cajun Chicken/Tofu Strips,
  134–35
Calories
    alcohol and intake of, 2
    carbon "food print" and, 47
    in dairy, 17–18
    defined, 33
    exercise and, 37
    fats and, 29
    fiber and, 19
    nutrients and, 2, 9, 10–11
    weight loss and, 33, 35, 36
Carbohydrates, 14, 17
Carrots
    Carrot Fruit Cup, 178
    Carrot Salad with Raisins, 222
    Coriander Carrots, 107
    Divine Carrot-Pumpkin Soup,
      104
    Lemon Asparagus and
      Carrots, 123
    Summer Vegetable Slaw, 97

Swiss Chard Rolls with Root
Vegetables, 93
Tofu and Root Vegetables, 63
Cheese
about: Neufchatel, 58;
quesadillas, 148; vegan pasta
sauce, 191
Creamy Feta Vinaigrette, 166
Fruit and Cheese Quesadillas,
148
Guava Cheddar Appetizer,
192
My Favorite Grilled Cheese
Sandwich, 144
Quick Chicken/Tofu
Mozzarella, 194–95
Zucchini Parmesan, 149
Chewing, 21
Chicken
about: fat/skin facts, 221; safe
cooking temperatures, 50;
thawing, 49
Cajun Chicken Strips, 134–35
Chicken Thighs Cacciatore,
184–85
Chicken with Portobello
Mushrooms and Roasted
Garlic, 85
Classic Chicken (or Tofu)
Parmesan, 162–63
Healthy Chicken Nuggets, 99
Healthy "Fried" Chicken, 220
Quick Chicken/Tofu
Mozzarella, 194–95
White Chicken Chili, 91
Yogurt Chicken Paprika,
68–69
Zesty Pecan Chicken and
Grapes, 119
Chickpeas. See Beans and
legumes
Chocolate
Chocolate Candy Substitute,
160
Chocolate/Carob Chip
Cookies, 128
Cholesterol, 19, 26, 29, 103, 177,
218

Citrus
about: lemon infusion for fish,
169; as superfood, 54
Ginger Lime Iced Tea, 140
Lemon-Almond Dressing,
145
Lemon Asparagus and
Carrots, 123
Lemon Pesto, 147
Lemon Sole with Capers, 157
Mustard Greens and Lemon
Sauté, 175
Orange Ginger Mixed
Vegetable Stir-Fry, 214–15
Orange Guacamole, 151
Orange Pilaf, 199
Orange-Pineapple Froth, 120
Tangy Lemon-Garlic Tomato
Dressing, 115
Yogurt Fruit Smoothie, 92
Classic Chicken (or Tofu)
Parmesan, 162–63
Cold Sesame Noodles, 215
Convenience foods, healthy, 56
Cooking
alcohol not burning off in, 57
ease of, 42–43
equipping kitchen for, 48–49
in microwave, 49–50, 109
safety, 49–50
sound food advice in seven
words, 43
support, 43
tricks and shortcuts, 50–51
Coriander Carrots, 107
Corn
about: popcorn, 165
Asian Popcorn, 164–65
Multigrain Cornbread, 143
Polenta, 205
Summer Vegetable Slaw, 97
Sweet Potato Corn Cakes
with Wasabi Cream, 102
Country-Style Omelet, 116
Couscous salad, 229
Cranberries. See Berries
Creamy Chickpea and Rosemary
Soup, 161

Creamy Feta Vinaigrette, 166
Cuban Black Beans and Rice, 103
Cuban Black Beans and Sweet
Potatoes, 167
Currants, 229
Curried Shrimp (or Tofu) and
Vegetables, 129
Curry, cooking with, 129
Curry powder, making, 179

Dairy
about, 17–18
buttermilk substitute, 143
calories in, 17–18
lactose intolerance and, 18,
38–39, 56
nutritional value, 17–18
Dates, Almond-Stuffed, 180
Dehydration, avoiding, 16
Dental issues, 2
Desserts. See Snacks (and
desserts)
Diabetes, diet and, 32–33
Diet. See Digestion; Nutrients;
Recovery diet
Digestion. See also Meals;
Nutrients
chewing and, 21
glycemic index (GI) and,
13–14
lactose intolerance and, 18,
38–39, 56
liver function and, 3–4
malabsorption and, 3, 11
maldigestion and, 2–3
malnutrition and, 1–3, 4
metabolism, alcohol and, 4,
9, 11
road to recovery, 4–5
Dinner
about: Choose My Plate
campaign, 55; eating
regularly, 15; vegetables at,
55
Almond-Encrusted Salmon
on Toast Points, 94–95
Apricot Rice, 169

Dinner—*continued*
Baked Halibut with Lemon, 168
Baked Sole Almondine, 65
Barbecue Sauce, 181
Blackened and Bleu Tilapia, 138
Broccoli and Arame in Tofu Cream Sauce, 83
Broccoli Pasta Toss, 95
Cajun Chicken/Tofu Strips, 134–35
Cashew-Garlic Ranch Dressing, 221
Chicken Thighs Cacciatore, 184–85
Chicken with Portobello Mushrooms and Roasted Garlic, 85
Chickpea Stew, 116–17
Classic Chicken (or Tofu) Parmesan, 162–63
Condensed Cream of Mushroom Soup, 228–29
Coriander Carrots, 107
Creamy Chickpea and Rosemary Soup, 161
Cuban Black Beans and Rice, 103
Cuban Black Beans and Sweet Potatoes, 167
Curried Shrimp (or Tofu) and Vegetables, 129
Easy Miso Noodle Soup, 155
Edamame Salad, 132
French Tarragon Green Beans, 195
Gingered Tofu and Bok Choy Stir-Fry, 165
Green Beans with Garlic, 191
Guava Cheddar Appetizer, 192
Healthy Chicken Nuggets, 99
Healthy "Fried" Chicken, 220
Herbed Quinoa with Sun-Dried Tomatoes, 109
Herbed Rice Pilaf, 185

Hot Vinaigrette for Greens, 137
Kale Pesto, 186–87
Kale Stuffed with Basmati Rice, 126–27
Lemon-Almond Dressing, 145
Lemon Asparagus and Carrots, 123
Lemon Sole with Capers, 157
Lentil Soup with Herbs and Lemon, 182–83
Lentil Stuffed Peppers, 106–7
Lima Bean Casserole, 75
Lovely Lentil Soup with Greens, 218–19
Marinara Sauce with Italian "Soysage," 67
Microwave Sole Florentine, 108–9
Mock Macaroni and Cheese, 190–91
Multigrain Cornbread, 143
Mustard Greens and Lemon Sauté, 175
Onion Rings, 213
Orange Guacamole, 151
Orange Pilaf, 199
Pan-Fried Green Beans, 225
Passion Beet Borscht, 133
Pasta and Spinach Casserole, 141
Pasta and Trout or Tempeh with Lemon Pesto, 147
Pasta Shells with Zucchini, 171
Pizza Sauce, 227
Polenta, 205
Portobello Sandwiches, 96–97
Quick Chicken/Tofu Mozzarella, 194–95
Quick Whole Wheat Pizza Dough, 226–27
Quinoa with Sautéed Garlic, 73
Ratatouille, 209
Red Beans and Rice, 193
Red Snapper with Peppers and Vinegar, 179

Rice with Black Beans and Ginger, 136
Risotto with Winter Squash, 173
Salmon Cakes with Mango Salsa, 72–73
Salmon with Fettuccine, 122–23
Seitan and Vegetables Stir-Fry, 70–71
Southwest Black Bean Burgers, 150–51
Spaghetti Squash and Vegetables, 201
Spicy Beef or Seitan and Cabbage, 203
Spinach Salad with Apple-Avocado Dressing, 101
Spinach Tofu Pie, 113
Split Pea Soup with Herbes de Provence, 125
Squash and Bulgur Pilaf, 135
Steak (or Seitan) Stroganoff, 105
Steamed Millet, 217
Stir-Fried Ginger Scallops or Tempeh with Vegetables, 88–89
Summer Vegetable Slaw, 97
Sweet and Sour Pork or Seitan Skillet, 77
Sweet and Sour Turkey Burgers, 174–75
Sweet Potato Crisps, 127
Sweet Potato Pancakes, 121
Sweet Red Salad with Strawberries and Beets, 187
Swiss Chard Rolls with Root Vegetables, 93
Tangy Lemon-Garlic Tomato Dressing, 115
Taste of Italy Baked Fish, 81
Tofu and Root Vegetables, 63
Traditional Stovetop Tuna (or Tofu) Noodle Casserole, 114
Tuna Panini, 100–101
Turkey or TVP Chili, 142–43
Turkish Lentil Soup, 211

Tuscan Pasta Fagioli, 131
Vegetable and Bean Chili,
    78–79
Vegetable Frittata, 87
Walnut Parsley Pesto, 111
White Bean Pistachio Salad,
    177
White Chicken Chili, 91
Whole Grain Noodles with
    Caraway Cabbage, 139
Whole Wheat Couscous
    Salad, 229
Winter Squash and Parsnip
    Purée, 223
Yogurt Chicken Paprika,
    68–69
Zesty Pecan Chicken and
    Grapes, 119
Zucchini Parmesan, 149
Dinner menus. *See specific Week
    menus (Week 1 through 12)*
Dips. *See* Sauces, dressings and
    dips
Divine Carrot-Pumpkin Soup,
    104
DIY Trail Mix, 66
Dressings. *See* Sauces, dressings
    and dips
Dry-roasting garlic, 85

Edamame
    about, 57
    Edamame Salad, 132
    Orange Ginger Mixed
        Vegetable Stir-Fry, 214–15
    Twisted Tabbouleh, 200–201
Eggplant
    Chickpea Stew, 116–17
    Ratatouille, 209
Eggs
    Country-Style Omelet, 116
    Egg White Pancakes, 146
    Tofu "Egg-less" Scramble
        instead of, 74
    Vegetable Frittata, 87
Empowering yourself, 41–43
Equipment, cooking, 48–49
Exercise, 36, 37

Expectations, vii–viii. *See also*
    Recovery diet goals

Fats and oils
    alcohol impacting, 4
    chicken fat facts, 221
    cholesterol and, 26, 29, 30,
        103, 177, 218
    good, bad, and ugly, 30
    importance of, 18
    nutritional value, 18
    omega-3 and -6 fatty acids, 20,
        30, 38, 115
    reducing intake, 29–30
    types of, 30
    undesired breakdown of, 4
    weight and. *See* Weight
        management
Fiber, 19–20
Fish and seafood
    about: environmental
        contaminants and safety,
        47; lemon infusion, 169;
        salmon, 54; as superfood, 54;
        thawing, 49
    Almond-Encrusted Salmon
        on Toast Points, 94–95
    Baked Halibut with Lemon,
        168
    Baked Sole Almondine, 65
    Blackened and Bleu Tilapia,
        138
    Curried Shrimp (or Tofu) and
        Vegetables, 129
    Lemon Sole with Capers, 157
    Microwave Sole Florentine,
        108–9
    Pasta and Trout or Tempeh
        with Lemon Pesto, 147
    Red Snapper with Peppers and
        Vinegar, 179
    Salmon Cakes with Mango
        Salsa, 72–73
    Salmon with Fettuccine,
        122–23
    Stir-Fried Ginger Scallops or
        Tempeh with Vegetables,
        88–89

Taste of Italy Baked Fish, 81
    Traditional Stovetop Tuna (or
        Tofu) Noodle Casserole, 114
    Tuna Panini, 100–101
Five spice powder, 77
Flaxseeds, about, 58, 115
Food. *See also* Cooking;
    Digestion; Meals; Nutrients;
    specific main ingredients
    choosing choice ingredients,
        46–47
    empowering yourself, 41–43
    fish safety and, 47
    healthy convenience, 56
    labels, reading/understanding,
        46
    in larger context, 41–43
    lightening your carbon "food
        print," 47
    menu planning, 51–52
    organic, 46–47
    at restaurants, 52
    safety, 49–50
    sex and, 51
    shopping for, 43–46
    superfoods, 54
Food groups, 17–19
French Tarragon Green Beans,
    195
French Toast, Stuffed, 158
Frittata, Vegetable, 87
Fruits. *See also specific fruits*
    about: baked, 225; frozen, 86;
        importance of, 17
    DIY Trail Mix, 66
    Fruit and Cheese Quesadillas,
        148
    Fruit Frenzy Sparkler
        Concentrate, 82
    Fruity Oatmeal Bars, 90
    Gourmet Sorbet, 86
    Homemade Fruit Pops,
        176–77
    Summer Fruit Cobbler,
        154–55
    Yogurt Fruit Salad, 98
    Yogurt Fruit Smoothie, 92

Garlic
    about: characteristics of, 97;
        dry-roasting, 85
    Cashew-Garlic Ranch
        Dressing, 221
    Chicken with Portobello
        Mushrooms and Roasted
        Garlic, 85
    Green Beans with Garlic, 191
    Quinoa with Sautéed Garlic,
        73
    Tangy Lemon-Garlic Tomato
        Dressing, 115
"Gee Whiz" Spread, 210
Ginger
    about: gingerroot, 63, 118
    Gingered Tofu and Bok Choy
        Stir-Fry, 165
    Ginger Lime Iced Tea, 140
    Ginger Pear Wheat Pancakes,
        118
    Orange Ginger Mixed
        Vegetable Stir-Fry, 214–15
Gluten-intolerance, 73
Glycemic index (GI), 13
Goals. See Recovery diet goals
Gourmet Sorbet, 86
Grains. See also Breads; Corn;
    Quinoa
    about, 17; bulgur, 135; fiber
        and, 19–20; steel cut oats, 59;
        as superfood, 54
    Berrylicious Yogurt Granola
        Parfait, 153
    DIY Trail Mix, 66
    Fruity Oatmeal Bars, 90
    Homemade Granola, 80
    Overnight Oatmeal, 62
    Squash and Bulgur Pilaf, 135
    Steamed Millet, 217
    Whole Wheat Couscous
        Salad, 229
Granola, 80, 153
"Grape meditation," 21–22
Green beans
    French Tarragon Green Beans,
        195

Green Beans with Garlic, 191
    Pan-Fried Green Beans, 225
    Summer Vegetable Slaw, 97
Greens. See also Kale; Salads;
    Spinach
    about: learning to love, 165; as
        superfoods, 54
    Gingered Tofu and Bok Choy
        Stir-Fry, 165
    Hot Vinaigrette for Greens,
        137
    Lovely Lentil Soup with
        Greens, 218–19
    Mustard Greens and Lemon
        Sauté, 175
    Swiss Chard Rolls with Root
        Vegetables, 93
Green Tea Smoothie, 152
Grilling safely, 50
Grocery shopping, 43–46
Guava Cheddar Appetizer, 192

Healthy Chicken Nuggets, 99
Heart disease and hypertension,
    25–30
    alcohol and, 25–26
    cholesterol (lipids) and, 26, 29,
        30, 103, 177, 218
    fat types and, 30
    lowering blood pressure,
        26–30
    reducing fat intake for, 29–30
    sodium and, 27–29
    tobacco, smoking and, 26–27
    understanding blood pressure
        readings, 27
Herbed Quinoa with Sun-Dried
    Tomatoes, 109
Herbed Rice Pilaf, 185
Herb gardens, 95
Herbs, swapping fresh for dried,
    151
Hummus, 206
Hydration, importance of, 16
Hypertension. See Heart disease
    and hypertension

Ideal body weight (IBW), 33–34
Ingredients. See also specific main
    ingredients
    choosing, 46–47
    grocery shopping, 43–46
    lightening your carbon "food
        print," 47
    measuring, 57
    reading nutrition labels, 46
    unusual, 57–60

Kale
    about, 127
    Kale Pesto, 186–87
    Kale Stuffed with Basmati
        Rice, 126–27
Kessler, David, 41–42
Kitchen. See Cooking; Food
Kiwis
    about: as superfood, 54
    Kiwi Banana Smoothie, 156
    Yogurt Fruit Smoothie, 92

Labels, reading and
    understanding, 46
Lactose intolerance, 18, 38–39, 56
Lemons. See Citrus
Lentils. See Beans and legumes
Lifestyle, diet and, 16–23
    creating new food memories,
        23
    fiber and, 19–20
    "grape meditation" and, 21–22
    importance of, 16–17
    real food and, 20
    roadmap to health, 17–19
    spirituality and, 23
    volunteering in food-related
        activities, 22
Lima Bean Casserole, 75
Liver
    alcohol impacting, 4
    functions of, 3–4
Liver disease, diet and, 31–32

Lunch
about: brown bagging it,
56; eating regularly, 15;
importance of, 15; leftovers
for, 55; as main meal, 55;
"relapse prevention bag" for,
15
Basic Lunch Wrap, 64
Black Bean Burritos, 84
Carrot Salad with Raisins, 222
Cashew Cream of Asparagus
Soup, 200
Cold Sesame Noodles, 215
Creamy Feta Vinaigrette, 166
Divine Carrot-Pumpkin Soup,
104
Easy Asian Dipping Sauce,
159
Fresh Mint Spring Rolls,
158–59
Hummus, 206
My Favorite Grilled Cheese
Sandwich, 144
Orange Ginger Mixed
Vegetable Stir-Fry, 214–15
Quinoa and Pumpkin Seed
Pilaf, 188–89
Simple Green Salad with
Vinaigrette, 198
Sweet Potato Corn Cakes
with Wasabi Cream, 102
Tempeh "Chicken" Salad, 170
Twisted Tabbouleh, 200–201
Lunch menus. See specific Week
menus (Week 1 through 12)

Malabsorption, 3, 11
Maldigestion, 2–3
Malnutrition, 1–3, 4
Mangoes
about: as superfood, 54
Mango Salsa, 72–73
Maple syrup, 113
Marinara Sauce with Italian
"Soysage," 67
Meals. See also Breakfast; Dinner;
Lunch; Snacks (and desserts)
chewing during, 21

eating regularly, 14–16
enjoying, 21
mindfulness during, 21
relapse prevention with, 14–16
Measuring ingredients, 57
Medical concerns and diet, 25–39
about: overview of, 25
diabetes, 32–33
heart disease and
hypertension, 25–30
liver disease, 31–32
pain management, 37–39
weight management, 33–37
Medications
dosage precautions, 6, 20
reducing side effects of, 34
timing of meals and, 32
Meditation, 21–22
Menu planning, 51–52, 61. See
also Recipes for recovery; specific
meals (Breakfast, Lunch, Dinner)
Metabolism, alcohol and, 4, 9, 11
Microwave
about: cooking in, 49–50, 109
Microwave Sole Florentine,
108–9
Millet, 217
Mint Spring Rolls, 158–59
Mochi, 58
Mood management, 12–16
blood sugar levels and, 12–14
carbohydrates and, 14
eating regularly for, 14–16
not getting hungry and, 14
Multigrain Cornbread, 143
Muscle mass, building, 34–35
Mushrooms
Chicken with Portobello
Mushrooms and Roasted
Garlic, 85
Condensed Cream of
Mushroom Soup, 228–29
Portobello Sandwiches, 96–97
Tofu "Egg-less" Scramble, 74
Mustard Greens and Lemon
Sauté, 175

No-Bake Oatmeal Love Cookies,
208
No-Bake Oatmeal Love Cookies,
Version "B," 216
Nutrients, 1–4, 9–12. See also
Digestion
alcohol and, 1–3, 4
carbohydrates, 14
choosing nutrient-dense foods,
11
common deficiencies, 3
defined, 2
density of, 10–11
Diet impacting, 5–6
fiber, 19–20
focusing on B vitamins, 11–12
food groups and, 17–19
food labeling basics, 46
importance of, 10
lifestyle and. See Lifestyle, diet
and
liver function and, 3–4
malabsorption and, 3, 11
maldigestion and, 2–3
phytochemicals, 12, 14, 17, 54,
74, 229
poor food intake and, 2
protein needs, 2
real food and, 20
replenishing, to reverse
damage, 9–12
Nutritional yeast flakes, 58
Nuts and seeds
about: almonds, 65; nut
butters, 58; protein from, 60;
as superfood, 54; toasting
nuts, 119; toasting seeds, 95
Almond-Encrusted Salmon
on Toast Points, 94–95
Almond-Stuffed Dates, 180
Asian Gingered Almonds, 207
Baked Sole Almondine, 65
Cashew Cream of Asparagus
Soup, 200
Cashew-Garlic Ranch
Dressing, 221
DIY Trail Mix, 66
Homemade Granola, 80

Nuts and seeds—*continued*
  Lemon-Almond Dressing, 145
  Quinoa and Pumpkin Seed
    Pilaf, 188–89
  Raspberry Almond Milk
    Frappe, 204
  Walnut Parsley Pesto, 111
  White Bean Pistachio Salad,
    177

Oatmeal
  about: steel cut, 59
  Fruity Oatmeal Bars, 90
  Homemade Granola, 80
  No-Bake Oatmeal Love
    Cookies, 208
  No-Bake Oatmeal Love
    Cookies, Version "B," 216
  Overnight Oatmeal, 62
Omega-3 and -6 fatty acids, 20,
  30, 38, 115
Onion Rings, 213
Oranges. *See* Citrus
Organic foods, 46–47
Overnight Oatmeal, 62

Pain management, 37–39
Pancakes
  about: creative toppings, 146
  Buckwheat Pancakes, 76
  Egg White Pancakes, 146
  Ginger Pear Wheat Pancakes,
    118
  Sweet Potato Pancakes, 121
Papaya, in Fruit Frenzy Sparkler
  Concentrate, 82
Parsnips. *See* Root vegetables
Passion Beet Borscht, 133
Pasta
  about: soba noodles, 155
  Broccoli Pasta Toss, 95
  Butternut Squash Tahini
    Sauce for, 191
  Cold Sesame Noodles, 215
  Easy Miso Noodle Soup, 155
  Kale Pesto, 186–87
  Marinara Sauce with Italian
    "Soysage," 67

Mock Macaroni and Cheese,
  190–91
Pasta and Spinach Casserole,
  141
Pasta and Trout or Tempeh
  with Lemon Pesto, 147
Pasta Shells with Zucchini,
  171
Salmon with Fettuccine,
  122–23
Traditional Stovetop Tuna (or
  Tofu) Noodle Casserole, 114
Tuscan Pasta Fagioli, 131
Walnut Parsley Pesto, 111
Whole Grain Noodles with
  Caraway Cabbage, 139
Peaches
  Fruit Frenzy Sparkler
    Concentrate, 82
  Summer Fruit Cobbler,
    154–55
  Yogurt Fruit Smoothie, 92
Pears
  Baked Pears, 224–25
  Ginger Pear Wheat Pancakes,
    118
  Spicy Cold Pears, 79
Peas. *See* Beans and legumes
Peppers
  Lentil Stuffed Peppers, 106–7
  Summer Vegetable Slaw, 97
Phytochemicals, 12, 14, 17, 54,
  74, 229
Pineapple
  Fruit Frenzy Sparkler
    Concentrate, 82
  Orange-Pineapple Froth, 120
  Pineapple-Banana Blast, 124
Pizza, 226–27
Polenta, 205
Pork
  about: safe cooking tempera-
    tures, 50; thawing, 49
  Sweet and Sour Pork or Seitan
    Skillet, 77
Portobellos. *See* Mushrooms
Potatoes. *See* Sweet potatoes
Pressure cookers, 48–49

Protein and Berry Pita, 196
Proteins
  benefits of diet high in, 31
  B vitamins and, 11
  calories and, 33
  disruption in digestion, 4
  disruption in digestion of, 3
  foods providing, 18, 30, 31,
    39, 60
  importance of, 5
  increased requirements for,
    1–2
  less meat and, 46
  liver and, 4, 31
  meatless meals and, 60
  milk, lactose intolerance and,
    39
  for muscle mass, 34–35
  recommended levels, 34–35
  seitan for, 59
  tempeh for, 59, 89
  tofu for, 39, 60
  TVP for, 142
Pumpkin. *See also* Nuts and seeds
  Divine Carrot-Pumpkin Soup,
    104

Quesadillas, 148
Quick Apple Crisp, 112–13
Quinoa
  about: 58; cooking, 109; for
    gluten-intolerant individuals,
    73; as superfood, 54
  Herbed Quinoa with Sun-
    Dried Tomatoes, 109
  Quinoa and Pumpkin Seed
    Pilaf, 188–89
  Quinoa Berry Breakfast, 88
  Quinoa with Sautéed Garlic,
    73
  Twisted Tabbouleh, 200–201

Raspberries. *See* Berries
Ratatouille, 209
Recipes for recovery. *See also*
  Breakfast; Dinner; Lunch;
  Snacks (and desserts); *specific
  main ingredients*

about: overview of, 53
brown bagging it, 56
daily diet, 54–56
healthy convenience foods
    and, 56
owning the meal plan, 56–57
protein from, 60. *See also*
    Proteins
standards for developing,
    53–54
unusual ingredients, 57–60
using menus, 61
vegetable preparation tips, 61
Week 1, 62–75
Week 2, 76–89
Week 3, 90–103
Week 4, 104–17
Week 5, 118–31
Week 6, 132–45
Week 7, 146–59
Week 8, 160–73
Week 9, 174–87
Week 10, 188–201
Week 11, 202–15
Week 12, 216–29
Recovery
    optimizing, 10
    road to, 4–5
Recovery diet. *See also* Digestion;
    Food; Nutrients; Recipes for
    recovery; *specific main ingredients*
    benefits of, 5–6
    "diet" as four letter word and,
        17
    empowering yourself, 41–43
    food in larger context, 41–43
    sound food advice in seven
        words, 43
Recovery diet goals
    healthy lifestyle, 16–23
    manage moods with foods,
        12–16
    replenish nutrients, reverse
        damage, 9–12
Red Beans and Rice, 193
Red Snapper with Peppers and
    Vinegar, 179
Regular meals and snacks, 14–16

Resources, 231–33
Restaurant food, 52
Rice
    about: cooking, 137; mochi, 58
    Apricot Rice, 169
    Cuban Black Beans and Rice,
        103
    Herbed Rice Pilaf, 185
    Kale Stuffed with Basmati
        Rice, 126–27
    Orange Pilaf, 199
    Red Beans and Rice, 193
    Rice with Black Beans and
        Ginger, 136
    Risotto with Winter Squash,
        173
Root vegetables. *See also* Beets;
    Carrots; Sweet potatoes
    Swiss Chard Rolls with Root
        Vegetables, 93
    Tofu and Root Vegetables, 63
    Winter Squash and Parsnip
        Purée, 223
Rutabaga. *See* Root vegetables

Safety, 49–50
Salads
    Carrot Salad with Raisins, 222
    Simple Green Salad with
        Vinaigrette, 198
    Spinach Salad with Apple-
        Avocado Dressing, 101
    Summer Vegetable Slaw, 97
    Sweet Red Salad with
        Strawberries and Beets, 187
    Tempeh "Chicken" Salad, 170
    White Bean Pistachio Salad,
        177
    Whole Wheat Couscous
        Salad, 229
    Yogurt Fruit Salad, 98
Salmon. *See* Fish and seafood
Sandwiches and wraps, 144
    Basic Lunch Wrap, 64
    Black Bean Burritos, 84
    My Favorite Grilled Cheese
        Sandwich, 144
    Portobello Sandwiches, 96–97

Protein and Berry Pita, 196
    Sweet and Sour Turkey
        Burgers, 174–75
    Tempeh "Chicken" Salad, 170
    Tuna Panini, 100–101
    Yogurt Fruit Salad, 98
Sauces, dressings and dips
    about: vegetarian
        Worcestershire sauce, 101;
        wasabi, 102
    Apple-Avocado Dressing, 101
    Barbecue Sauce, 181
    Butternut Squash Tahini
        Sauce, 191
    Cashew-Garlic Ranch
        Dressing, 221
    Creamy Feta Vinaigrette, 166
    Easy Asian Dipping Sauce,
        159
    "Gee Whiz" Spread, 210
    Hot Artichoke Spinach Dip,
        202–3
    Hot Vinaigrette for Greens,
        137
    Kale Pesto, 186–87
    Lemon-Almond Dressing,
        145
    Lemon Pesto, 147
    Mango Salsa, 72–73
    Marinara Sauce with Italian
        "Soysage," 67
    Pizza Sauce, 227
    Tangy Lemon-Garlic Tomato
        Dressing, 115
    Walnut Parsley Pesto, 111
Scallops, in Stir-Fried Ginger
    Scallops with Vegetables, 88–89
Sea vegetables
    about, 59
    Broccoli and Arame in Tofu
        Cream Sauce, 83
    Simple, Easy Arame, 83
Seeds. *See* Nuts and seeds
Seitan
    about, 59; protein from, 60
    Seitan and Vegetables Stir-Fry,
        70–71

Seitan—*continued*
    Spicy Beef or Seitan and
        Cabbage, 203
    Steak (or Seitan) Stroganoff,
        105
    Sweet and Sour Pork or Seitan
        Skillet, 77
Sex, food and, 51
Shopping for food, 43–46
Shortcuts and tricks, 50–51
Smoothies. *See* Beverages
Snack menus. *See specific Week
  menus (Week 1 through 12)*
Snacks (and desserts)
    about: baked fruit, 225;
        craving sweets, 18–19;
        creative dessert substitutions,
        173; eating regularly,
        14–16; ice pop tools, 177;
        importance of, 15–16, 55;
        relapse prevention with,
        15–16; simple ideas for, 55
    Almond-Stuffed Dates, 180
    Apple Bread Pudding, 196–97
    Asian Gingered Almonds, 207
    Asian Popcorn, 164–65
    Baked Pears, 224–25
    Basic Banana Smoothie, 212
    Berrylicious Yogurt Granola
        Parfait, 153
    Carrot Fruit Cup, 178
    Chocolate Candy Substitute,
        160
    Chocolate/Carob Chip
        Cookies, 128
    DIY Trail Mix, 66
    Fruit Frenzy Sparkler
        Concentrate, 82
    Fruity Oatmeal Bars, 90
    "Gee Whiz" Spread, 210
    Ginger Lime Iced Tea, 140
    Gourmet Sorbet, 86
    Homemade Fruit Pops, 176–77
    Hot Artichoke Spinach Dip,
        202–3
    Kiwi Banana Smoothie, 156
    No-Bake Oatmeal Love
        Cookies, 208

    No-Bake Oatmeal Love
        Cookies, Version "B," 216
    Orange-Pineapple Froth, 120
    Pineapple-Banana Blast, 124
    Quick Apple Crisp, 112–13
    Raspberry Almond Milk
        Frappe, 204
    Sneaky Apple Cookies, 172
    Spicy Cold Pears, 79
    Summer Fruit Cobbler,
        154–55
    Yogurt Fruit Smoothie, 92
Sneaky Apple Cookies, 172
Sodium intake, 27–29
Sorbet, 86
Soups and stews
    about: miso, 58
    Cashew Cream of Asparagus
        Soup, 200
    Chickpea Stew, 116–17
    Condensed Cream of
        Mushroom Soup, 228–29
    Creamy Chickpea and
        Rosemary Soup, 161
    Divine Carrot-Pumpkin Soup,
        104
    Easy Miso Noodle Soup, 155
    Lentil Soup with Herbs and
        Lemon, 182–83
    Lovely Lentil Soup with
        Greens, 218–19
    Passion Beet Borscht, 133
    Split Pea Soup with Herbes de
        Provence, 125
    Turkey or TVP Chili, 142–43
    Turkish Lentil Soup, 211
    Vegetable and Bean Chili,
        78–79
    White Chicken Chili, 91
    Winter Squash and Parsnip
        Purée, 223
Southwest Black Bean Burgers,
  150–51
Soy products. *See also* Edamame;
  Seitan; Tempeh; Tofu
    about: miso, 58; protein from,
        60; tamari, shoyu, and soy
        sauce, 59

"Soysage"
    about, 59, 67
    Marinara Sauce with Italian
        "Soysage," 67
Spicy Cold Pears, 79
Spinach
    about: as superfood, 54
    Hot Artichoke Spinach Dip,
        202–3
    Pasta and Spinach Casserole,
        141
    Spinach Salad with Apple-
        Avocado Dressing, 101
    Spinach Tofu Pie, 113
Spirituality, 23
Split Pea Soup with Herbes de
  Provence, 125
Sports drinks, 16
Spring rolls, 158–59
Squash
    about: butternut, 54;
        summer and winter, 209; as
        superfood, 54
    Butternut Squash Tahini
        Sauce, 191
    Mock Macaroni and Cheese,
        190–91
    Pasta Shells with Zucchini,
        171
    Ratatouille, 209
    Risotto with Winter Squash,
        173
    Spaghetti Squash and
        Vegetables, 201
    Squash and Bulgur Pilaf, 135
    Vegetable and Bean Chili,
        78–79
    Winter Squash and Parsnip
        Purée, 223
    Zucchini Parmesan, 149
Steak. *See* Beef
Steamed Millet, 217
Steaming vegetables, 61, 123
Stir-Fried Ginger Scallops or
  Tempeh with Vegetables, 88–89
Strawberries. *See* Berries
Sucanat, 59
Summer Fruit Cobbler, 154–55

Summer Vegetable Slaw, 97
Superfoods, 54
Sweet and Sour Pork or Seitan
   Skillet, 77
Sweet and Sour Turkey Burgers,
   174–75
Sweeteners, 59, 113
Sweet potatoes
   about: as superfood, 54; white
      potatoes vs., 14
   Cuban Black Beans and Sweet
      Potatoes, 167
   Sweet Potato Corn Cakes
      with Wasabi Cream, 102
   Sweet Potato Crisps, 127
   Sweet Potato Pancakes, 121
   Swiss Chard Rolls with Root
      Vegetables, 93
   Tofu and Root Vegetables, 63
   Vegetable Frittata, 87
Sweets, about, 18–19. See also
   Snacks (and desserts)
Swiss Chard Rolls with Root
   Vegetables, 93

Tabbouleh, 200–201
Tangy Lemon-Garlic Tomato
   Dressing, 115
Taste of Italy Baked Fish, 81
Tempeh
   about, 60, 89; marinating and
      sautéing, 147; protein from,
      60
   Pasta and Trout or Tempeh
      with Lemon Pesto, 147
   Stir-Fried Ginger Scallops or
      Tempeh with Vegetables,
      88–89
   Tempeh "Chicken" Salad, 170
Textured vegetable protein (TVP)
   about, 142
   TVP Chili, 142–43
Thiamin, 3, 11
Toasting
   nuts, 119
   seeds, 95

Tofu
   about, 39, 60; characteristics
      of, 39; nutritional value, 39,
      60; storing, 60; types of, 60
   Cajun Tofu Strips, 134–35
   Classic Chicken (or Tofu)
      Parmesan, 162–63
   Curried Shrimp (or Tofu) and
      Vegetables, 129
   Gingered Tofu and Bok Choy
      Stir-Fry, 165
   Quick Chicken/Tofu
      Mozzarella, 194–95
   Spinach Tofu Pie, 113
   Tofu and Root Vegetables, 63
   Tofu "Egg-less" Scramble, 74
   Tofu Smoothie, 110
   Traditional Stovetop Tuna (or
      Tofu) Noodle Casserole, 114
Tomatoes
   about: paste, 105; peeling, 117;
      as superfood, 54
   Country-Style Omelet, 116
   Herbed Quinoa with Sun-
      Dried Tomatoes, 109
   Marinara Sauce with Italian
      "Soysage," 67
   Pizza Sauce, 227
   Tangy Lemon-Garlic Tomato
      Dressing, 115
   Vegetable and Bean Chili,
      78–79
Traditional Stovetop Tuna (or
   Tofu) Noodle Casserole, 114
Trail mix, 66
Tricks and shortcuts, 50–51
Tuna. See Fish and seafood
Turkey
   about: ground, 175; safe
      cooking temperatures, 50
   Sweet and Sour Turkey
      Burgers, 174–75
   Turkey Chili, 142–43
Turkish Lentil Soup, 211
Turnips. See Root vegetables
Tuscan Pasta Fagioli, 131

Vegetables. See also Root
   vegetables; specific vegetables
   about: cooked vs. raw, 12;
      customizing dishes, 61;
      importance of, 17, 55;
      preparing, 61; sea vegetables,
      59; steaming, 61, 123; variety
      of, 61
   Orange Ginger Mixed
      Vegetable Stir-Fry, 214–15
   Seitan and Vegetables Stir-Fry,
      70–71
   Vegetable and Bean Chili,
      78–79
   Vegetable Frittata, 87
Volunteering in food-related
   activities, 22

Waist circumference (WC), 34
Walnuts. See Nuts and seeds
Wasabi, 102
Watermelon, as superfood, 54
Week 1 menus, 62–75
   Sunday, 62–63
   Monday, 64–65
   Tuesday, 66–67
   Wednesday, 68–69
   Thursday, 70–71
   Friday, 72–73
   Saturday, 74–75
Week 2 menus, 76–89
   Sunday, 76–77
   Monday, 78–79
   Tuesday, 80–81
   Wednesday, 82–83
   Thursday, 84–85
   Friday, 86–87
   Saturday, 88–89
Week 3 menus, 90–103
   Sunday, 90–91
   Monday, 92–93
   Tuesday, 94–95
   Wednesday, 96–97
   Thursday, 98–99
   Friday, 100–101
   Saturday, 102–3

Week 4 menus, 104–17
    Sunday, 104–5
    Monday, 106–7
    Tuesday, 108–9
    Wednesday, 110–11
    Thursday, 112–13
    Friday, 114–15
    Saturday, 116–17
Week 5 menus, 118–31
    Sunday, 118–19
    Monday, 120–21
    Tuesday, 122–23
    Wednesday, 124–25
    Thursday, 126–27
    Friday, 128–29
    Saturday, 130–31
Week 6 menus, 132–45
    Sunday, 132–33
    Monday, 134–35
    Tuesday, 136–37
    Wednesday, 138–39
    Thursday, 140–41
    Friday, 142–43
    Saturday, 144–45
Week 7 menus, 146–59
    Sunday, 146–47
    Monday, 148–49
    Tuesday, 150–51
    Wednesday, 152–53
    Thursday, 154–55
    Friday, 156–57
    Saturday, 158–59
Week 8 menus, 160–73
    Sunday, 160–61
    Monday, 162–63
    Tuesday, 164–65
    Wednesday, 166–67
    Thursday, 168–69
    Friday, 170–71
    Saturday, 172–73
Week 9 menus, 174–87
    Sunday, 174–75
    Monday, 176–77
    Tuesday, 178–79
    Wednesday, 180–81
    Thursday, 182–83
    Friday, 184–85
    Saturday, 186–87

Week 10 menus, 188–201
    Sunday, 188–89
    Monday, 190–91
    Tuesday, 192–93
    Wednesday, 194–95
    Thursday, 196–97
    Friday, 198–99
    Saturday, 200–201
Week 11 menus, 202–15
    Sunday, 202–3
    Monday, 204–5
    Tuesday, 206–7
    Wednesday, 208–9
    Thursday, 210–11
    Friday, 212–13
    Saturday, 214–15
Week 12 menus, 216–29
    Sunday, 216–17
    Monday, 218–19
    Tuesday, 220–21
    Wednesday, 222–23
    Thursday, 224–25
    Friday, 226–27
    Saturday, 228–29
Weight management, 33–37
    best "diet," 35
    body mass index (BMI) and, 34
    building muscle mass, 34–35
    calories and, 33, 35, 36
    exercise and, 36, 37
    ideal body weight (IBW), 33–34
    overweight vs. overfat, 34
    simple science of (weight-loss tips), 35–37
    waist circumference (WC) and, 34
White Bean Pistachio Salad, 177
White Chicken Chili, 91
Whole Grain Noodles with Caraway Cabbage, 139
Whole Wheat Biscuits, 130
Whole Wheat Couscous Salad, 229
Worcestershire sauce, vegetarian, 101

Yeast flakes, nutritional, 58
Yogurt
    about: as superfood, 54
    Berrylicious Yogurt Granola Parfait, 153
    Yogurt Chicken Paprika, 68–69
    Yogurt Fruit Salad, 98
    Yogurt Fruit Smoothie, 92

Zesty Pecan Chicken and Grapes, 119
Zucchini. *See* Squash